When I first met Alex I had never heard of the island, and nor had he. Now, thirty-five years on, it is all I know, and all I want to know. On journeys to the mainland, to the shops and to visit the children and their children, I am excited to be going on an adventure and mightily relieved to come home.

We grew our five children here, in this wild place, this place of shipwrecks and wind-battered shores, where the roads follow ancient drover tracks and snake around lochs and between hills where the rock is firm and steady; where people drop in for a blether about nothing in particular and where women still bring plates of sandwiches and pots of warming soup to ceilidhs in the village hall.

Island Wife

Island Wife

living on the edge of the wild

Judy Fairbairns

www.tworoadsbooks.com

First published in Great Britain in 2013 by Two Roads
An imprint of Hodder & Stoughton
An Hachette UK company

1

Copyright © Judy Fairbairns 2013

A CIP catalogue record for this title is available from the British Library

Hardback ISBN 978 1 444 75958 7
Ebook ISBN 978 1 444 75961 7

Printed and bound by CPI Group (UK) Ltd, Croydon, CR0 4YY

Hodder & Stoughton policy is to use papers that are natural, renewable
and recyclable products and made from wood grown in sustainable
forests. The logging and manufacturing processes are expected to
conform to the environmental regulations of the country of origin.

Two Roads
Hodder & Stoughton Ltd
338 Euston Road
London NW1 3BH

This book is dedicated to my children. You are the beacons that lit my way back home, however deep the storm. I never knew I could love like this.

The farmer wants a wife
The farmer wants a wife
Eee Aye Addy-Oh
The farmer wants a wife

Traditional

Tapsalteerie
Topsy-turvy

Scottish, seventeenth century – origin uncertain

Contents

Preface: The Island   1

1. Alex   3
2. Lock Up Your Daughters   9
3. I Do   16
4. Bryn and Cassie   22
5. A Little Rebellion   35
6. Land Girl   40
7. Looking Towards the Island   49
8. Tapsalteerie   59
9. Bookings and Boilers   64
10. The Stock Valuation   72
11. Different Languages   79
12. Fly and Callie   85
13. Jake   94
14. Granny-at-the-Gate   102
15. Alpha Beta and the Whale   111
16. Eagles, Tourists and the Bait Barrel   122
17. A Full Hand   129
18. Women and Dreams   139
19. Gobbler   144

20. First Rites   151
21. Holidays   161
22. Cracks Appearing   173
23. Christmas at Tapsalteerie   182
24. Isobel the Hen   188
25. Girl Friday   195
26. Men in Uniforms   204
27. The Man Who Looks After the Whales   213
28. Winter Peace   221
29. Boarding School   231
30. Duchess   240
31. Catering and the Co-op   249
32. Blue Days   255
33. Alex's Accident   262
34. The Recording Studio   266
35. Exams and Teenagers   277
36. Through the Narrows   286
37. Leaving Tapsalteerie   294
38. Dissolving   304
39. Sail and Return   313
40. Restoration (Work)   323
41. The Exhibition   332
42. New Beginnings   342

    Epilogue   346
    Acknowledgements   349

Preface
The Island

⌒

The island is not like other places. It has a different heart-beat. I felt it the first time I stepped onto the black rocks of the shore, and something deep inside me knew I was home. Even if I had never been here before, couldn't even pronounce the names of the villages, it didn't matter one jot. This was journey's end and its beginning.

Last night the moon was full and bright and pushing into the bedroom as if there wasn't enough room for her outside. She squeezed between the half-closed curtains and lay across the bed till the duvet grew heavy and hot across my feet and I had to get up. There are no street lights here to interrupt the nights or to confuse the birds. When it is light, we rise and go about our work, and when it is dark, we sleep. Only it's not dark. Not when there's a full moon turning the whole world a bright limey green, so that even my eyelids glow, and I just have to give up and go downstairs and into the yard, barefoot as a child, to see it. On such nights the moon is a big round grapefruit, smack bang in the middle of the sky, and the sea-loch is a green soup. The black hills, not yet softened with summer foliage, are sharp edged like broken teeth. Owls hoot and hunt in the darkness, and somewhere down there on the shore oystercatchers call out in frantic trills that rise from the silence, quickening my own heart, and then, just as swiftly, falling away into the night.

The little burn tumbles down the hillside and disappears under the road, where it falls into a deep pool. I throw my potato peelings into that pool. Old bones too, and crab shells when we are lucky enough to have crab to eat. Sending it all back to the sea is what I say, like a thank you.

Once I found a tup, a young ram, upside down in the burn. He was too heavy and the gulley too narrow for him to right himself and what I saw first were his four hooves sticking straight up behind a chaos of brambles. The clear spring water ran over his nose, and his eyes were wide open. I wondered how long he had fought to hold his head up, to stay alive. They had to haul him out with chains and a digger. I saw him go by on the trailer, legs still rigid, destined for a big hole in the ground.

I drink the last of my tea and tiptoe back upstairs . . .

1

Alex

When I first met Alex I had never heard of the island, and nor had he. Now, thirty-five years on, it is all I know, and all I want to know. On journeys to the mainland, to the shops and to visit the children and their children, I am excited to be going on an adventure and mightily relieved to come home. On the mainland, I put on my mainland shoes and I keep moving to prevent being trampled by the crowds. On the island, I would struggle to get anywhere near a trampling opportunity.

We grew our five children here, in this wild place, this place of shipwrecks and wind-battered shores, where the roads follow ancient drover tracks and snake around lochs and between hills where the rock is firm and steady; where people drop in for a blether about nothing in particular and where women still bring plates of sandwiches and pots of warming soup to ceilidhs in the village hall. We watched Disney on open spools at the Christmas party and sang

3

favourite carols; ate ice cream and jelly in festive grease-papered bowls. Everyone came, from the old folk to the newborns, all dressed up in party clothes. Then silence was called and we all listened hard for the jingle of sleigh bells and in he came at last – Santa in his farmers' wellie boots, with a heavy sack on his back, bursting with gifts. Mobile phones were still a dream and only a few islanders had a television. We didn't at Tapsalteerie. Not all the way up that long bumpy track to where the stones are ancient and you can still believe in the little people; to where old stories spin webs among the heather, and the dew sparkles like diamonds on the first grass; and where the land runs out into the great Atlantic Ocean, wild and icy clear and full of secrets she will never tell.

I take a swallow of hot black coffee. Alex makes good coffee, warming a cup for me on the little aga, so it's all ready for when I come down. He also sleeps soundly at night, unlike me, and wakes refreshed to dress in the early light with the curtains firmly closed in case anyone catches him naked.

The tide is high this morning and the air quite still. I can see a lot of the loch from the bedroom window, once the curtains are open. Sometimes, the otter is out fishing, teaching her cubs, or I might see the sea eagle balancing on his favourite perch, almost at the top of the tallest pine below our neighbour's field. I usually hear before I see. The gulls and crows tell me, with their cawing and shrieking as they dive at the huge bird, baiting him, telling him to leave. Apart from the odd twist of his head at their coming, he ignores their taunts. I can see the big white tag around his neck, which would tell me, if my binoculars were powerful enough, how old he is. Sometimes when he flies over the house the tag crackles in the wind, like gunfire, and I wonder it doesn't drive him mad, so close to his ear. Something silent around his foot would have been kinder.

His wingspan is over ten foot and I remember the surprise of him one day as I drove back from the village. He dropped down from the pines and into the road, flying straight towards me. I could see how huge he was from such close quarters and I stalled the car, leaping out to watch him. He gracefully cut through the air just above my head and I could feel his tail wind ruffling my hair.

Hallo, you wonder! I said. One of Tommy's sheep peered at me through the fence.

Not you, I smiled. No offence.

I am working today, I tell Alex, the word sticking for a moment, new in my throat. After all, work is scrubbing floors and ironing things you only just ironed, and baking high-rise buns for others to eat.

Working? Alex queries, as he arrives balancing a slice of home-made white atop his regulation double-egg breakfast.

You spend all day messing around with paints! He scratches at a few of the paint spatters on the window with his knife.

I raise my chin and remind him of the exhibition date, that I have only half the canvases ready and that there are only a few short weeks left. It's my first exhibition on the island; my first exhibition anywhere for that matter.

What's this one going to be? he asks, revolving a canvas till it's gone full circle.

I squint at it, at its bright blue ground with a few squiggly pencilled outlines.

I have no idea, I reply. Would you like a side plate for that bread?

There is already a peppering of crumbs on the table. He shakes his head, scoots the crumbs onto the floor, a floor he never sweeps. I really have tried to tame him over the years, this wild man of the sea, but he has faithfully resisted me. He would rather break his fast on the transom of a yacht, fully canvassed up and on a long reach, than bother with such whimsies as side plates.

Granny will be turning in her grave, I say, quite pointlessly.

When she lived here with Granddad it was a lovely little chintzy home with pretty plates and shiny silver laid across gingham tablecloths with napkins to match. Even though the napkins now languish in the drawer, the lines made by Granny's iron are still bold and straight. They moved here shortly after we did, Alex's parents, as if that was just the way of things, settling in one end of the stone gatehouse to the Tapsalteerie estate. Now it's just me and Alex here. The children have moved south and the old people north, to heaven.

What's the trip today? I ask Alex.

An eight-hour whale-watch, he says. Forty folk from the RSPB on a jolly. Should be fun!

I consider forty people trapped together on a boat for eight hours. It doesn't sound like fun to me.

You have egg on your face, I tell him, as he gets up to leave.

I know, he grins. Elevenses.

When we first hatched this whale-watching idea, over thirty years ago, Alex was the only skipper, with no crew to help man his small and slow-moving boat. Every day, fair or foul, he would set off from the pier below Tapsalteerie House and turn the bow into the waters of the North Atlantic in search of Leviathan. In the springtime he would head for the islands where the puffins make their burrows and hatch their young, and where guillemots, shags, razorbills and terns made their nests on skinny ledges high up the guano-caked cliff-face, turning the sky into a tumble of flight and an ear-splitting noise. Later in the summer, he would head north to where the shearwater bob in their hundreds and gannets burst the sea open as they dive for food. Every day, lives were changed aboard that little boat, as it trundled among the scattering of islands, peppered with wild orchids, sea grass and wild thyme. No one came back the same, not with the sights they had seen, with the salty air filling their lungs, and the sounds and the silence making a new music in their hearts, and it was Alex who led them to it, who made it happen. Some folk said there were no whales here. But Alex knew better, and he could always find them, when others could not.

Now Tapsalteerie belongs to another and our son runs the whale-watch, from a different pier on a big, powerful boat with a fully trained crew, and Alex employed as a skipper. Without this daily fix, the old sea dog would fade away to dust in no time, for the call of the sea is louder in him than any other call and will not be denied. Wild or calm, screaming abuse or singing a lullaby, pulled by the moon and glittering with diamonds in the sunlight, she draws him like a mistress, and we have learned, the sea and I, to share him, over time, although it was me who paid the higher price.

2

Lock Up Your Daughters

~

We met at the twenty-first birthday party of a mutual friend, although Alex had already seen me once before, a year or so earlier. With the stage lights blinding me to all but the stage, I never knew he existed at all.

While he was sipping his pre-theatre cocktail, on some bar stool beside his then girlfriend, I was aaahing and ooohing through my vocal exercises in the Green Room. As the couple took their seats in the front row of the Upper Circle, I was being squeezed into my whale-bone corsets and hooped skirt and marched off to make-up. I was seventeen and the lead in a week-long run of the musical, *Lock Up Your Daughters*. Considering my parents' protective attitude towards me, the irony of the title did not escape anyone's notice. This was Saturday night – the last night – by which time I had perfected the sauce in my songs, the flirty sparkle in my eyes and the final passionate kiss with the lead man, who enjoyed it rather more than I did and had to be sternly removed from my cherry-flavoured lip gloss every night. The audience loved it, cheering through every curtain call, and Alex was bewitched.

By the time Alex rocked up to the birthday party with his two mates, the evening was fizzing with champagne and chattering guests. Someone was playing the blues on a little upright piano and I sat on top of it in my extremely short dress with bell sleeves, and my black vinyl boots reaching right up to my knickers. I was singing Billie Holiday and Alex could hardly miss me.

He says his heart flipped. He decided that night that he would make me his girl.

I watched him come through the doorway. Dinner jacket, too big. Hair to his shoulders. Beard. My mother would have a blue fit.

As I rounded off the last notes of 'I'll be Seeing You', he vanished into the crowd.

By the time he asked me out for dinner, I had already accepted four other invitations, one of them from a young man with a black Ferrari. By then I was finding it increasingly hard to see straight, which didn't bode well for later on. Of all the men, Alex was the most intriguing. He was older, stood out from the others with their expensively cut jackets and their clever talk. He also looked more and more like my safest choice, considering the storm now gathering in my belly. As the room began to revolve even faster, he and his friends gently gathered me into a rather snappy red sports car and I settled back in the seat, breathing in the leather. As Alex climbed in beside me, I gave him a weak smile, and threw up all over him.

The next day was Sunday, and I had to catch the train back to the depths of Buckinghamshire, where I was working as a nanny.

Alex is going to drive me down, I told my mother.

Alex? Her voice was thin, sharp.

I nodded, wishing immediately that I hadn't. Inside, a steel band was warming up and my mouth tasted feral.

If he isn't here by 3 p.m., she said, firmly, I'm taking you to the train!

Her shriek brought me to the window at precisely ten to.

You didn't tell me he had long hair AND a beard! She drew back from the glass as if both might be catching.

He does?

I had forgotten.

When he held out her hand to shake hers, on the doorstep, she made as if to slap his face.

During the three-hour journey I learned all about Alex. About his travels to America, his work scraping boat hulls on the beach in Big Sur, sleeping rough and living on his wits. His work in a lumber camp high up in Canada, where the temperatures plummeted to minus 40°C and the gas cylinders exploded. Travelling through the Yucatan, through the desert, the jeep collided with a swarm of butterflies that clogged the radiator and stopped them dead. Of the subsequent heat by day and the terrible cold at night, and nothing but sand for miles. Of the people he met along the way, who bathed his fevers and cooked his meals, and of the day he awoke to find his jeep without wheels and all his belongings

11

gone into the night. He had returned to this country when his father was taken ill and could no longer manage to run the two-hundred-acre arable farm in Norfolk.

You didn't want to come back? I said, although I wasn't really asking.

He shook his head. You do what you have to, for your family.

I lasted longer in that nanny job than in any other.

The trouble with you, young lady, my mother said, is that you don't want to do anything at all!

And she was right. I didn't, thus far. I'd learned to type and write shorthand very fast, but that meant being a secretary. I looked at those who had been secretaries for years and knew I wasn't going to end up like them – those perfumed, tightly corseted spinsters – not at any price. Some of my friends found work abroad, which both excited and terrified me. Some went to colleges or universities to study important things like forensic science or hairdressing, but no matter what my parents or tutors suggested, nothing appealed to me, except for one thing. All that ever held me in its thrall was the thought of escape.

And so, listless and bored, I spent my days, in between jobs, lying on my bed in my lonely room with the yellow-flowered wallpaper, listening to *Abbey Road* on a loop, and dreaming of some fantasy suitor with wild hair and wilder beard, and of our happy gurgling babies; of my long flowing dresses, and my cosy wooden beach home, and of long evenings engrossed in conversations about life and love and the universe and how lucky we were, our eyes twinkling and all our bills paid by someone else.

My parents must have agonised over me, their first-born, the eldest of five, a strange fish who never swam with the shoal. Rules were everything in our house. I was too wild for them, and decided I had been dumped in these leafy suburbs by some daft stork that had lost its bearings.

I knew the kind of home I should have been born to. There, daughters ran barefoot and tousled, helping themselves to each other's clothes, pens, jewellery and snacks from the fridge without asking. I always had to ask. Their shoes, when they wore them, might be scuffed and their school bag raggedy. They chattered to the adults and were listened to, and not corrected at all on their diction, or their volume control, or the length of the skirt they were wearing, or the crumbs spraying from their full mouths.

Let me be Penny, I would pray into my pillow, who is like a deer on the sports field, where I was always stuck in goal because of my asthma. Or Jill, who can watch telly anytime she likes, and is always asked out at weekends; or Mary, although I would need to meet Mary's mother first.

In the suburbs, whichever way I turned, there was only wasteland.

Now I had a face to give the suitor of my daydreams.

For over the weeks that followed, Alex would drive down overnight to see me for a day and a half, before driving all the way back, and each time I saw him I liked him more. I was easy with him, I was myself, and he made me feel precious and cherished and clever and funny. Once we met in a hotel in London, and I was genuinely terrified that one of my mother's friends would spring out from behind a pillar with a loud 'Aha!' as I signed my name on the hotel register as Alex's wife.

Silly girl! Alex said affectionately, as he took my hand.

We didn't go down for dinner, but ordered room service. By now I was quite certain the Mother Police were downstairs, and besides, I only wanted to talk to Alex. When the knock came on the door, I dived off the bed to hide. The waiter, catching sight of me as he laid down the tray of food, smiled politely.

Madam, he said, with a little bow.

After he had gone, the ridiculousness of my performance quite broke the ice, and I was still laughing as Alex took me in his arms and kissed me softly on the mouth over and over until I forgot my mother altogether.

Then one Easter, when I was home for the long weekend, he asked me out for dinner. He arrived in his black Morris truck, the one he used on the farm. It was equipped with a short-wave radio, so that the farm workers could contact him if necessary. I didn't really understand, at that point, how cutting edge the farm had become under his leadership, for Alex was an innovator, an entrepreneur and he was managing his two-hundred acres in completely new ways, breaking the rules as Alex always does. He grew daffodils for Covent Garden and designed a bulb steriliser that changed the whole flower market around. He dried corn, cured onions so the skins turned brown. He grew peas and beans for Bird's Eye, and spinach for Sandringham. He sank bores in the ground to irrigate the potatoes when others lost their crops to the drought. If an idea for improvement came into Alex's head, then Alex brought it out into the light. I had never in my life met such a man, and my girlish heart was overflowing with what I guessed just might be love.

What do you fancy? he asked, scanning the menu.

I chose beef ragout and ate the whole thing, gravy and all, with my fingers, and he never said a word. Later, much, much later, we sat in the darkened driveway and he asked me to tell him more about me. Faltering at first, I began to open up, gradually, bit by bit. He was like no one else I had ever known. Ten years my senior, and with a whole lifetime already lived, he was gentle with me, patient and, above all, interested in what I had to say. He was the only man, since I was fourteen, who didn't feel he had the right to dive into my knickers after a hurried name swap, and it made me soft and vulnerable and I didn't mind it one bit. When he told me he had fallen in love with me, I knew I felt the same way.

Will you marry me? he asked, and my eyes swam.

It was well after curfew when someone gave the curtains a parental switch, spilling light onto the bonnet of the truck. I shivered.

Yes, I said. I will.

3

I Do

A few months later we married in the little church where I
had once been the smallest choir girl and where I had
read the lesson on important days, standing on a wood block.

My elocution lessons got me there. My diction was
perfect. I could wrap my mouth round any phrase I chose to
wrap it round, especially if there was an audience with ears
to catch it. In those days churches were full, and not just at
Christmas and Easter. The choir was twenty strong and on
Fridays we practised before the capable hands of a choirmas-
ter, whose baton swiped the air fast as a bluebottle.

Are you awake back there, second sopranos?

Yes, we squeaked, dragging ourselves to attention.

The lectern, upon which the great black Bible sat, with its
swirly writing, was shaped like an eagle in flight. When I was
practising 'In the Beginning, was the Word, and the Word
was with God, and the Word was God' my father stood at
the back of the church calling out encouragement, raising

his chin so I would raise mine, and teaching me how to throw my words right to the back. After the service people fluttered around me, telling me how well I read, and I basked in the glory, forgetting God completely.

On the day of our Edwardian-themed wedding, my father and I travelled from home in a horse and landau. The early afternoon was fair, and the horse ancient, and nothing mattered that day. My mother had spent all morning helping me to 'frill up', plying me with little sips of champagne to steady my nerves as she fixed my hair. She looked elegant, as she always did, dressed in fine cloth, tailored especially for this grand occasion, with shoes that matched her hand-bag that matched her hat. I felt like a princess sitting beside my father as we swayed beneath a canopy of lime trees, the air full of a June fragrance, wild birdsong and the clip-clop of the horseshoes on the road. Being alone with him was a rare treat. As we neared the church, we heard the bells ring-ing out to the whole world that I was about to begin living happily ever after. My dress, made by Alex's sister, was cream silk with dusky pink ribbons in artful places. It had long sleeves with little ruffles of lace at the cuffs and the same lace at the neck. My long auburn hair fell loose down my back, and on my head I wore a hat created from the same material as the dress. I was nineteen years and three months old and I held tightly onto my father's strong arm, but I wasn't nervous about marrying Alex; not at all. There was not a doubt in my mind that we were meant for each other, even though sometimes I read different messages in the eyes of others.

Although my friends cooed and clapped their hands in delight when I showed them my sapphire set in diamonds, some of them must have had their doubts, although they said nothing – unlike Alex's friends, who had plenty to say. He was committing his life to me, and I may have been pretty and bubbly and fun to be around, but was not wife material, dear boy, not at all. I was just a slip of a thing, with absolutely no experience of real life at all.

My father, the vet, was proud of me though, I knew it, could see it in his face as helped me down from the landau. It never crossed my mind that my parents might be filled with apprehension at this whirlwind romance; at the fact that I was so young – young enough for curfew rules, despite the engagement ring on my finger.

My three sisters and Alex's were the bridesmaids. They wore flowers in their hair, and their excited whispers darted around our heads as we gathered in the porch.

Quiet now, girls! said the verger, and then, Good luck!

On his signal, the organist began to play 'The Arrival of the Queen of Sheba' and the congregation rose to their feet.

After the ceremony, Alex held my hand very tightly as we walked back down the row of guests. He looked resplendent in a green Edwardian frock-coat and beaver top hat, although he didn't wear that inside the church. Alex knew the rules for a gentleman. He always held the door open for me, even the car door, and I had not been treated like such a lady by any previous beau. Outside, all the farm workers had formed an arch with their sugar beet hoes and I laughed with delight to see their faces. They were all squeezed into their Sunday best, their weathered faces lined with hard work, their eyes merry with fun. By this time I was already very fond of them all, and our times together would become my life, for I was now the farmer's wife. They had come all the way into town for us, to see us wed, and I was much moved.

I didn't know they were coming! I whispered to Alex, as the photographer shuffled us into a group.

They wouldn't have missed this, even if they had to walk, he chuckled.

I pictured the group tramping the Acle Straight, their hoes over their shoulders like pikes, in their tight-fitting suits, the women in unfamiliar heels . . .

No, I said. I suppose they wouldn't.

Some of these men and women had worked for Alex's parents and some lived in tithed cottages at the far end of the little village. Now they worked for 'the youngster' as they called Alex, and so, by definition, for me too, although I couldn't imagine telling someone older than me what to do.

I would learn, eventually.

I first met Alex's parents in their little thatched house as a dinner guest, and a future daughter-in-law. They were all politeness and I was all good manners and it looked like we might just get along famously, although I can now see they may have concealed their real feelings. After all, their only son had chosen, rather suddenly, a town girl ten years his junior with absolutely no idea of what it might mean to take on the role of farmer's wife. And I no longer wonder at the nursery rhyme. I know exactly why the farmer wants a wife and so did Alex's mother. It was in the lines of her face and the constant working of her hands, hands that could turn nothing into something, every day, year after year. Alex looked just like her, but nothing like his father, who could not have been more opposite to his wife. He was a quiet and gentle soul, had bred fine horses before I met him, and I could just imagine him soothing a troubled mare with his low soft voice, this gentleman farmer who was never in a hurry. Alex's mother was his antithesis. Where he was long and wiry, she was small and round. Where he faltered, she took control. When he drew breath, it was she who spoke. In-between the many tasks of her days, she found time to paint flowers, delicately petalled in soft water colours, and I could recognise every one. For Alex's mother, the petals had to look like the real thing and she was often disappointed in the result. Later in her life she would stop painting altogether, as she gradually lost belief in her talent. It was safer not to keep trying. That way there was no disappointment.

Her tongue, like my own mother's tongue, could be sharp. Neither woman had found life easy. They grew up in war-torn times, times when women were expected to get on with it, basically – whatever 'it' might be – with selfless commitment and a strong sense of duty and most certainly without any fuss or grumbling. What about me? was a question you would only ask your pillow, and then when quite alone and in your smallest whisper. Our men come first, naturally, then our children and then us, with our big loving hearts always open, our front steps scrubbed and no sitting down till the afternoon, after all the ironing is done. Everyone knows that.

*　　*　　*

As Alex and I climbed aboard the landau behind the driver and his dozing old horse, I threw my bouquet into the crowd, and Alex's sister caught it. We couldn't wait to get away from the crowd, to be alone. Alex had parked his sports car just around the corner, and, after folding me and my stout petticoats into the passenger seat, we headed off in a northerly direction.

We just have to stop at the next garage, grinned Alex, a conspiratorial glint in his eye.

That grin thrilled me. I could feel it run down my back.

He disappeared for a moment of two, and returned pulling a light trailer. When I saw what was strapped to its flatbed, my heart sank. It was his sailing dinghy.

Where I had been thinking long beach walks and picnics among the dunes, he was already on a far reach, heading for the horizon. As he secured the trailer, his face in the rearview told me he had convenient amnesia.

I don't like sailing, Alex, I had told him, and not just once.

The panic rose in me and I almost ran. Then I remembered my stout petticoats and the vows I had just made. I let the pictures move through my head and right on out, the silly dreams of long romantic moonlit walks, the sharing of newspapers, the slow gentle days. I knew he wouldn't sail without me. He didn't want to do anything without me. I was already his everything.

As we pulled out into the road, I looked across at his happy face through my white misery. All those rainbows.

My husband. A stranger.

4

Bryn and Cassie

⤳

As the little dinghy gathered enough speed to fly across the bay, the centreboard shattered with a sharp crack. After the initial shock, I fought to keep in the grin, as Alex grabbed at twists and splinters, his face pale with disbelief. We were miles offshore by now on the ebb tide, and the village in the distance looked like Toytown. He was looking for a miracle, and I dutifully looked too, albeit with little enthusiasm. Reality was a very long muddy walk back to the hotel, dragging a heavy boat, and after that? No more sailing. Although I felt guilty about my level of glee, I felt it anyway.

We dragged the boat to a little island and pulled her onto the shore. We had a picnic lunch with us and a bottle of champagne and the sun was shining. The tall maram grass offered ample privacy for a honeymoon lunch.

Halfway down the bottle, Alex's hands began to wander.

I'm covered in mud! I exclaimed, as if that would ever have stopped him. I was no good at such things, coming as I did from a life with as many rules about ladylike behaviour as there were minutes in a year. We could wait till bedtime, I said feebly, taking a last peek over the tips of grass. We could have a bath, dinner, a bit of romance, work up to it, you know . . .

Even buried beneath my husband, with the sandflies biting my bottom, I kept my ears open.

There could be birdwatchers, I protested. You never know about birdwatchers until it's too late, when they pop up from behind a tuft and train their Zeiss binoculars on your behaviour patterns.

Let's give 'em something to write in their notebooks, then! Alex grinned, kissing me all over till I giggled like a schoolgirl and tipped him into the spiky maram, the sun hot on my back.

Back in the hotel, hours later, I took a long soak and fell into the lumpy old bed that rose like the Grampian hills in the middle and left each of us in our own valley. At dinner, we were actors in different plays. Mine was a celebration, but for Alex it was a wake, the champagne moments all but forgotten now the reality of his broken boat had sunk in. As I listened to him sleep on the other side, I cried into my pillow for my mummy, like the little girl who had gone to stay a weekend with a school friend on her father's farm. So homesick was I, so terrified of going to sleep, that I had to be brought home late the first night. But this was not a weekend, and I was no child. No matter how hard I cried for my mummy this time, there was no chance of going home. This time it was for life.

* * *

I lived a whole lifetime before I met you, Alex told me.

While I swapped sweeties in the junior playground, he sold his first sailing dinghy to buy a one-way ticket to Canada. As a young émigré, he boarded the ship for a six-week journey across the Atlantic. I am sure, being Alex, he would far rather have packed a few lunches and taken off up the River Yare and out to sea in his little dinghy with the sun in his face and the wind at his back. Perhaps his mummy stayed his eager hand and lucky she did, for a serious storm halfway across almost did it for the big ship. Alex and his friend were the only ones left standing when everyone fell into their sick bunks, so had free run of the bar and the games deck. He docked in Montreal with empty pockets and a head full of ideas. Car deliveries paid well and offered free travel, in comfort, from one state to another; waiting at tables, at which he became very professional, saw him charming the Canadians with his proper English accent and filling his pockets with substantial tips every night. Moving to Vancouver and broke again, he took work on the railways, shucking coal into sacks in the driving sleet and rain.

That first Christmas he spent alone and broke in an empty youth hostel. In the New Year he was offered work at a lumber camp way up north of Prince George Sound, in an isolated desolate place where it snowed all the time. His job was to 'watch the hog', a highly dangerous task and one for the new boy. Standing high above the machinery, with a long pole in his hands, he had to clear any blockages that might halt the massive circular saw blades from their work. He wore no safety gear, no harness and the blades had no protection guards around them. The rig ran twenty-four hours a day, for if it stopped, even for a few seconds, the metal would freeze and fracture from the biting cold, a regular 30° below zero. There were wooden huts for the workers that were comfortable enough, despite having to share the bunks with bedbugs and pubic crabs, and there was always a mountainous supply of food for the hungry men. Steaks the size of doormats, pancakes, American style, with real bacon, eggs and maple syrup were served up every day. Alex was in heaven.

When the temperature plummeted to minus 40°, the gas tanks threatened to explode and the machinery ground to a permanent halt. Someone decided to airlift the men out, leaving Alex and his friend to keep an eye on things – although on *what* is a question I might have asked had it been me. Alex no longer had to clean the dodgy latrines as the water was now an icecap, and the cooking gear had blown up as the temperature continued to drop. As their blood began to freeze and they wondered if they would ever get out of there, a chopper finally arrived to pluck them from a chilly grave.

After the ice, he travelled into the sun, to California, Mexico, British Honduras, living by his wits, learning how to work hard for little pay, how to cross a desert in an open jeep, how to keep his profile low once his visa expired, how to live on the skimpiest diet, wearing the same tattered clothes, free and wild and uncluttered.

Then his father fell ill and suddenly he was on a plane bound for home.

That was eight years ago, and now I have moved in. Bouncing down the metal steps of the number 34 bus, day return please, and minding the puddles so they don't splatter my stockings with brown dots, I walk into this two-hundred acres of prime arable land with its loyal team of workers. There are seven men full-time – a parcel of twinkling rogues if I ever met one. Mostly Alex employs a regular gang of five women from the village, and on occasions when the daffodils need picking, or the onions sorting he might call in up to thirty more. And these women are earthy, rough and ready, mothers and wives as tough as their leathery skin. As I learn about hard physical work, grumbling and whining and complaining as much as I dare, there is an awakening in me around these folk. Nothing, for them, is worth grumbling about. You could be dead tomorrow, they wheeze, puffing on Capstan Full Strength. I had never thought of that.

Gradually, my typewriter hands grow tough and rough, and when they bleed in the cold, a pot of lard is pushed under my nose.

Rub it in hard! they said. That'll sort it right out.

After unwrinkling my middle-class nose, I do; and it does, and I smile at myself. I am getting the hang of this farmer's wife thing, now, and I am also enjoying it. I have my own role, my own part to play.

Two months later, there is a baby on the way.

What? How is this possible? I ask myself. I can't have a baby! I am still a baby myself!

Myself snorts.

As the sickness gives way to a glorious inner peace and the most pleasant of music playing in my heart, I begin to build my fantasy. My baby will be a boy, of course, and a happy one. He will be beautiful, a good feeder, he will sleep all the way through the nights and fill my days with joy and laughter as we grow to know each other, forming a bond that no one could ever break. The birth will be natural, the labour short. I will breastfeed, of course, and have plenty of cash for my own choice of baby clothes. What's-his-name and I will visit the grandparents often, meet with other young mothers and babies in sunny gardens over tea and chitchat, and Alex will adore his new son and want to learn everything about him so that he is almost as involved as I am. We will spend hours choosing his name, and when we have chosen it we will smile together with our secret, and we will talk long into the night over all our plans for our new family, all the outings we will take, all the fun we will share together.

First, we must decorate the nursery!

It's far too early for that, says Alex and I think he may be right, even if I am crestfallen.

We could buy the pram and the cradle, perhaps?

No, he says. It's tempting fate.

I buy a book on names and study it till the pages threaten to fall out with exhaustion.

We can't agree on a single name.

The baby takes two days to travel twelve inches, finally making his entrance with a loud squawk. Alex never leaves my side. As the pains rise, I squeeze his hand with my own, crying out at the agony of it all. His face is lined with worry.

Is she alright? I hear him ask the midwife.

She will be, comes the reply.

Afterwards, Alex tells me how it was for him, watching

the ugly pain rack my young body. How he felt the fear and how the hours dragged into days and then into cold black nights. By day two he is frightened for my life, and then, suddenly, the baby's head crowns and with a last surge of strength, I bring forth our son.

Together we hold him. Together we cry. At last, it is over.

The old black lab, on the other side of the bedroom door, can bear it no longer. She butts it open, leaps onto the bed and licks the tiny red face.

Oh let her! says the district nurse, a farmer's wife herself, as she tugs at the bloodied sheets and rolls them into a ball. There's nothing like a rasping tongue to get the blood moving!

The nursery is ready now, but I don't want my baby out of my sight. My baby. I watch as the nurse pops him into his pale blue Babygro and swaddles him tightly in a shawl. I am in silent awe of this new life, born of me, of us.

Nurse him, she says, as she guides his open mouth to my engorged nipple. It will make him feel safe.

The baby starts to suck and is almost drowned in a torrent of yellow milk. The nurse smiles as he chokes and recovers.

Do you have a name? she asks.

I think so, I tell her, and look over at Alex, who nods his head.

Bryn, he says.

That's not a name! My mother is horrified. I shall call him Alasdair.

And I shall call him Sebastian, says the other mother, equally miffed.

Even in their shared dismay at our choice of name for our firstborn, the mothers cannot quite agree.

From the very start, I am not who I planned to be. I am hysterical, tearful, fussing and spooked by everything. Dangers lurk in every corner and I find none of the bovine peace I had read about, or met in more experienced women, that sun-warmed cud-chewing motherhood I imagined was part of the deal. I am on edge the whole time, sleepless and overwrought, and my baby picks it up. After a few days my mother arrives, despite Alex's attempts to keep her away. I am a mess and she knows it and at a time like this a girl needs her mother. She brings helpful gifts and sometimes my little sisters, who all jump on the bed to marvel at this tiny new boy, ever so slowly growing to fit his zero-sized baby suits.

But still the baby cries, and one night Alex takes charge. He moves Bryn into the nursery and shuts the door.

Let him cry, he says, and wraps me in his arms. He is soon asleep.

I lie awake, my mind and body in meltdown. All my instincts tell me to go to my child. Breast milk soaks the sheets. I lie in a misery I never knew till now. I am exhausted, torn, doubting and sore.

One desperate day, when he has cried for hours, rejecting my voice, my arms, the milk in my breasts; when I can no longer take the stupid useless failure of a woman that I am, I shake him and he slips from my hands, hitting his head on the table corner as he goes down. Distraught and disbelieving, I gather him up. He is quiet now, white and shocked. But I don't want him to be quiet.

Oh God, let him scream again! I pray, my eyes hot with tears, and I hold him close till his breathing comes in soft, sweet pants. When I tell Alex, he is gentle, but I know he will be watching me. I am glad he works on the farm and that he can pop home at any time.

The following week I visit a doctor who specialises in troubled mothers like me, with troubled babies, like Bryn; babies who burst into a world they don't much like the look of. She feeds me tea and reassurance in the sunshine of her wide green garden as I admit to my crime.

She smiles encouragement and sends me home, more confident, and deeply relieved to know I have done no lasting damage.

A few nights later, our own doctor calls.

I have a note here from Social Services, he says. Your baby is to be taken into care while you undergo psychiatric treatment, which I believe is nonsense. Would you like me to stop this happening?

I cannot believe my ears. How could she do that so secretively, with such falsehood in her mouth and in her kindly eyes?

Yes, please, stop it, I whisper, the shock is like needles in my heart.

Gradually my strength returns, and my shattered confidence begins to heal. Bryn learns to feed at regular hours, and the farmhouse settles into a sort of routine. Alex encourages me to be relaxed with motherhood, as he is relaxed with fatherhood, if changing the odd nappy counts as fatherhood. I have yet to drink tea in sunny gardens with other mums, but there is still time for such things. I spend all morning washing terry-towelling nappies and drying them on the washing line. I feed my little boy, dress and undress him, watch him stretch and change and all the time I learn to love in a way I never knew before and one that fills me completely. Now, for the first time, here is a life I would give my own to protect. No hesitation. No question.

When he is a few weeks old, Alex suggests we go off to Wales on holiday.

No way, I say, without hesitation. My body is wrecked and I can just about cope at home with all the kit I could possibly need around me.

That night, Alex looks into my eyes. He knows I am in there, somewhere.

I love you, he says. I will take care of you forever. Do you know that?

I know it, I say.

We leave the next morning. There is no room for the Moses basket, other than squashed in the 'very back', which is too far away from me in the front seat. In between the 'very back' and me are the entire contents of the nursery and the bathroom, and balanced atop all this are two Labradors in their beds. They look like extras in the pea-green-boat story.

Bryn travels at my feet in a fruit box.

A what? shrieks my mother. That is appalling! She says the word as if I might not hear every syllable.

As we belt along motorway after motorway, I request a stop to change Bryn's nappy.

Alex doesn't do stops.

No, he says. Can't you do it while we drive on?

There's no water to wash him.

Use the orange squash, he says.

And I do.

The holiday is just what we need. The little lighthouse-keeper's cottage with no phone, no knocks on the door; the wide empty beaches, where we walk and talk in the soft salty breeze, and above all, Alex away from the demands of the farm. Giving all his time to me.

Back home again, I decide I must brave the drive into town. I settle Bryn in the Moses basket and put him on the back seat of William, my old and beloved Morris Traveller. He is racing green, which sounds altogether too fast for me, with shiny wood framing the double back doors.

It takes me fifteen minutes to get out of the driveway and onto the road, stalling and lurching as if I'd never driven before, my heart beating like a drum.

Calm down, I tell myself in the mirror, and proceed to drive the whole twenty-three miles in second gear, gripping the wheel with ice-white fingers.

Can I leave my baby with you? I ask the nice lady at reception.

Of course!

She beams, thrusting her face into the basket. I dash for the underwear department.

Extra large . . . yes . . . control pants . . . yes . . . nursing brassieres with reinforced . . . yes . . .

Twenty minutes later, and well on my way home, I remember Bryn, who is still in reception.

*   *   *

The following year Cassie is born, also at home, and her birth is over in just a few hours. Alex is beside me once again. I am more experienced this time and know the ropes, although his hand still takes a few days to stop hurting. Afterwards, he brings me toast and champagne and Bryn, in his arms, to meet his new sister. Bryn is an independent little boy now, with a beautiful face and blonde curls. He should have been a girl, says my mother, with that face.

Cassie is a bigger baby, and more peaceful. But then so am I. She sleeps well, feeds well, is happy to lie in her pram under the almond tree in all weathers, wrapped in furs and feathers and gurgling at the sky.

Where's Cassie? asks my mother one evening as we wash teacups and light the fire. It is snowing hard and we have closed the curtains for the night.

I grab the torch. I would never find the pram in this dark with all that snow swirling in my eyes.

And so we have our pigeon pair. They are both baptised and celebrated, their souls in safe hands. Our little family is complete.

I want ten children, says Alex.

Well, not with me, you don't. You married the wrong woman. Oh, I've seen the right sort of woman, the peaceful cud-chewing mothers with natural instincts and big laps and soft soothing voices, but I am not one of them.

I am more a bundle of live wires with a storm approaching.

By the time the children are toddling, I know for sure that my mother-in-law lives far too close by. She pops in most days to

33

tweak my plumbago and deadhead my geraniums. It is true that they used to be hers before she left the big farmhouse for a tiny cottage a mile down the road and a short mile is just near enough to justify all this popping in. She arrives without knocking and she brings with her gifts and baking and wholesome advice along with her secateurs.

You don't need another vacuum cleaner, she says. This one has plenty of life in it yet.

I don't like that sort. I can hear the whine in my voice.

Oh diddums, she snorts.

She is a superb cook. She is also a superb dressmaker, flower-arranger, organiser of events, maker of teddy bears and other assorted soft toys, of cakes, of preserves. She has met most people and the ones she hasn't met are probably riff-raff anyway. She can paint, skin rabbits and pickle walnuts. She can preserve eggs in aspic, carrots in sand and fruit in jars. She can blanch vegetables, cure hams, press tongues, take cuttings, graft roses, make perfect loaves and turn beech leaves blue. She can knit anything you ask her to and makes wonderful clothing for the children. We are the envy of the whole playgroup.

She can turn nothing into something overnight.

She is also a mother-in-law, mine, and I have taken away her only son, her beloved.

We step carefully into our new relationship, she and I.

Will you teach me all these things? I ask her.

With pleasure, she says.

And she does.

When she isn't looking, I buy a new vacuum cleaner.

5

A Little Rebellion

~

Monday is washday.

Sundays are for church, roast beef, loud classical music and bad tempers.

Mondays are for washing, and Tuesdays are for ironing and folding and putting away in the right places.

For Alex, the right place is on the floor. Any floor will do, as he is not fussy. Another right place is the back of his chair in the bedroom – until, that is, it grows exhausted with being the right place for all his clothing, and falls over. This gives me permission to wash it all. Sometimes I tip the chair over myself.

The day dawns cold and wet. This could upset me, but I am not downcast. The prospect of yanking my new twin-tub machine out from under the big basins (both deep enough to bathe a whole pony) in the washhouse and turning on the taps to fill the tub can send tiny thrills down my spine and see me leaving the second half of my piece of toast. The big brass taps yell HOT and COLD and I need the monkey wrench to open them. Only the COLD one works, which today feels very unfair as the air inside is colder than a fridge.

Stop complaining, girl, I tell myself. You might have had to stagger down to the river bank to scrub this lot on a big stone, braced against a tiger attack.

Once upon a time, this washhouse would have been a bustle of laundry maids in crisp white aprons and caps, but now it is just me in my voluminous over-trousers, a duffle coat and fisherman's socks inside my gumboots.

In the first days of being Mrs Someone, I love it all, for I am playing house, and if you were to wander by, you would hear me singing carefree washerwoman songs in time to the slosh-slosh rhythm of the paddles. I take great care in the rinsing process, and make sure nothing gets tangled in the spinner. A girl could wreck her husband's close-quarter wear easily as this part of the process is fraught with dangers. A careless unfankling of a complicated knot of underclothing could result in very long pants and very short socks. But, as the wash morning creeps into the afternoon, when my back is yelling for mercy and my chilblains pulse hot as red larva and my toes have lost all sense of themselves, the dark clouds gather.

Now, with two babies, I am on terry-towelling duty every day, whether I like it or not, for disposable nappies are not yet on the shop shelves. And I do like it, in principle – as many modern mothers do. But still, all that soaking in buckets, the washing at terrifying temperatures, the pegging out in a frost for extra whitening. All that silent, brainless, thankless work.

Winters can be long for those of us who have to work at close quarters to the cold – like me, in that freezing laundry room with ill-fitting windows and a North-Easterly shooting under the old door and hours to wait before COLD becomes tepid, never mind HOT.

What am I doing out here? I ask myself.

The following Monday I make my decision. It's my own decision, made entirely by me – perhaps the second of my life.

I will move the twin-tub into the kitchen. It has wheels after all, so the designer must have imagined that a bit of movement might go on. The kitchen is cosy and I can fill the tub from the hot tap that says HOT and means it, and I can do other jobs at the same time. It makes perfect sense, and as soon as Alex has taken himself off to lead his farm hands into battle with hoes and ploughshares and the like, I am rounding the corner to the washhouse. It is well below freezing in here and I marvel at my stupidity to date.

I puff and haul, pant and shove the little twin-tub along the concrete path and over the sills. It fits snugly before the kitchen sink and I pull out the hoses, connect them and turn on the taps. While the drum fills, I make myself a cup of coffee. This freedom feels quite heady. I add the bubbles, sort the first wash and begin the cycle. I feel light as air, not least because I am. My duffle coat and over trousers are on their pegs and my gumboots underneath.

The whole thing is almost done by lunchtime when Alex returns home.

What's that? he asks. He has never been good at identifying white goods.

My washing machine! I say, a little unsure of his mood. His face looks stern. Perhaps there was trouble in the fields.

What's it doing in here?

My heart sinks. Washing? I offer, tentatively.

Oh no! No chance!

What? Why not? And I start to babble and stutter about the cold and the tap that doesn't work and the efficiency of multi-tasking . . . but he is not listening.

It's too noisy. I can't stand the racket. The washhouse is for laundry.

This is the first time I begin to wonder about the fairness of the marriage contract. I have walked up the aisle of my own free will, agreed. I have promised to love, honour and obey – which, with hindsight, was rather keen of me. Actually, this whole wife thing is really challenging, and demands more energy than the Good Lord is allocating me each day. In the early days of just we two, we would curl up together over the Sunday papers, sipping hot cocoa and discussing life or music or who next to invite for dinner, but now there are three of us: him, me and our relationship. Add to that two babies making constant demands on my time and patience and the result is chaos.

How did things change so fast? Once the day had been divisible into bite-sized chunks, fitting into a cosy pattern; now it is ripped apart like an old jumper.

Once Monday was washday and Tuesday for ironing and putting away. Days were for work and nights for sleeping. Now days and nights are one, and I don't know my way around this any longer. And, on top of it all, my white knight is turning off-white and becoming grumpy and jealous any time my eyes are not exclusively on him when friends come for dinner, or we are invited out, or we visit the local steak bar.

Your neckline is too low. Your eyes are too black. Your dress is too short.

I want to remind him of the girl he swooned over not so long before, with her high-rise dress and tarty black boots, her eyes black as the moon's backside, and her cherry mouth wide open with song.

But I don't.

You knew all this before you married me, I say to myself as he rises from his cheese sandwich. If you didn't like it then, why didn't you say so? It's a bit late now, with two babies under the belt, so to speak, and a marriage contract filed away in the council offices. And while we're on the subject, there are a few things I would have you change about yourself!

In my imaginary conversations, he always turns around.

What things? he asks, showing a genuine interest. I clear my throat. Pick my words carefully.

I would have you bath every day, instead of once a week. I would have you wash your beard every night, instead of just on bath days. I would have you brush your teeth twice a day and visit the dentist regularly.

There! I said it all and with a gentle firmness.

Trouble is, he has already gone back out into the fields and I am left watching the gap widen between us, and, for the life of me, I can't explain why.

6

Land Girl

‿⟋

While the dropped stitches of my daily routine outnumber the neat ones, the wild pattern of the seasons refuses to be ignored.

Every autumn we have to grade the potatoes into the sacks for market. A long belt driven by an old engine runs the length of the huge draughty barn, with old-timers Jeffrey and Roy at each end of it. It is their job to make sure the paper sacks fill equally before tying them off with wire twists and humping them onto the pallets, each one holding a ton. The rest of us flank the belt, be-gloved and dressed up like guys awaiting a bonfire. Warm woolly mitts, jumpers, hats and scarves do little to keep out the cold. Our feet in thick socks and warm boots keep us clear of the concrete, but without regular stamping the chilblains always find a place to land.

Get the bugger going, Jeff! Molly, one of our regulars, yells from somewhere about a mile down the barn. As Jeffrey kicks the old motor into life and the belt, the 'lumper', begins to shunt out the rhythm we will dance to for the rest of the day, voices rise to be heard over the racket and the banter begins. Experienced hands begin to flick pebbles onto the ground, to pick out any rotten potatoes, to show off any mutant shapes, and I watch and learn. Songs spill into the air, jokes are called out, and laughter is all around us. Suddenly Molly shrieks like a banshee and everyone looks towards her as a matchbox flies into the air over her head. As it lands, I can see the tail sticking out.

Jeffrey, you old sod! she screams, her unlit cigarette dangling in her mouth. As I watch the terrified mouse scurry into a darkened corner, I feel my own fears go with it. In that moment, everything I had believed about hard work disappears into the dark. Never before have I seen work as a task to be shared, and not only shared, but made light on its feet with humour and pranks as if it were something wonderful and not a life sentence.

In those stark early days of my adult life me and the hands worked together and laughed and teased each other, and I have them to thank for my very first real sense of belonging.

Over the next few years, Alex has ideas for development. Alex always has ideas for development and I am right beside him. Together we create a working farm museum complete with sturdy draught horses, Suffolk Punches, to work the equipment, a craft and coffee shop, a fresh vegetable store, a pick-your-own business and open days that draw thousands. And every day I am learning more and more, my self-confidence growing strong and heady. I know me, in this world according to Alex. My skin fits. I can do so many things now. From making the odd fairy cake, dusted lightly with sugar, for the coffee shop, I've graduated to making jams for the freshly baked scones. I can recognise vegetables from their leaves, and I know about crop rotation and which time of year is for ploughing. Now, happily, I am always caked in shit, or slime, snot or stour. I squelch and skid my way through beet and sprout fields, onions and King Edward potatoes, as the wind bites into my skin and chafes my eyeballs till they shine with light. I inhale the piss and muck of sweet-stabled horses with hot breath and wide feet, and the whickering of them sings through my dreams. I walk them out to first grass in the spring, three of them roped, two outriders and me, all together in a line like Windmill girls, until they smell it, the sharp sweet green that rushes up their velvet noses and into their hearts, and with a pull of powerful chests and legs I am lifted off my feet and sailed down the track towards the open gate. As they bend their thick necks to graze, ropes dangling free, I laugh out loud at the madness of spring.

We have built up this empire, the two of us, and it is done. We are a team. The main farm still grows intensive commercial vegetables, cereals and flowers, but now our tractors are like buildings on wheels and all of the equipment state-of-the-art. Two mechanics work full-time in the workshop, and a complex irrigation system feeds the crops till they grow to astonishing size. We make a fortune one winter on potatoes. We dry onions, sterilise bulbs for export; there are massive corn-drying bins, some weaner pigs for fattening, as well as peacocks, hens, geese, rare breeds, public toilets, two secretaries and a donkey. The Suffolk Punches work the land set aside for auld-time farming, and pull the wagons for the rides. A few years on and there are five of them: two barren old mares, one brood mare, Annie and her yearling filly at foot. We borrow a local stallion for a day to cover Annie and to put her in foal, so we can call ourselves breeders.

The stallion comes out of the trailer sounding like Zeus in a very bad mood, his huge feet making sparks on the ramp. He is a pounding god of a beast, with a thick neck, snorts of steam pumping out of his nostrils, his rolling eyes wild, his balls massive.

Good luck Annie, I whisper, reversing into the empty stable and closing the half door. She suddenly looks very small and I fear for her back, although God did design them both, so I am hoping that this little part of the whole world is safely in His hands, for the afternoon, anyway.

He's not shod! yells the wiry man on the other end of his halter rope, reading my mind.

Silver linings . . .

One year we decide to enter our horses in the local show. We will enter as a farm wagon, old style, piled with stooks instead of bales, with ribbons and plaits in the horses' manes and tails.

We will wear old farm smocks and boots and use the old harness that refuses to shine however much I worry it with Neatsfoot Oil and a scrim rag. Beaten, I decide it will look more farmer-ish against the high shine of the drays' trace harness, with their brass bridle swingers glinting atop the high black heads of the brewery shires.

My mother comes with us to look after Bryn and Cassie, while we unpack the horses and settle them in. It's a boiling hot afternoon when we arrive along with lines of other horse trailers, all shapes, all sizes. The middle-sized trailers led by gleaming Range Rovers all turn left. Around these trailers there seems to be a lot of fuss. There is always a woman at the wheel. A fierce, sharp-faced sort of woman with a waxed hat on her head and scary red lips.

Emileeeee! she barks. Oh Gawd! she wails. Bloody Hell! And so on. And Emileee, who is as skinny as her mother is four-square, crumples and looks at her small riding boots which are possibly the only safe things to look at, while her mother curses her way into the Light Horse enclosure.

We are turning right, into the loafish end of the field, where the wooden stables rise high and there are tinkers and diddicoys and trailers painted like canal barges. Here there is chat and laughter, although we can still hear the strident voices of the Light Horse Mothers on the warm breeze.

I think we are supposed to walk in sedately, I whisper to Alex as we judder and bounce the wrong way round the cones. He looks very handsome in his old-fashioned farming smock, his face brown as a berry and his eyes sparkling. I sit proudly beside him, while the children wedge themselves among the stooks of barley straw. We are now full in the public eye, in a huge ring and with not much idea of what we should be doing. Alex seems confident enough. He manages to wheel in the pounding abundance of horse flesh, round it on itself and point it in the right direction. Bryn and Cassie are squealing with delight, and I must grip the tails of their smocks tightly to prevent them spinning into the air. With bells jingling and tassels bobbing, Alex aims us mid-field, calling to the horses, as the panicky-eyed boys yank the big gates wide for us to leave the ring.

Cassie takes to the horses like she has always known them. Pint-sized and fearless she walks among them, while I have to pull myself firmly together, soothing and crooning and blowing softly to calm myself, not the horses, knowing that one quick turn to the right could flatten my spindly legs or my baby girl like a Shrove Tuesday pancake.

Not Cassie, though. Cassie knows nothing of fear.

Leave her be, soothes the old horseman, as we both watch her march about beneath the round swelling of their bellies. They whicker at her, bend their necks and she chortles and pushes at their huge faces, or hugs their soft muzzles tight in her chubby arms.

One morning at 6 a.m., I hear her outside on the concrete pushing her little trolley over the bumps and chattering away to herself. The next time I surface, there is silence outside and my heart slams into my throat. I know just where she is.

All the horses are in one field, a way from the house, and fed twice daily with nuts and hay while we wait for the late spring grass to flesh up a bit more. The ground beneath their feet is closed and cold, and they are more than ready for their breakfast each morning. Annie now has her little filly foal with her, and the yearling, Brindy, is coming into season, so she is nippy and volatile.

The feed bucket is missing from its place in the porch and so are Cassie's little red boots. Her trolley stands abandoned by the open gate. I throw a jacket over my nightwear, push my bare feet into my wellies and head for the field.

She is there, as I feared, a toddler in pyjamas and little red boots, dragging the bucket through twenty moving legs. In her other hand is a wooden spoon from the stone jar in the kitchen. She must have pushed a chair over to reach it. The horses are dancing hungrily around her, each one trying to nosedive into the bucket.

Baggirl Annie! shouts Cassie, swatting at Annie's legs with the bowl of the spoon. Annie, surprised, jerks back. Now Cassie swings around at them all.

Get back! she yells, and to my amazement they all do just that. She tips the pellets into a tiny mound and seconds later I am right beside her.

Good girl! I say, to all girls present.

As we move quietly away, Annie squeals at Brindy and nips her rump, upsetting all the others and causing an uprising and a rearing and a bucking as they come together with squeals and snorts and explode apart, tails riding high, to gallop away across the field like sudden thunder. As they disappear into the skyline, I lift my half-naked Amazon over the fence.

With the old mares, we take wagon rides up the long straight track between two fields, turning at the bell mouth where the land meets the sky, and back down again to the yard.

One Open Day, when the sun is warm and wagon rides are in everyone's mind, the relief horseman is absent.

Can you take the rides? asks Alex, only he isn't really asking. Alex believes I am Superwoman.

No, I say, all aproned up and baking cakes for the teashop. But I will. Alex knows I will.

Thank you lass, he says softly, and my heart melts.

I choose Duchess. She is the big calm chestnut with doe eyes and a soft snuffly nose. I feel slightly more in charge of her.

You can do it, grins the old horseman, having left his own wagon to help me tack up. Horse knows the way.

I take the five shillings apiece and load up, feeling terrified and hoping it doesn't show.

Off you go! the horseman chortles, patting Duchess on her shiny rump. She starts forward with a squeal.

Don't feel insulted, I whisper in her ear. I hate it when men do that to me, too.

I am fully laden as we bumble out of our parking space. Most of the load is a fat family who insist on sitting together down one side of the wagon. I know that Duchess is level, as is the horizon, but the rest of us are most definitely not. I call the horse to a stop and separate the family; they grump and whine at me as they shift their weight around, rocking the tiny granny and the skinny Chinese couple and their baby about quite a bit.

Now we are balanced and I click my tongue and we are off again, slow and sedate, gentle and swaying like an old ship in a calm warm sea.

From nowhere a load of kids arrive on bikes, yelling and whooping and startling Duchess from her stupor and into a trot from which she will not be tempted. The Chinese couple are loving it, and so is the tiny granny as she clutches onto her carpet bag and squeaks as we bob along, the air flying past our faces. The clopping rhythm makes music with the sun-baked ground. I don't bother about the fat family. They could probably do with losing a lunch or two.

As we bounce back into the yard, the old horseman has his face set on D for disapproval.

Too fast, he mutters as he moves his wagon out.

Duchess snorts at his receding back.

7

Looking Towards the Island

⌒

Alex grows restless, and, to be honest, so do I – although not for the same reasons. Over five years we have built up this thriving multi-level farm and there is nowhere else to expand. And there is a second unrest in Alex: the strong dislike of commercialism. I realise that sounds weird, considering the successful venture we now run together, but it is the bit after the harvesting that makes him uncomfortable and often angry. The middleman is beginning to skim off more and more wealth for himself. He will offer one price and treble it at resale, and if one farmer in the area agrees to it we are all trapped, for we need this middleman, however bad a taste he may leave in our mouths. What's more, health and safety rules are hitting the ground and stifling all individuality, and that's enough in itself to send both of us up a tree.

As Alex grows morose and frustrated, my own unsettled feelings rise like the choppy North Sea inside me, and

I no longer feel my feet on the ground. Dreams of wild places, a wilder ocean, a new start in the sharp clear air of Scotland dog my nights and wake me with indigestion. We are, in short, hemmed in – by the new busy road outside our gates, the parents, the abundance of paperwork, the rules, and the constraints of running such a big and varied business. Neither Alex nor I have ever lasted long inside others' boundaries. I ran away, or got expelled, and he bought a one-way ticket for the other side of the world. Neither of us is going to stop now. We find it increasingly hard to breathe and our relationship struggles for an even keel. What we need is a fresh start, far away from any risk of me turning into my mother, or of his getting anywhere near my plumbago. I think I honestly believe that if we leave the farm, we might also leave the build-up of angst and sore places.

We can, in short, begin all over again – just me and Alex and the babes. We can find a piece of unclaimed land, stick our flag in and wait for the music to reach heart-stopping pitch. We can build a homestead with high fences and deep wells for pure clean water. Alex will smile lovingly at me as I stand square and proud behind a mound of home-made scones and my breast will swell with pride for my man, my protection against any and all dangers, such as bandits or mothers. Together we will overcome, grow strong together and our farm will be the biggest and best for miles around. We will be a force to be reckoned with. We will leave this farm to someone else.

I send off for glossy brochures of far-off estates in wild places.

How do you feel about leaving all this? I ask Alex one evening. He has just come off the phone.

My parents have found a place for us to see, he grins. We can leave tomorrow early.

Where is it? I ask, my head spinning.

It's an island off the West Coast of Scotland. The folks are up there in their camper van.

As I pack for the journey I can feel the extraordinariness of things.

One visit to the island is all it takes for our hearts to be captured. It is really that simple. We make an offer, all seated around the big kitchen table sipping tea and sharing cake, and it is accepted with a firm handshake. That's how deals are done up here. A man's word is his honour, and honour is at the top of all lists.

Now we just have to sell the farm! says Alex, sounding a lot more confident than he feels. And it is not just the farm. To keep us sane, as we worked every minute of every hour, Alex bought a yacht with enough room for us to stay in and very big sails. I must confess, I have learned to love the wild spindrift in my face and the freedom of the open sea. Bryn and Cassie are as happy on the ocean as they are on land, and they play along the decks all day, clipped firmly to the rails with karabiners and a length of hemp rope. But this boat is for someone who has time to play, and Alex knows that his next one, the one he will buy for our new life, will need to be a powerful working boat and able to generate an income.

*   *   *

Saying goodbye to the horses will be hard. It is not that they are the only living things around to be loved and looked after, but there is an untameable wildness to horses, an ancient knowing that is wider and deeper and stronger than any human can understand, and I have been touched by them. First, we sell Annie with her foal and the yearling. They are quickly chosen for their breeding and the future inside each one of them, but the two old mares will be tinned food for dogs unless we are very careful.

We give one to the old horseman, as a friend to graze his field and to cheer his old age, and the other, Duchess, we will take with us, wherever we go.

Although I am euphoric with this leaving, there is also a sadness in me. Together, we have taken two-hundred acres of arable land and turned it into a huge venture. A large area of land is worked with the old horse-drawn methods. From planting to harvest time, with help from the old horse-men who found a new lease of life in their retirements, we have it down to a fine art. A working agricultural museum, complete with steam-driven machinery, is open to the public. We have a forge for shoeing horses, a fresh produce shop selling our own vegetables and preserves, a craft shop brimful of local work and a coffee shop that keeps me baking every day. On open days, we can count thousands on our little farm, and I am proud of that – proud of Alex, for it is his vision that brought it all into the daylight; proud of myself, for I took to it, as if it were always within me. Even though this life was new to me, it was already there, some-where deep in my bones, and I can feel the wildness growing inside me as a tree with roots and branches wide enough and high enough to scrape the sky. Even though I don't know the words yet, the melody sings to me like a boy in a cathedral and I know myself in a way I never did when I lived by timetables and directions. Now I wake with the first birds and rest as the sun goes down and there is a rhythm and a sense to my days. Now I know I need to be the blood and guts of a thing, the driver of the bus and never more the passenger. If I walk now, along a pavement, my legs ache from the lack of give. When I move through the town, I am astonished at how people dress, so unlike themselves, how they move along on skyscraper heels, their bodies arched like question marks with a crying in their backs at the end of every day.

We have chosen Scotland, the land of my mother and her forebears, and our family holidays for years, where we tramped through endless glens and up sides of steep mountains with our father in his fore-and-aft, his steel toe capped boots, his pockets full of barley sugars for our ten-minute breaks every hour. Where water tastes like it came from heaven and not the holding tank in the loft; the land of Irn-Bru, Puff Candy and floury breakfast baps. I can already hear the lilt of the pipes across the misty glen as I stir the porridge for breakfast. I watch my Alex stride along a rugged rocky shoreline, his newly washed beard flapping in the breeze. I see our many children running fast and free, their cheeks pink, their feet bare. There are no dangers, no fast roads, no hum of traffic, and there is no crime. My husband smiles at me over a warming nip of peaty malt and I watch the firelight flicker in his eyes. I am his lady love, his sunshine, and he is my broad-backed protector, my knight, my hero.

It will be tough to say goodbye to my parents, to my family, but I am no longer homesick, and my head is dream-filled with possibilities. After all, it's only Scotland, not the Amazon jungle. And besides, leaving all parents behind makes it fair.

Goodbye! I say to my parents.

Goodbye! I say to my in-laws.

My parents hug me tight, their eyes bright with tears and something else – apprehension.

My in-laws tell me they are coming too.

What happened, Alex? Did you not make it clear to them?

He says it is all a big misunderstanding. To myself, I wonder.

His mother knits me a shawl. To keep you warm, she says, as if she knows I have a chill.

We arrive in a blustery October, and, although we don't yet know it, we are heading into the coldest winter on record. If I thought my laundry cave and my chilblains, big as oysters, were the worst that could befall a nice middle-class girl, I was much mistaken. But for now it is still only October and a bit blustery, and we are pioneers, remember.

We stand on the top deck of the rusty old car ferry, hair whipping in the wind, watching seagulls hang over the warmth of the big black funnel, and our two toddlers in matching Norwegian wool. Alex and I are wearing the same pattern. I thought we looked cute in the shop. I check the other passengers for smirks for we now resemble the family Von Trapp crossing the border into our new life. If the wind wasn't whipping the very breath out of my mouth, I would surely burst into song. What I actually do is swing to the rail and throw up.

Seasickness, Alex tells two little upturned faces, pale with concern.

But he is wrong. Somewhere deep in the dark of me, tiny as a pinhead, Jake is beginning.

On the lower deck are all the vehicles. Mine is a big Landrover stacked to the roof with all our worldly goods, over which two hysterical cats leap and yowl as they have done for the last 500 miles.

Give them this pill, says Jock, the vet confidently, handing me two white discs the size of small Frisbees. It'll knock them out for the journey.

Impossible, I reply. I will have to unpeel the cat to get that inside of it.

Crumble it, he says, as if I am a bit stupid. Vets that say such things have obviously never tried it. Animals always know when you have crumbled chemical poison into their food.

I grab one cat, clamp it between my thighs and shove the pill into its maw, knowing it won't be staying there.

First, it yowls, emitting gobbets of white bubbly froth. Next it snaps its jaws tight on my fingers, and I yowl, wrenching my hand away in attempt to shake off the cat which scoots across the lino and bumps into the wall. While I am busy counting fingers, he barfs up a frothy mess of chalky bits and bile. I dive for it, scoop up the mess and try again.

The other cat, hiding beneath the sofa, growls quietly at me, its eyes wide. By the time it is all over and done with, they are both reeling like drunks and I am exhausted, bleeding and late. I push them into the back of the Landrover and into their beds from where they glare at me – or they would, if they could keep their eyeballs under control.

I check the lime-spreader in my rear view.

Lime-spreader? You are joking. Tell me you're joking.

Alex leans over the table on his fists.

I'm not joking, he says. We might need one up there, and I am already pulling the horse-box.

I have never pulled a load, I point out. I have only ever driven as far as my mother's and I did those twenty-three miles in second gear.

You'll be fine, he says; pick it up in no time.

I am hysterical after one short mile. The cats, due to sleep for nine hours, are now wide awake and rigid with fear. They scream at every car that passes and lunge about, falling down between things, head first. I would laugh if I could loosen the clench in my jaws.

I make my next brave decision, pulling into a lay-by on some country lane. I unhook the spreader. Without the load I can move in a straight line, cats permitting. Alex makes a call to a farmer friend. He will collect the lime-spreader another time.

The rest of the journey is long and tense. Everyone drives too fast – except me, much to Alex's frustration.

We are supposed to be in convoy, he says.

At one motorway stop, Alex unlatches the door of the horse-box. Duchess whinnies and blinks back at the sudden sunlight.

What are you doing? I yell, as a stream of cars whizz by my legs. Alex pushes past Duchess' chestnut rump and disappears into the box. He unhooks her lead rope and talks her gently backwards down the ramp.

Letting her out for a walk, he says, only I had already guessed that.

Are you crazy? I indicated the non-stop rush of traffic and almost lose my arm.

She'll be fine, he says and begins to walk her up the skinniest sliver of green between the road and a tangle of scruffy dust-covered trees. I just can't bear to look.

Duchess, however, is delighted to be free, and only mildly concerned by the cars careening past her flanks, as she jiggles about on the bit of grass that now looks like a postage stamp under her huge feet.

Come on girl! clicks Alex, breaking into a trot beside her. And off they go, bouncing along together, inches from certain death. Cars slow, and delighted people peer through windows, stick up their thumbs.

Hours later we arrive at the ferry terminal, breathless, intact and together. Alex is surprisingly relaxed about the lime-spreader. I open the flaps of the horse-box so that Duchess can smell the sea. She whickers at me and my heart melts in those big gentle eyes.

It's not the same sea, I tell her. You'll be seeing this one every day, for it will surround you, surround us all.

As they load us onto the open deck, I look back to the

houses dotted around the bay and peppering the hills that rise from the harbour to the sky.

Tea, lass? asks Alex, pushing a steaming mug into my hand. I see adventure in his eyes, and I know it's in my own.

Where's the island, Dad? Where's the island? The children jig and pull at his sleeves.

Over that way, he says.

And we all turn to look.

8

Tapsalteerie

⌒

The Tapsalteerie estate is now completely ours, Alex's and mine, and my heart is fizzing with excitement. Owning a whole estate sounds so grand, and the name has such a jaunty dance to it. It is probably just as well I don't yet know what it means.

As we slide through the silent village on an autumn evening, I know they all expect us, have talked of nothing else for days, maybe weeks. There is only one estate up this road, after all. It's not quite the reception I had dreamed of, with the pipers and the red carpet. Where I saw all the villagers pulling open their doors and bouncing out, stamping their boots and swishing their tartan skirts to welcome us, curtains twitch and doors are firmly closed against the evening chill. No matter. They're bound to love us eventually. Everyone does.

It's huge this place, spreading itself across over 1,200 acres, six whole miles of it coastline, and the rest flat green parks and rocky hills covered in heather, scrub hazels, rowans too – which, I am told, are good for keeping witches away.

The witches I know would just gather the fruits and boil them up in a jelly pan.

The big house, where we will live, stands tall and granite strong, a distance back from the shore and overlooking a wide lawn and an expanse of green field dotted with the white backs of the sheep, for which we are now responsible. Not that either of us has a clue about sheep. One end of the house has a turret, making it more of a castle than a mere house, and there are three floors, thirteen bedrooms, four bathrooms, huge reception rooms for all the receiving we will be doing, a big front hall, a cellar and an acre of kitchen complete with a four-oven Aga. There is a walk-in larder with a high ceiling, sprigged with big iron hooks for hanging big beasts, and netting on the window to keep the smaller ones out. Fireplaces are in most rooms, and all of them funnel a chill into the empty space. The windows are old and draughty and there is no sign of double-glazing. The frames are pulpy with decay, all the carpets are stained and thin and the kitchen lino curls like a Dead Sea Scroll.

In the absence of any furniture, Alex brings in a couple of rounds of wood from the woodshed. One for him and one for me.

There! he says, with a big grin, and sits himself down. The lino cracks once and then lies quietly down beneath him.

I can hear the children running through the house, along the long landings, up the servants' stairs and down the gentry stairs with the curving walnut banister and ornate newel posts.

Wheeeeeeee! they call to each other, silent when hiding and squealing when discovered, then more running and laughing as they burst into the kitchen for a drink and a biscuit. This is a child's heaven, I can see that. They can be missing for days without ever going outside the thick stone walls.

Vampires! shrieks Cassie, bursting out of the dusty, spidery dark of the wine cellar. I retrieve a fossilised bat from the lumpy stone floor.

Lunch! I say, waving the crispy cadaver under her nose and she is gone shrieking like a banshee back into the depths of the house.

When we first saw Tapsalteerie, it was like walking into a storybook and there were stars in my eyes. It was also the height of summer. Any sense I ever had abandoned me completely as I wandered through the big rooms, stared out at the rising tide and listened to the gulls keening as the fish roll in. I heard the pipes, felt the wild fresh clean wind against my face, and tasted the salt on my tongue. I saw, like the children, places to hide, places to play, and never did I wonder if the fireplaces worked, or where the fuel would come from. I marvelled at the deep old porcelain bath on ornate legs with big brass taps and not once did I think it would take two tanks full of hot water to achieve half-full and tepid. I saw no outside mud moving in, nor bats, slugs, mice or rats. This was heaven for me and I wanted it, even though I had to agree to turn the house into a guesthouse and run the estate cottages as holiday accommodation in the summer months. Alex had already begun his search for a boat to take people out to the little islands to see the puffins, and I would stay home with Bryn, Cassie and the little one now making himself known under my home-made smock. I would answer the door, answer the phone, and answer the questions. I would learn to cook dinners, breakfasts, wait at table, drive the children to school and back again, do the shopping, clean the house, all the usual things women do around the home.

It felt like a dream to me in this magical place, with views way out to the little isles across a wild ocean whose every breath I can breathe, whose songs I can learn, whose dancing can take me high as the geese into a sky that has no stopping.

A few months after that first look, the estate is ours, and our bank account is empty. Not a single bawbee left for Coulter's Candy. That's ok. We don't need anything. We already have it. We have bought ourselves a dream.

The house looks ten times bigger than I remembered and the garden, seen first in full bloom, now looks dank and empty. The wild roses that so caught my eye last time are now tucked in firmly for the winter. Azaleas and rhododendrons are bloomless, and the grass is rank and yellowing and missing its last cut of the summer. The boiler is out and the kitchen cold as ice. We flick light switches, but the light fittings have all been taken and all we can see by torchlight are bare wires sticking out of holes in ceilings and walls. Upstairs, we discover that all the beds have gone too, although we had asked for them to be left for us, as our furniture will not arrive for another week or so. Alex decides we will drive down to the village pub for food and hopefully the loan of some quilts and pillows, and a pot or two for heating water. They offer us free rooms for the night, but we are fine, Alex says, confidently. Full of chips and a warming whisky or two, we bump home to the cold dark castle that is all our own and fall asleep altogether in one room, cuddled up close, our heads full of adventures and dreams like all good pioneers.

In the morning we wake to the birds. The day is cold but fair, and I call the kids to the window to watch the deer nuzzling the grass on the lawn. It is a sight for the gasping, your first deer on your own lawn, so close you could almost touch him. In the flat lands we came from, Nature is kept on a tight leash. She is fenced in and fed chemicals for her own good and timed and planned and organised until she explodes with a powerful and dangerous rage. Here, we can't but listen to her, humbled by her strength and grace.

But for now hot coffee and a resounding breakfast is the order of the day. We must haul timber and chop wood for fires and look around all the estate and the cottages, making lists. And then we can head for the island 'town' to buy lights and pots and food stocks and whatever we will need for this beginning.

9

Bookings and Boilers

It is hard to imagine we will ever be ready for the Easter invasion of tourists. Yet we take bookings. I listen to myself, with growing alarm, describing the beauties of the property, ignoring the dodgy roof and the areas of mouldy damp – and that's just the big house. There are seven holiday cottages to turn around as well – and by turn around, I mean the full 360°. When I wax lyrical about the master bedroom in the big house, I have to look away from the creeping mould on the walls and the window held in place with a broom-handle, hoping the disbelief doesn't come through in my voice. I also cannot look Alex in the eye as I paint my imagery and spin my spin. The fact that he knows it's all bullshit too is no help at all. It feels doubly bad.

Is the bedside table in between the twins or is there one for each bed? quavers an elderly voice down the wires.

I look around the room at the stains on the carpet. The wet patch on the wall is coming back and the window glass is rattling. There is no other furniture and the wires still stick out through the ghastly wallpaper like insect feelers.

Yes, I say.

Which? she asks.

All of it! I say with a flourish, although I have forgotten the question.

Three bedside tables, then?

Yes, three, I tell her.

Bryn comes in with a dead mouse in his hand and lays it carefully on the bed.

I'd like to book in August! The voice yanks me back.

Lovely, I say. And Bryn beams with delight.

I lower the stinking mouse gently into my apron pocket, and we all go downstairs to book Mrs Thing in for August.

Don't worry lass, Alex says. We'll be ready in time. It'll be fine.

For Alex, it will always be fine. He chose me, after all, and I am always thorough in any task I undertake.

Bloody-minded, more like! he tells me. But he knows I will never stop till this is done, no matter how much I might want to.

Each cottage has its own personality, its own place on the estate, purpose-built for the workers and their families. The gardener's cottage stands above what was once a lovely walled garden with fruit trees and unusual shrubs and flowers. Now it is a tangle of overgrowth, but it still has a certain beauty to it, or we decide it does, for we have no time to devote to reclaiming its salad days. There is a cottage on the shore, for the fisherman, one in the woods for the gamekeeper, and two at the farmsteadings, a series of barns incorporating a byre for the milk cow, two haylofts, a dip tank for the sheep and a harness room. One modern wooden house, looking just like a Swiss cuckoo clock, stands at the tip of an inlet. This one is the largest and the one in the best condition, so we begin with the others. Every day, as the temperature begins to fall, we spend chilly days scraping what looks like linguine off the windowsills, pull fungus from between the cracks in the kitchen lino and lay poison for the vermin. Alex fills in miles of pot-holes in the tracks so that our potential guests don't disappear down one of them forever, and we cut and drag and burn and clear rhododendrons, ivy and hazel scrub, all threatening to move indoors. There is furniture in all the places, but a lot of it is wonky and some of the mattresses are damp and stained. There are walls and doors to paint, fireplaces to repair, water systems to make fast to their precarious moorings in lofts and a serious attack required on the rodent population. There are curtains to make, rats and bats to remove from cisterns, carpets to patch or replace, chairs to recover and repair and on and on into weeks, into the cold, into despair and out again. It feels like everything is almost dead and we are the only ones with training in CPR, and still the winter wages its war on us, freezing our fingers, choking the breath in our throats, doing everything it can to bring us down.

All through this, the children fly free as in a storybook, climbing trees and building dams across the burns, or leaning into the wind until they tumble to the ground in a laughter of limbs. Their lips are mostly blue, their fingers freeze, their wellies fill with icy water, and they fall into bed every night to sleep soundly till the new day dawns, while Alex and I sit under a mound of blankets beside the Aga.

Are we mad? he asks me one night, when the radio play had ended. It was about a family surviving a nuclear bomb. I had found myself relating to more of it than I would like.

Of course! I say, just as he expects me too. If I stopped to ask myself what I really think, we could be in big trouble.

I try a smile, and the crack in my lips tears open.

The three furniture lorries arrive from the South a good ten days after we do, by which time Alex and I are tired of sleeping on the floor and ready to be re-acquainted with old friends. Their journey is fraught with difficulties, the first of which is that the vehicles are too high to fit onto the new ferry with a roof, which is exactly as Alex warned them. They drive around to the smaller open ferry, a distance of 80 miles, and find they are too long for it. All this time our four freezers full of meat and vegetables from the farm are gently thawing out, but by now the lorry drivers are too fed up to care. Three days later they bump up the drive, white-faced and wide-eyed as if they have just arrived on the moon. With bad grace, they confound me, rushing each piece of furniture at me so fast, I cannot keep up with directions. We find the grandfather clock in the bathroom and the bookcases in the cellar. Much of the veneers are damaged, but we have little energy left for a fight. Alex has to cart the now stinking contents of the freezers down to the sea for the crabs to eat, but first we must remove each piece of meat, each measure of peas, or beans, sprouts and leeks, fruit for jamming, soups and stews, from their polythene bags. I will never need to buy polythene bags again.

We manhandle the empty freezers against the back wall of the garage.

One night, exhausted and a little despondent, we share a bar meal at the pub. As the beer hits the spot, we find ourselves smiling. At least we are here, and the heavy work on the cottages is all done, bar the cosmetics. Now we can begin on the big house.

By this time the in-laws have moved to the island and, although I never thought I would admit it, are proving to be an essential part of this renovation, if we can really call it that, for there is more repair than renew going on as we have little or no spare cash.

Granny-at-the-Gate, as she is now known, works like a Trojan, arriving each morning with her thermos of coffee, her feet in snow boots and the rest of her swaddled in as many layers as she can apply without losing her balance. She spends hours scraping off mould and muck and chipping old clinker off dog grates and stoves, and polishing them till they gleam with promise, although no one is sure if they will provide any warmth. She makes new curtains, tablecloths, napkins for the guests and chair covers for the old armchairs. Her dedication to our future is what keeps me going when all I want to do is cancel it. Granddad does his bit too, amusing one child at a time.

I can't cope with more, he says.

I know the feeling, old chap.

The grandparents' own house at the gate is a mile away at

the end or the beginning of the rough track to the big house. We have to drive past it whenever we go out or come in, and it seems to me that Granny always has her eyes on the window. She has written out a big sign saying STOP! and if I pretend I don't see and sail on by, to begin the bumping, gear-wrenching climb up the track to the big house, then there is all hell to pay.

I had some rock buns for you! she snaps. Silly girl, always in too much of a rush!

I swallow the unfairness of her remark, but I say nothing. There would be no point. Granny says what she feels, after all, and it's not up for discussion. I am roundly ticked off over the phone, and then again when the family get to hear of my thoughtlessness.

The second floor of the house will be for the guests in the summer. The rooms are big, with wonderful sea views and a bathroom each. The ceilings are high and corniced and the fireplaces wide as caves. We dare not light a fire inside them, as heaven knows when the last one burned in any of these grates. We hide the carpet stains with carefully placed rugs, and paint everything that doesn't move. We travel to the mainland to buy light fittings for all the dangling wires and Granny makes endless lampshades in the right colours for the right rooms. The upper floor is where we will live. It's only a two mile hike up the stairs to the rooms that housed all those maids and butlers in the days when maids and butlers were secured for the benefit of the gentry. I am sure we will love it, although forgetting a thing and having to go back upstairs for it is not something I want to do too often.

Our leg muscles grow strong and I write lists. One for upstairs and one for downstairs, There are no rugs left for our quarters, and little furniture, but we don't need much, and besides, the only person who puts anything away is me. Everyone else just drops things, leaving drawers and cupboards for the spiders. There is a little bathroom up there too, although it takes forever to suck up the hot water. None of the radiators work, which is not surprising at this altitude. It's hard enough just to breathe.

We should bleed them, Alex, I say, meaning he should, as I have no idea what I am talking about.

Put on another jumper, he says.

If I put on another jumper, I will not be able to bend my arms, I say, bending my arms with some difficulty.

His conscience gets the better of him one day. I think it was my red nose that did it.

The radiators are beyond repair, he tells me. We need a whole new system.

It's not even a conversation for Alex.

In the kitchen the Aga thrums merrily, pumping out heat and goodly things like bread and stews and warming soups. I even manage cakes and buns now and again, although it seems that with an Aga cooking is an uneven process, so nothing browns uniformly. A cake can look quite artistic. One side is for us, the other for the birds, and the birds will need to take care not to blunt their beaks. Notwithstanding this quirk, I become good friends with this Aga. The one down south was solid fuel and a moody creature. Oil is dependable and much more expensive, although that small point is not yet important to me. However, it bothers Alex a lot, for this Aga does nothing but the cooking. The water is heated by a smart looking oil-fired boiler in the washroom next door, a boiler that fires up on time every day and roars like a lion till the water in the big tanks rises to hot. I love the boiler, for its clean work, its dependability, and that reassuring click just before take-off.

We have to turn the boiler off, Alex says one morning, as he peers at a load of figures on a notepad.

I feel I have just been punched in the gut.

You can't do that! I protest pointlessly.

I can, he says. It costs a fortune to run. We can look into an alternative once we have made some money. You know there is none to spare now.

He swings into the washroom and flicks up the switch.

He comes back, puts his hands on my shoulders. I have to make things work for the family, he tells me, and drops a kiss on my mouth, as if that makes it all okay.

I hear my own sob in the terrible silence of the moment, but, by the time it has travelled up into my mouth, Alex is out and heading for the hill.

10

The Stock Valuation

‿‿

It is the custom when buying a hill farm on the West Coast to purchase the stock separately. A few weeks after we settle in, and find our way around the coastline and the miles of plumbing, the stock valuation takes place. It seems that this is how things are done on the island. The new owner agrees to take over the resident animals, having had a wee look at them first, of course. There is a shaking of hands to seal the deal and at some point after taking over the estate, an official comes in to value each beast for the new owners. The delay is never explained, for it is not for the likes of us to know. On the West Coast there are clocks, and there is, indeed, such a concept as Time, but it is relative, and not to anything I have known before in England. 'Tomorrow' could be any number of tomorrows depending on where you are when you say it. 'Later' could turn up in six months and please don't expect an explanation, never mind an apology.

For the valuation we must gather in all the livestock, including John the Bull and Shaggy Maggie the Highland Coo, who hasn't been seen for months now. The Valuer will check every one of them for defects, ailments, good points and bad, assessing each one and expecting the buyer to agree. His word, after all, is final, and the only word to be had around these parts.

We enlist help from the other crofters and farmers for the day, having brought the cows down from the hill and into the fields around the steadings. The vet is also required to be there for any medical queries and also because he enjoys a good day out with the lads. He can lean against the wall, puffing on his pipe, while the 'boys' heave, lift, flip and crog the two-hundred-odd Cheviot sheep. They will all be covered in green slime by the day's end. In anticipation, they arrive in waterproof leggings, their jackets tied with orange binder twine around their waists.

We all gather at 9.30 sharp. Me, Alex and ten men.

Be there first thing! the Valuer had chirped down the phone.

First thing is different up here, it seems. Something to do with ferry timetables.

It is now half ten.

He'll have stopped off to visit, says one crofter, hawking. The gobbet lands between his feet.

Or the pub! chuckles another, his dark woolly hat pulled down over his ears.

I grin. Even I know the pub doesn't open till eleven.

Eventually he rolls up, a dapper middle-aged man in a porkpie hat and a loudly checked squire's jacket with leather patching on the elbows. His cravat is a bright buttery yellow. I think he looks like the Mad Hatter. All the crofters welcome him with manly back slaps and honks of laughter and sly remarks about his timing, for they know him of old. Anytime there is any valuation, he and they will come together just like this. He is also the local auctioneer at the stock market on the mainland, and they will all be dependent on the swing and crack of his hammer.

As I look upon this country scene, I feel very much an outsider, vulnerable to any manner of skulduggery. I wonder if Alex does too.

We'll start with the hogs, announces the Valuer, spinning on his shiny heel and making sure he steers well clear of the shit. His clipboard is tucked firmly underneath his arm. A few of the ten good men and true scuttle after him.

Hogs? I wonder to myself, but I don't say anything. My voice would sound silly, squeaky, among all this manly grunting. I wait for the hogs to enter stage right.

Ah! Virgins! It is the year-old female lambs, not yet mothers, who are hogs, an ugly name for such pretty creatures, white, still, and quite clean looking. Next year they will be gimmers, another daft name if I ever heard one.

To begin with, the process is quite straightforward. One man grabs a beast, crogs her, tipping her up to expose her belly so that her legs stick straight up from each corner. She now looks like the blueprint for a set of Highland bagpipes. Teeth, tits, eyes, ears, legs, feet and privates are poked at and tweaked whilst she silently endures each indignity.

Twenty pounds! barks the Mad Hatter and the little sheep is flipped upright and booted back out into the world.

Just before the gimmers make their debut, out comes the whisky bottle. I can see my mother, back in the civilised world, looking at her watch and tutting quietly. This is the first of many this day and by the end of it I am amazed that anyone can still speak, let alone remain upstanding. The Valuer makes more and more of his decisions from where he leans against the cleanest bit of wall, while the others, including the animals, get filthier, smellier and wetter, as they slip and slide about in the muck and the piss.

Sheep are not attractive creatures, never really clean and very, very stupid. Some of the older ewes are very heavy with twins and their bellies are swollen and tight. These girls move carefully, their slow eyes taking in the bustle and swirl of the big barn. They are not flipped like the virgins, but respectfully tipped backwards against a manly chest as though into an armchair. I rub their heads as they trundle past.

You look tired, I tell them. I know how you feel. Only I hope mine is just the one.

When it comes to the cows, there is no talk of crogging. Flipping Big John on his back would require two cranes and a paratrooper regiment, and the cows themselves are of the wild variety. There is no Daisy Moo in this herd, with her gentle cud-chewing personality and a fondness for Old Mrs Brown's cherry cakes. These cows are fast and bad-tempered, growling and mean. The black curls and the big eyes are a hoodwink, in my opinion. A couple of bonks with that solid head and a trample or two and you'd be down in the bog never to be seen again. The talk would be that you ran off with a dark stranger and didn't they always know you would?

Big John is first into the crush, a narrow walkway of steel piping with a gate at the end. John pushes his head through the gate and someone drops the lever that secures him fast by the neck. He might pull a bit, but John is a peaceful fellow, although his size is pretty scary at such close quarters. His shoulders are broad and strong, his head as big as a coffee table and his balls are massive. I have never seen anything so huge attached to any living creature. They could feed my family for a week with a nice onion gravy and some root veg. As if he hears my thoughts, he fixes his beady eyes upon me and roars loudly, clanging his nose ring against the bars of the crush.

He fancies you, lass! yells one crofter, tipsy and winking, his nose pulsing scarlet.

As the whisky disappears, so does the day, and finally the valuation is completed. Someone has already walked out with dogs and whistles to take the sheep back to their hill grazing, and the cows are on their way. John, quiet peaceable John, decided he didn't want to stand around in the yard waiting for release, so he hopped over the five-barred gate, which is now a three-barred gate, and trotted away up the hill. We never did find Shaggy Maggie.

*　　*　　*

When the final bill arrives through the door, Alex has a fit, and pays up. To disagree at this point would be to start all over again, which would be too much to face. Besides, we know it was a conspiracy. Everything is a conspiracy when you are English, an incomer, a white settler and, worse, the new owner of an estate.

We can do this; I know we can. We can learn to laugh at ourselves, as they do so readily, because we must look funny to them. A young couple, clueless about pretty much everything they are planning to take on, and buying all that land, all that property. Of course we look like the filthy rich, and no amount of in-depth, serious persuading will change their minds one tiny jot.

Alex does keep telling everyone he has links with Scotland and is therefore one of them, which goes some way towards a cautious friendship with the local drinkers, but Scotland is beside itself with nationalism, its history blackened by greedy English bastards, and all of us from south of Coldstream are to blame.

I understand enough about this place already to know that they will decide what and who we are, not us. They will tease and wind up and kid on and drive you crazy if you let it get to you, I tell Alex. These are West Coasters. Just let them do it. It will be much more peaceful that way. Let them think what they like.

But Alex cannot do this. He knows who he is and he will make sure they do too.

His visits to the pub, although infrequent, are always interesting. When I go, there are winks and nudges and extramarital suggestions. Sometimes the nonsense of this can remind me that I am a woman, and of the joy there is in being one, and the smile in it all as well as the grind. When they see Alex coming, they swing around on their bar stools, take a deep breath, and turn their minds to mischief.

11

Different Languages

~

I know it's not good to bottle things up inside. I know what it leads to, because I am there already.

I call my parents. My father's voice sounds like home.

Hallo Dad, how are you?

He tells me of the garden, of the early bulbs chitting, the frost on the spider webs, the new delivery of wood.

I want to say, I miss you Dad, but I don't; I can't. I made my bed, didn't I?

Later I try to explain how I feel to Alex.

Being too busy to give any real time to a relationship is like not watering a potato crop, I say to him, using his own language. If I explain how I feel in my own, the wires in his brain twist and knot and he just has to dash out for air. I have a few short moments to get the words right, using the right tone of voice and picking the right moment.

You can just imagine how often that happens.

I wouldn't NOT water a potato crop, he replies and looks at me as if I am short on marbles.

When he has left, I do what I always do. I stare out the window and pretend I can fly.

Gradually there grows a sort of rhythm to things. Since the dismissal of the boiler, Thursday is now officially washday, whereas before any old day could be washday, depending on the level of demand elsewhere.

If, for example, a cow needs bringing in from way out on the hill, or some sheep need moving, or if the electrician suddenly turns up after weeks of wheedling by telephone, then that urgent and immediate job automatically takes the day, claims it as its own.

But Thursday now has an importance it never had before. For on Thursdays the boiler is lit – for a few precious hours at least – and thus Wednesday night is vibrant with a wild anticipation. I could get quite merry of a Wednesday night, if I wasn't so pregnant and so terribly cold.

Come Thursday morning, I am already drunk with anticipation. I am up early and flipping that switch with a flourish and loving the click, the pause and then the roar of the beast pulsing into life. I picture my pregnant bulk wallowing in a whole bath full of hot scented water. Today I can bathe the children, wash their hair, their clothes, my hair, the house. Oh the wonder of it!

I prefer to forget that the tank takes two hours to fill, and that even on a Thursday I have to ration the warm water as scrupulously as a quartermaster.

But I can do this. I set two big preserving pans of water

80

onto the Aga, which – thankfully – is allowed to remain alight, and lug steaming buckets upstairs. I wash jeans and coloureds on cold and dunk the children in the big scullery sinks, which is where they are dunked every other night so they suspect nothing.

At five, there is a knocking at the door. Someone wants to come in.

Alex scuttles out of the room. He doesn't do visitors. And nor, on a Thursday at five, do I. Not when I've just run the bath I've been waiting for all week.

Bugger off! I say, as I open the door, but my mouth says, Hallo! Come in!

Traitor.

I offer them tea and cake, which is why they have come anyway. While the visitors talk twaddle over my jam and scones, I almost explode with frustration at every cooling second that passes.

Much later, as I stamp upstairs to bed, after a short and unpleasantly tepid scrub down, I am feeling very sorry for myself. To add to my misery, Alex has managed to avoid his weekly wash, as the water was cold – my fault for making people so welcome. It will now be another week of not washing, and sleeping inches from my nose, a point that only seems to bother me. I pull on my night layers and settle beneath our 75-tog duvet, filled with ducks, geese, hens and any other feathered creature I could persuade in, and turn the pages of my book with gloved fingers.

My feet are bloodless and frozen even inside my football socks and my knees are purple and yellow in equal parts. My nose is red, and my bottom is the entire colour wheel. I know this, as I just saw it in the bathroom mirror, when I wrenched down my sensible drawers with all possible speed in a bid to be naked for the shortest possible time. There it spread, like a mountain range, vast and pocked as orange peel. I was horribly shocked. The last time I saw it, it looked pert and racy in small frilly pants. It also sat in quite a different geographical location, and looked, well, eye catching, as I moved along. Now it's just a soft landing.

Do you think I'm beautiful? I ask Alex, who is reading a science-fiction magazine.

No, he says, not beautiful. Pretty, yes. Come here.

He tells me I am his world; that he loves me so much. I have left my life, my family, to join his. I support him in all his plans. I am cook, cleaner, nurse, mentor, secretary, mother and wife. I should feel wonderful, being all these things, people tell me so. But I don't feel wonderful at all. I feel sad and cold, tired and dejected.

Slow down! says Alex as I hurtle round the kitchen units and bash my hip on the corner of the heavy kitchen table.

I weep. It's only a bump, but I weep.

I call my mother and she growls. I know she aches for me, but it doesn't help blaming Alex. I wasn't forced here, I tell her, I chose to come. But the space between my decision and what is happening now is a whole country, and neither she nor I speak the language.

The house is draughty as a colander; all the windows rattle in their frames like loose teeth, despite the wooden wedges and duct tape. Cold winds lift the carpets as they whistle through the fabric of a house whose ceilings are as high as tightropes in the big top. There are holes in skirtings, in floorboards and even in windowpanes. It is a battle already lost to retain any warmth within its walls. We block keyholes with newspaper and stuff old clothes under doors; we stuff up all unused chimneys and board them over. We seal off doors, then whole areas of the house, leaving the resident wildlife to freeze without hope of escape. We hang heavy drapes across corridors and around stairwells. Polythene covers every window, not many of which would open anyway without falling into the garden.

And the temperature drops further. The wine in the cellar freezes. The water inside the lavatory bowls freezes and the kids have pissing matches every morning. Cassie invariably wins.

I hear their chuckles every morning as I stick my nose out from under the bedclothes, and I marvel at their resilience.

When I go downstairs, they will be already tucking into big bowls of cereal, scantily dressed, barefoot and laughing. For them, this is one big game they can play every day, adventure after adventure.

We delay plans to open the hotel the following August, in recognition of Jake's arrival at the end of June. I would rather have had the year off, but Alex says we have to bring in revenue. I am to go over to the mainland for this birthing, as there is a five-year gap since Cassie and time enough, it seems, for all sorts of complications to arise. For now, however, apart from feeling tired and heavy and wondering how on earth I will cope with a hotel and a new baby, I am as fit as a flea. Besides, August is as far away as it is possible to be, or so I kid myself. We don't even have a snowdrop through the ground yet and pissing competitions still herald the start of each new day. Each evening we sit by the Aga and listen to music on the radio, or read, and share snippets of our day, while the old stable clock tick-tocks on the wall and the dogs snore in their beds. Way up high, the children sleep peacefully – at least, I presume so. They could, in fact, be hosting the Oscars up there and we wouldn't hear a thing.

The violin begins. A concerto – Mendelssohn, I think. I just know it gives me goose bumps, whoever wrote it. The wine is warming and the glass sparkles as I tip it to the light. I draw up my legs against the floor draught and tuck the blanket around them. Across the kitchen, in his old rocker, Alex is reading up on bees. There are a million things I want to say, to talk through, as I imagine other couples do, things they disagree on perhaps, important issues in a shared life, but I don't know how to begin. We are only on safe ground when we stick to ordinary things.

Wood cutting tomorrow! says Alex. Good forecast too!

He lights a smoke and puffs contentedly.

My eyes watch him.

I am not broken, they say. Not yet.

12

Fly and Callie

⌒

Fly is our first collie and we most certainly need her. Sheep won't come when you whistle. What they will do is swing round in a communal panic and run until the land stops, which could be four estates over, and no one will offer to bring them back for you. It's just going to be you blundering through treacherous bogs, facing dangers unknown in the swirling mist, and all your wiles no match for the unbelievable stupidity of the woolly-jumper-carriers. If one turns left, they all turn left – even if there is no left.

But with a good dog you stand a chance.

Fly is five years old and a dog from the Borders. She is no longer any use for the high hills of home, which makes her perfect for the gentle roll of our couple of island hummocks.

At least we think that was what her former owner was trying to tell us. Border folk speak in tongues.

Her name's Fly, says the leathery faced farmer who could be a hundred and fifty and is probably forty-five.

Whit like's thon hill?

Alex's face is a blank.

Bitch's only fit for 'in-by' now.

Lighter by £300, we load a bemused liver and white collie with eyes of chocolate into the back of the Landrover and head back up north. It is clear from very early on that Fly has absolutely no clue what her friffly well-spoken English master is saying to her. She hunkers down and stares up at him, her eyes bright and keen, just waiting for some sense to dawn, while Alex sputters and whistles and beeps and squeaks at her, as he was taught to do in the Borders.

One day they set off together, Alex tooting and Fly slinking along at his heels, watching his face, which is quite pink with exertion, to look for a heft of sheep, missing from the shore for some days now. There have been recent reports of sheep being lifted by men in boats, never to be seen again, and Alex is worried. No farmer can afford to lose any of his stock, when they represent a substantial part of his income. As I watch them head up the hill, I see Fly falter, turn and head down towards the shore. Alex, pacing along in his own world, hasn't noticed.

Oops.

Half an hour later, the laird is back, but there is no sign of Fly.

Bloody waste of money, that dog, grumps Alex into his coffee.

Some time later, when he has gone about some other business, and I am kneading enough dough for the next two days, I see some sheep teeter around the corner coming up from the shore. They blink like idiots and rush forward in sudden spurts.

There is a dog at their backs and no mistake. Sure enough, with her belly almost on the ground and her eyes watching for any escape attempts, Fly appears, gently guiding the little group up to the house and into the yard, where she holds them in a corner resting her face on her paws.

I think I'll listen to her from now on, says Alex.

That first February, the weather is appalling. Driving sleet and bitter winds rage on day after day and we stay indoors as much as possible. This is calving weather, dire and spiteful. Blizzards and high-velocity winds careen across the hills and bend the trees into bizarre shapes like old women with curvature of the spine. Angry waves lash the rocks along the shores, throwing up mountains of freezing spume, and the waiting grass cowers, still in the dark safety of the brittle ground. Only gulls fly and all the rest of God's creatures are either dead, hibernating or indoors. But out there on the hill, in the teeth of all this punishment, the cows are calving. Every morning Alex must take food to the herd and check the newborns and their mothers.

There's a calf missing, I'm sure of it, Alex tells me one breakfast. That young heifer shows all signs of having calved, but there is no calf to be seen.

He pats Fly on her soft head.

You and me'll need to find her today lass, he says softly and she shuffles her bum nearer so she can put her nose in his lap. They may not understand what each other say, but there is no doubting there's already a bond between them.

They are gone all morning and the weather never softens one tiny bit. I am beginning to wonder if the glass in the kitchen windows can take much more of a battering. I manage to save Alex some lunch from small grabbing hands, but it is not till almost 3 o'clock that the little red tractor bumps around the corner and into view. There is something flat and dark on the trailer bed. I hope it's not the calf. A calf is money to the farmer and every one counts.

Call the vet, says Alex. Ask him what to do with a seriously hypothermic calf. There's no milk on the mother, so she'll be a pet. Fly found her curled up in a tangle of bracken and briars, hidden there by the mother.

Fly wags her sodden muddy tail. Poor love, she must be starving. Alex feeds her and rubs her dry while I call the vet.

Run a big deep bath, says the vet, and immerse the calf in it. Keep the temperature steady.

How long for? I ask, but I know it's a stupid question.

As long as it takes, he says, patiently.

Ok, I say, stepping smartly up to the mark.

Alex has to light the boiler now, even though it is nowhere near Thursday, and for just a second I wonder about staying out all night myself, in my jim-jams, curled up in a briar patch. As the water heats and the boiler roars, Alex rubs at the calf with barley straw to encourage the blood to thaw and begin moving.

When the water is hot enough, we lift the calf, now hardly moving at all, and as cold as ice, and gently lower her into the big guest bath with brass fittings and white tiles and surrounded by a light blue carpet. The water immediately turns black with mud and blood. We take it in turns to hold up her head so she doesn't drown, while the other boils kettles and tops up the warmth. Aching hours later, the calf opens her eyes and watches us watching her. Her heartbeat is steadier now, and she is no longer gasping scratchy breaths as if her throat were an open wound. The inside of her frozen mouth now feels warm. We lift her, wrapped in a load of the biggest guest towels and carry her downstairs to where Alex has constructed a square of hay bales in front of the Aga. He fixes a warming lamp to the back of a chair and directs it into the centre of the nest. We fill a plastic lemonade bottle with high-energy powdered calf milk and affix the teat to the neck.

Open wide!

No thanks.

For three long days and nights we force milk down a resisting throat as the calf fights us all the way, jerking away her head, refusing to swallow. Sticky yellow milk is every-where and we all smell of it. It seems to be an impossible task, and as we lose hope, the calf looks like she is losing what little she ever had of a life on this earth.

On day four, she suddenly gets the message and takes her first weak suck and swallow. Gradually she grows a little stronger and takes a bit more each time we feed, which is every four hours, day or night. We can hardly speak for exhaustion and it takes all my strength to keep hold of the bottle as the life flows back into the limbs of the little black calf. She is strong now, and hungry, and if I don't pay atten-tion and hold tight to my end of the bottle, the whole thing might disappear down her throat.

All this time the family still need to eat, and I must become a gymnast. I must bend like a paperclip over the calf, with pots of this and pans of that, in order to produce the stews and soups and the endless loaves of bread for a hungry world, but I do have to watch my centre of gravity. A little too far over and I would never get back again. Sometimes, the calf thinks it is feed time and lifts her head up to butt at my swelling chest. I smile, although unlike a human baby, this one could toss me into the soup cauldron with one loving nudge.

Bryn and Cassie are enchanted with their leggy little pet, who still needs turning every few hours to avoid a twist in her gut, as she has made no attempt to stand.

Perhaps her legs are buggered, Alex says, shaking his head.

No, no! I say, only because the thought of looking after a legless pet for many years to come fills me with horror. She'll walk again, you'll see.

Gradually the calf begins to stand, shakily at first, but at least she is taking some action instead of just letting her long limbs flop and skid about underneath her like four useless sticks. As the spring weather warms the land just a bit, Alex moves the calf out into the barn, and fixes the bales and the light overhead. It takes me a week on my hands and knees to return the Aga forecourt to its original state, and even longer to remember to stand straight over a pot of soup.

We call her Cally, and I have no idea why. She grows daily and is now well on her feet and blaa-ing like a ship arriving in port every time she spots any one of us. She will only stop this interminable racket when someone is playing with her, or feeding her, and the former only happens when the children come home from school. I have no time for play these days, and besides, the thought of Cally cavorting through the guest rooms while I make beds and paint over mould and patch tears makes my head spin. As the new grass peeks through, we move her out into the paddock with the other calves, and it is here where she shows how different she is from her peers; those whose mothers had four legs and big flanks to shelter against, not to mention the right sort of milk.

I wonder, as I look at her, if she shrunk in the bathwater. She was in it for hours, after all. Look at her! She's dumpy and ungainly, all squashed up like a rectangle on legs, chasing the others about like a dog, her tail sticking straight up as a radio aerial. Sometimes she cavorts alone while the other calves bunch together and watch.

They're sniggering at you. I say it under my breath so she doesn't hear. But she is one of those untouched by playground sniggerings. She gallops straight for the group, her little hooves shuddering the ground, and veers away at the very last second, spinning mud into their faces. The sniggerers scatter like leaves in a sudden breeze. When the children call Cally, she alone hurtles across to the gate and blares at them while the other calves stand silent. They take her into her night pen with no rein or halter. These are her siblings. Why would she run away? At weekends she is always loose, following them here and there, watching them build tree houses, or dens, and scrabbling in the mud with them, to see if she can find whatever it is they are looking for. She goes with them on shore walks and picnics and pinches sandwiches from their paper bags, running away with them in her mouth in a game of chase. She attends outdoor birthday parties and startles the living daylights out of visitors with her noisy rush at their car doors.

She's friendly! I call out, as if she were a German Shepherd. Their faces are a picture.

Sometimes, if I am not watching carefully, Cally will come into the kitchen and help herself to a drink from the dog bowl, most of which overflows with the excitement. Then she paws at the water, which flips it completely. Now we have a burn running across the lino. If there is a packet of muesli, or biscuits, or sugar perhaps, left on the side, she will snatch it down and bury her nose in the depths of the bag, emerging with a huge snotty sneeze. Within minutes the kitchen is demolished, the floor streaked with mud, the air full of white dust and the bin toppled over, its contents trampled through and scattered. I find her skidding in the mire on her spillikin legs, snorting and coughing out the sweet, floury gloop, and I chase her out into the garden, where she hightails it across the lawn with a cheeky blaa. There is a yoghurt top stuck to one hoof.

A bit close, I warn her silently, as she bounces over to the bee hives. With sudden jerks, she rebounds backwards as if shot and veers off at great speed in the opposite direction.

Serves you right, I tell her later, as I rub honey into the lumps on her nose.

As she grows, we must distance ourselves from her, moving her out onto the hill with the others. When we walk by, she always looks over and there is a memory in her eyes. It's hard not to run to her, to hug her neck as we did so many times before. Later, when she is loaded with the others for market, we watch in silence as she walks up the ramp and into the darkness. When all the others have been sold, she will be left behind, the runt, a joke, useless for breeding. She will be loaded onto a meat wagon and no one will ever know she was once an honoured guest at birthday parties; a clown who came back from the dead and who entertained us and made us laugh until our sides ached and the tears rolled down our cheeks.

13

Jake

⌢

In July, Jake is born, and he chooses Wimbledon week to make his appearance. He is also ten days late, which is the first and last time Jake is late for anything in his life.

Because I am now an island dweller, and years have passed since I birthed my last child, I must cross the water to the maternity home on a hilltop overlooking the harbour. An old lying-in hospital, it is staffed by old nurses who were young there once and know a thing or two about delivering babies safely into the world. It is not modern, nor equipped with fancy birthing gadgets, but there is a wealth of wisdom and common sense in those starched white uniforms. The humour is raw in such a place, sharp and clever and for the ears of women only. It is a necessary support bandage, for we have all left our dignity at the door as we came in.

I have to go over on my due date, even though the due date is only a guess. Them's the rules. I waddle in on a hot sunny day and am apportioned my bed in a big light room with bay windows and a wide sweep of a view. From here I can watch the ferries and fishing boats go in and out of the harbour and the tiny people wander along the promenade. I can see gulls floating over the quayside and watch them squabble and bicker over abandoned scraps of fish. The nurses are more like mothers – well, mothers in storybooks: bosomy warm women with laugh lines and soothing hands and gentle reassurance. Even the resident doctor is a woman, and there is a grace and a peace about her that puts all of us at ease, for I am not here alone. There is a nervous young first-time mother-to-be, whose nervous young husband arrives early for each visiting. They sit together in a silken silence, holding each other's hands like scared kids on their first day at school. I can hear their occasional soft murmurings across the room. Another inmate is a girl who looks to be around fourteen and far too young for motherdom. Her own mother is her only visitor.

Are you excited about your baby? I ask her, when she introduces me to her mum.

Na, she says. I'm no keeping it.

Her mother is nodding. She has no wedding ring on her hand and I wonder if this is a pattern repeating itself. It will not have been easy for her, bringing up her daughter alone, not if she is poor, which is how it looks to me. I rub my own swollen belly, my own baby who is so very welcome, and will be so very loved by his father and his mother. I smile at them, stuck for words.

Others come and go, arriving in the night, shouting and yelling a lot and grinning like Cheshire cats at breakfast. We reach out feather fingers to touch the soft skin on a new face. We marvel, as we always do, at such a miracle and the beauty of it.

Each day after check-ups, I wander downstairs to the big sitting room, dotted with big old easy chairs. Wimbledon is always on the screen, and nurses pop in for a quick look on their way to and from the wards.

How's the women's doubles? Who won?

What about that Swedish guy? How is he doing?

And off they fly, with a chuckle or a groan, their rubber-soled shoes squeaking for a good few minutes after they disappear.

I am having the best holiday of my life. For the first time since I got married, I am wandering about slowly with the sun warming me and no demands on my time at all. I can go here, if I choose, or there, or neither way at all, and there is no one asking me questions. Where are you going? What for? When will you be back?

It's bliss.

One day, as I am fast becoming part of the furniture here and have developed somewhat of a daily routine, I am on my morning wanderings from bed to bed, after the doctor's rounds. Each woman sits up, in her pretty nightie, bought especially for the hospital, her pillows plumped up like clouds behind her head, her hands folded over the mound of her belly. Someone mentions the trams in Edinburgh and it brings back to me a story my mother told me; a funny story about herself. I get to an amusing part and begin to laugh. The pressure of the laugh causes a rupture and my waters break. At first it just feels like my legs are suddenly warm, and then I realise what is happening. As the puddle spreads beneath me, I get an uncontrollable attack of the giggles. The others join in and someone calls for the nurse.

Will you sit down, she says, steering me by the elbow back down onto my bed, or we will all drown in here! Her eyes are merry with laughter as she turns down the covers.

Where is your plastic sheet? she asks me.

In the cupboard, I tell her, still giggling and pushing out water. With the others.

The others? she queries, her eyebrows disappearing into her fringe.

Six plastic sheets fall out onto her white shoes.

You naughty girl, she tuts, and moves me aside to tuck one quickly under the sheet. I am astonished at this flood coming from me. Must be half a swimming pool across this floor by now.

Well, I tell her, they are buggers to sleep on.

Sleeping, my girl, is out of the question for a while now. You girls, no one to move across this floor or it'll be Armageddon!

And she is whirling out of the door to find mops and buckets and to get the delivery room ready for Jake and me.

It is not an easy birth, and I am not conscious for a lot of it, drugged to the eyeballs and screaming with the pain as if it was my first time. Alex manages to catch a ferry over and goes through it all beside me, his fingers once again numb from my desperate squeezing. I fight it all the way, the birthing, the nurses, the instruments, and the air is thick with expletives. One nurse fans the air as if to shoo them away.

My but the swearing on this girl! says another as she deftly sweeps a sick bowl into place just in time. You wouldn't think to look at her, would you?

Oh how little you know me, ladies.

I had forgotten it all, this birthing thing.

But no matter how much I may scream or thump the nurse or tell her I don't want a baby after all, thanks all the same, it's way too late for that now, way too late for regrets.

You agreed to upstairs-inside, remember, chuckles the thumped midwife.

But even though labour is long and hard, takes far too long and all my remaining energy; even though I am drenched in sweat, drugged and delirious, torn and stretched, once I hear the PUSH! word, I give one last bloodcurdling yell and little Jake shoots out into the world, covered in blood and slime and looking like a tadpole.

Isn't he beautiful?

The rose-tints come with the job. It is Nature's way. Your own baby is a stunner, everyone else's a prune, though you don't tell them, of course.

As I recover and practise night feeds and how to get into a bath without splitting in half, the nervous young mother goes into labour. Two hours later, the young girl follows suit and as I wander into the nursery to feed Jake in the night, I hear the cries and groans and soft murmurings of the nurses in both delivery rooms, and I have a word or two with God.

The next morning I am due to return home and I'm excited as I carefully dress and collect my wash things from the bedside cabinet. The girl is back with her baby, a healthy bouncing girl, although the adoption team will collect her later in the day. She sits high on a rubber ring to ease the pain of the stitches. She is pale and quiet.

Your baby is cute, I tell her, although I don't know why. I know she doesn't want it.

The girl just shrugs and looks blank.

There is no sign of the young married couple.

I see an ambulance arrive at the front door.

New inmate? I ask a passing nurse. She shakes her head, looks grim. I know it's not good. The second labour room is quiet now and the atmosphere in the little hospital downcast and heavy.

I watch the incubator going into the ambulance and the nurses helping the young mum up the steps. I see her husband hold her and the agony in their faces. For a little while the engine ticks over and I wonder why it isn't already gone, speeding down the road to Glasgow where all will be made well again. Then everything stops. It's over. When Alex arrives, we feel awkward and too lucky with our new boy, his strong lungs and his easy hunger. I think of the rejected baby upstairs and how cruel life can be. The young mum looks up as I walk past the open doors, and gives me a little smile.

Such grace.

At home there are no nurses, no trolley-dollies bringing lunch, no help with the lonely night feeds, no women joshing, easing troubles, sharing them. Alex does what he can – more than that – but every morning he has children to take to school and then a day at sea with the passengers. It is full summer now, and the cottages are busy. He has to call for help from the women in the village. As for me, I cannot sit down and wonder if I ever will again. I soak my ripped hindquarters in an hourly bath of Epsom salts. My breasts arrive in the room ten minutes before the rest of me, and they are so heavy that I must take special care when walking downstairs. They have also set like breezeblocks, and if this new baby so much as snuffles in his sleep, their pumps leap into action, soaking all my top layers within seconds, no matter how many breast pads I shove into my massive nursing bra. If I am out somewhere, I can see people's eyes trying not to pop out of their heads.

And then I start to cry, for days and days and days.

Baby blues, dear, says the midwife sensibly, as if I will feel much better just knowing this. It's quite normal. Coochy coo! Such a pretty boy!

Alex looks at me, and the memory of Bryn and the baby blues hovers in the space between us.

It won't happen again, I tell him.

I know, he says, I know it won't. But I do wonder how you will cope.

He looks lost.

Ask me how, Alex, ask me and I will tell you.

But he just keeps looking lost, rubbing my back and finishing with a pat.

He knows I am stretched to my limit. My interior is wrecked and my nights filled with bloodcurdling screams. My feet are puffy, I have piles, backache and loose teeth. I am so tired that there's not a minute in the day where I don't ache to fall asleep in a chair – if I could sit down, that is.

Alex does his very best, and is wonderful with Bryn and Cassie, taking them out on the boat, off on the quad bike to check the lambs, and down to the grandparents for tea and cake. However, around me he is lost, I can tell, and it stops his natural flow. It seems that he knew me once, when I hitched my wagon to his star, and then, somehow, I changed. But don't all women change once we have babies, once the reality of motherhood kicks us in the gut and brings us firmly to the ground?

If he asks me once more how I am feeling, when it is glaringly obvious I am falling apart, it just might be his last question.

I want him to hold me, and yet when he does I push him away. He comes to me with his heart on a platter and I turn my back. He thinks that showing love this way is enough and I know it isn't, although neither of us knows how to put it right.

We are both of us lonely.

14

Granny-at-the-Gate

～

Although Jake is only a few weeks old, and I'm still below par, we must press on with our preparations to open the house as a sort-of hotel in August. The first blow comes when I discover that the food delivery vans will, on absolutely no account, drive up to the back door. I discover this after I have given my first order to the store on the mainland.

When will you deliver? I ask brightly, as if I knew this feeding-guest-thing like a pro.

Depends where ye stay lass! says the man, sucking at his teeth.

I tell him.

He lets his breath go with a whoosh.

Och, no, hen! he gasps. No up there! The boys'll just dump it at the gate! Then he chuckles, as if it's funny.

The boys are old men. There was I picturing two skinny lads with a big truck under their butts, when the truth is a man a bit younger than my dad, with 'Tracy' tattooed up one of his bare arms. He whistles that well-whistled tuneless tune known to all workmen, as he dumps my orders outside Granny's house, box on top of box, and only just off the road, so that all passing vehicles can soak the wobbly tower with puddle water. Gulls enjoy pecking at the block of cheddar as it sweats inside its polythene wrap, and walkers, not yet acquainted with Granny, are not averse to popping the odd strawberry into their mouths as they wander by. By the time I come down on the afternoon school run, there are menu changes to be made.

The strawberries are mush, Mum! Cassie giggles, firing one at Bryn's head and beginning a fight.

Granny is outraged. Don't worry, she says, waggling a limp Cos lettuce at me. I'll sort them out.

The next delivery day, she is watching through the plants in her conservatory. As the lorry screeches to a halt and the driver jumps down to open the back doors, she marches out looking dangerous, tea towel flapping at the air.

Not there, stupid! she yells, as the man lumps down a box of tinned grapefruit onto the yellow backs of the bananas.

But even she cannot always be watching, and no amount of requests to the man with whistling teeth at HQ makes one jot of difference.

I can't be responsible for the drivers, he says, in all seriousness.

Why not? I query. They are your drivers!

Aye lass, but I can't see what they're up to on the island, now can I? I'm no clairvorint!

This time we both chuckle, but not at the same joke.

103

One day, when it's lashing with rain, the driver decides not to leave the boxes in the rain, a decision to be greatly admired and one that shows signs of intelligence, not apparent till now. He slows beyond Granny's gate, and begins to reverse into the rise of her gravel drive. I wish I had been there. No one, not even the Holy Father himself, is allowed to reverse up Granny's gravel. The lorry spins its huge wheels, sending a shower of stones into the air and digging a big hole. This, in turn, causes a small landslide and a large part of the driveway slips down into the road. The driver is about to realise his mistake.

Within seconds, a ferociously indignant midget barrels out of the house and up to the driver's door. She thwacks at the metal with her fists, screeching insults at the bemused driver, who now has a quandary on his hands. Does he get out to be beaten to a pulp by an angry woman, or does he drive back to the depot with all my groceries, thus facing the wrath of the man with whistling teeth?

In the end he waits for her to calm a little, and opens the door gingerly.

He never so much as walks on the gravel ever again.

Once he has been sent packing, Granny calls me on the CB radio, our regular source of contact.

Are you there, over? Her tone is high-pitched, tense.

It takes me ten minutes to cross the kitchen.

Come in Granny, over?

She is quite beside herself with rage.

That stupid idiot has just dumped . . . oh you should see the mess the soft fruits are in, and my driveway . . . honestly, I am raging!

I can tell. The radio is shaking in its wall bracket.

I've got them shut in the garage now, she says.

What, the soft fruits or the stupid idiot?

I sigh. So it won't be Strawberries with Cointreau Cream on the menu tonight after all.

Thanks Granny. I'll be down soon to collect it all.

And thank you for caring so much, I whisper in the silence of my heart. For all your outspoken words that sometimes pierce like swords, you are a wonderful support. You may be small and dangerous, you may tweak my plumbago and reserve the largest cake for Alex; you may tell me things I don't want to hear and knit me jumpers I will never wear, but in the storm that is my life, you are a shelter that can be trusted.

So, its Strawberry Stramash tonight people and you'll love it. Do I have cream?

Of course I have cream. I have Blossom, don't I? Blossom, the dairy cow – an Ayrshire with a huge milk bag and a bemused look in her eyes, as though her life is one big puzzle. Every day she gives us gallons of frothy warm milk from which we get thick yellow cream and farmhouse butter, and we are learning how to milk her as we learn everything else at Tapsalteerie – the hard way. There is one right way to pull on the teats of a cow and ten wrong ways. All the wrong ways lead to a bad-tempered snorting beast with sore teats and one of her mucky hooves in the milk bucket just as soon as she can get her aim straight. It takes much practice with aching hands and dextrous fingers to bring down the liquid ivory.

Alex is the milkmaid, most of the time. He even has a three-legged stool.

What shall we do with all this milk? I ask him, as most of it goes down the drain.

Perhaps we could sell it, Alex says, and he calls the pub to see if they are interested.

They are. Collecting forty-ounce bottles from their optics, we wash them out and fill them with milk, delivering them each morning on the school run. The pub guests watch me deliver the bottles to the kitchen, and smile. This might explain the delicate whisky flavour on their bran flakes that morning. When I stop to collect other children on the way to school, I know their parents sniff the air inside the Landrover. Apart from the usual hum of sheep, dogs and other things we don't investigate too closely, the whiff of whisky so early in the day might well unnerve them. I just grin. They will think what they like, whatever I say.

The milk is warm! marvels one pub guest who has intercepted me on my dash to the kitchens. I must be quick as the engine is running, the kids are loose and they move like greased lightning once a dastardly plan forms in their minds. As she pulls back her hand, I hover just long enough to be polite, my third eye on the Landrover, where someone's leg has just appeared at head level. If the school bag is still clamped to the rest of this child's body, school books and pencils and healthy snacks are now presumably all underfoot.

Yes, straight from the cow, this morning! I tell her. Her little boy peers up at me.

A cow? he says, his face all screwed up.

He thinks it comes from a shop, laughs his mother.

I laugh too. So did she.

When it is time to churn the butter, the big kitchen clears in a twinkling. One minute it is thrumming with life, the next quiet as the grave.

I know it's a boring job, I say into the empty room, all this turning of the paddles, but you are all quite happy to spread the stuff onto your slices of fresh baked bread!

If the weather is sticky and humid, the churning process is cut in half. I make butter balls and float them in iced water, as I used to watch my mother do; only she took her butter from a packet.

The guests marvel at me. Well, I am proving to be rather marvellous by now. I make yoghurt too and rice puddings, crème caramel and other creamy treats that will send you into paradise and put inches on your waist overnight.

New guests arrive this afternoon and I am a little less terrified than at first. Although we are quite new to house guests, we have had good experience catering for visitors and know a thing or two about this and that. I have old Rona working for me in the house, Rona with her wicked sense of humour and her ability to make everything amusing even when I might find it quite impossible. Rona keeps me going, helps me to get over myself. She also knows about all sorts of important things, such as how to lay tables correctly, which is a great relief as I can never remember.

Alex has written the advertising for the house. Apparently we are a private family-run hotel, serving gourmet food, using fresh produce, and with everything home-made in our kitchens.

I pin this description up on the wall to remind me that I am a whole lot grander than I thought. Here I stand, quite alone, in the one and only kitchen, kneading dough or simmering a redcurrant *coulisse*, while Jake gurgles at the ceiling from his Moses basket on the table. Underneath, Bryn and Cassie have built a complex cardboard labyrinth. One of the dogs has been coerced into it and, from the chomping sounds, is being fed something delicious, possibly the hors d'oeuvres. I am glad the guests never get to see this.

Welcome to you both! Colonel Henderson, Mrs Henderson.

They look shaken. Mrs Henderson's tam-o'-shanter is sliding over her brow. I am not fazed by their faces. All guests arrive looking shaken.

Good journey? I ask, my head on one side like a robin.

Well, apart from that track. The Colonel wafts a hand over his shoulder.

Mrs H is standing with her mouth open.

I know. I give them my biggest smile. Isn't it wonderful and wild? So rustic and so . . . different! Some people never leave the tarmac, and look at you two intrepid adventurers!

This nearly always works.

By now the Hendersons are puzzled, the beginnings of a grin pulling at their mouths, and they obviously think I am amazing, for their eyes never leave my face. And they are loving the waft of baking I brought with me into the front hall. I guide them into the big drawing room where I have already placed a welcome tray with pretty teacups, matching plates and a pile of warm scones. The tea is made with leaves and fresh spring water and is all ready to pour.

How do I know when to boil the kettle? Am I psychic? No indeed; it is the Granny-at the-Gate who tells me.

Are you there, over?

Hallo Granny-at-the-Gate.

They're on their way. Stuffy pair of old trouts by the looks of it. You should see her hat! Good luck!

I cringe, and look towards the kitchen door. Of course, they can't hear, they are still on their way, but I have the uncomfortable feeling that one day, the subject of Granny's careless comments will be standing right beside me and we will both be at least ten paces away from the volume knob.

But this time, they don't hear. And by dinner time, after spending a pleasant hour or two in their grand bedroom in the turret with panoramic views and an en suite bathroom, they are in love with the track – pot-holes and all. Although for the life of them they can't say why.

I bring the same wing-and-a-prayer attitude to my cooking life, learning and developing skills as each new situation arises. I came into this marriage able to bake a Victoria sponge and fairy cakes, and nothing else, so it has all been learned on the run. Now I face a daily changing menu of three courses for up to sixteen people at a sitting. Either I become proficient and quickly, or I poison folk in large numbers. It's not as if there is anywhere else to go, apart from the pub serving high teas up to 7 o'clock. There are places in the town, but it's a long old drive, and besides, two trips over the pot-holes are enough for anyone to have to face.

Everything that can be home-made is home-made, just as it was in the flatlands coffee shop, from the mayonnaise to the preserves, from pâtés to breads, from shortbread to puddings, from soups to sauces. We serve fresh fish, shellfish, venison, beef and lamb – not all of it from the estate, but all of it from the island. We pride ourselves on all this home produce, although sometimes, when I am pricked to bleeding by wild brambles, or tired of hiking up hill and down dale in search of wild rhubarb, red currants or crimson sea gooseberries, my pride flops a bit. By the seat of our pants, we convince people we have done all this for years. It's in the blood, this island hotel lark. By painting over the cracks in walls or in pastry cases, we show them we are pros. We have learned how to bring old furniture back to life with beeswax and aching elbows. We have learned what flowers to pick and how to arrange them. We have worked out what wood burns best in the grate and we can fold napkins into any shape you want. We can feed vegans, skin deer and make butter. And best of all, we can change direction at the first shift of the wind and take full advantage of a new course, filling our sails and racing into the wild with a whoop and a cry, while the rest of the world is wondering what happened.

We are building a dream that others can share, but it isn't their dream, it's ours, and I know exactly why.

No one else in their right mind would ever take this on.

15

Alpha Beta and the Whale

~~

After much searching, Alex at last finds his work boat, in which he can run trips to the little islands. She is a functional little boat, with room for passengers and a good reliable engine. It isn't out of choice that Alex buys such a craft, but common sense. Everything must work for us up here. There is no time for any frou-frou, and at least he will be able to venture out into the wide open sea, even without a classic wooden yacht beneath his feet and the sails overhead filled with an energetic Southerly. Even a motor boat is better than no boat at all, and he will get the hang of small-talking his passengers.

Fishing Boat For Sale, the advert said, and Alex took off to see her.

Enter Nina.

This little wooden fishing smack has one engine and many leaks. She has come all the way from Shetland, where the weather is unlike anywhere else in the world. The waves are mountainous and the winds can break windows and remove roofs at the drop of a hat. Nina, by definition therefore, must be up for anything. I am not surprised she has sustained a few leaks and one or two loose screws. What girl wouldn't?

Alex collects the boat from the mainland and chugs her slowly back to where he has sunk an old cast-iron stove, full of concrete blocks, into the watery depths of the inlet as a mooring. There is a jaunty orange buoy at the end of a long chain all ready to hold Nina fast as the tide ebbs and flows around her black hull.

Alex paints her up and plugs the leaks with caulking and tar. The little stove is repaired and cleaned, the galley scrubbed of rust and grime, and soon the little boat is shiny and new again and only Alex knows how much paint it took to fill in all the cracks. He brings her over to the old pier and ties her up to two iron rings sunk into the stones.

He is ready for business.

Granny-at-the-Gate has hand-painted signs pointing visitors up to the pier.

Come with us into the magic of the islands! See puffins, basking sharks, gannets diving, sea eagles soaring! Bring waterproofs and lunch. Tea and coffee on board.

And there she is, every morning around 9.30 a.m., flapping her arm seawards and answering questions through rolled-down windows.

Yes, off you go, about two miles, follow the signs! Hurry up, you're late! Here, take this to the boat please!

And a surprised visitor is handed a large tin of shortbread.

Granny sticks her finger under the driver's nose.

No pinching! she warns.

No one dares.

Alex has fitted a CB to the boat, so the three of us are back in the marriage now and each of us can hear everything the others say.

Be careful Granny, I whisper to myself. There would be no point saying it to her, nor to Alex. Neither of them would feel the need.

It takes almost three hours to putter out to the islands as Nina is slow and old. Perhaps it is for the best, as she might just rattle apart were she required to move faster, but it feels interminable to Alex as they slide up one side of every wave and back down the other for miles. The engine belches black smoke and, if the wind luffs round behind them, the visitors standing in the open air all disappear into a dark cloud, to emerge coughing, their eyes streaming. When it rains, a few of them can shelter in the wheelhouse, but only if Alex is in the mood for being squashed into a corner and asked daft questions, the same daft questions every single trip.

Bring waterproofs, we tell everyone, good ones mind. Flimsy see-through fit-in-your-pocket waterproofs are as much good as a man-size tissue out here where the rain blatters your skin and the wind would whip you over the side if your fingers weren't white with holding onto the rails. Caught out in such weather with another two hours of elderly chugging, even when you can see the land, and have been able to for quite some time, toughens up even the most adventurous of travellers.

But it is all worthwhile when they slide under a sky full of nesting seabirds that swoop away from high granite cliffs, dipping into the waves for fish, and rising back into the push of the winds to feed their young. There must be hundreds of nests, balanced on skinny ledges and made of a few sticks and a lot of guano, set solid as concrete and stinking like an old barrel of fish bait. Young chicks lean out, calling for their parents, who know exactly which of the many nests is their own. I never see a parent dithering in front of a line of open-mouthed chicks as I do when looking for my kids in the school playground. No, they fly straight in and straight out and get it right every time. Further along, where the rocks are covered with a luscious green carpet of grass, the puffins build their burrows like rabbits. If we lie quietly down and wait, we will see these comical birds suddenly pop out from a black hole, and blink at the brightness of the day. Leaning forward into the wind, they dive over the cliff and float down into the waves, in search of sand eels. Here is one with a beak full, unsure at first, as we might be too close to his burrow, then landing, and scurrying down into the ground to feed the chicks. Way up high, the gannets, white and gold against the flat sky, fold their wings and dive into the wild waters at a tremendous speed, cutting through the waves like knives. Wild grasses and rare flowers bob their heads in a wind that always blows around these cliffs.

Keep away from the edge, Alex warns the passengers. It is a very long way down and the edges of the cliffs are crumbling; crumbling with the punch and batter of the winds and the grabbing of the waves. The sea never sleeps. She is always plucking at the shore like a fretful old woman worrying at the bobbles on her cardigan.

* * *

Fishermen call.

Do you take fishermen? they ask.

Alex nods. It's cash after all, even if he has no idea about sea fishing. They can teach him. Granny gets another sign-board out.

Sea-fishing trips. Book now!

Alex is nothing if not enterprising, although that's not what others call it.

Barmy! says Granny, baking extra shortbread and making sure she has plenty of flags marked 'Alex'.

What do you fish for? someone asks me on the phone.

Everything, I say, hoping he won't ask me for a list.

Skate? Shark? White fish?

Yep, all of them, I say, remembering the bedside tables.

Got the gear, or do we bring our own?

Oh. Er . . .

I think quickly.

Bring your own if you have it! I say cheerfully.

Ok, that's fine, we will.

As the demand for trips of all types increases, Alex realises he must let Nina go and find a faster, more modern fibre-glass boat, preferably with a younger engine and absolutely no leaks. Nina is sold to a man from an island even further away from civilisation, who will cherish her for his own pleasure. I can almost hear the old girl sigh with relief, as she will no longer be rammed forward at her fullest tilt every single day, come hell or high water. Then Alex finds Alpha Beta, who changes everything.

115

Although a plastic boat makes sense for this business, Alex is not a man of plastic boats. Instead of sanding and rubbing and planing, he only has to wipe off any trouble with a damp rag, repairing scuffs with something from a toothpaste tube. But, on a positive note, there is no winter maintenance, and no personality to get to know – or so Alex thought at first. But Alpha Beta has a very big personality, two big fast engines and a large viewing deck. She can get to the small isles in less than half the time and she can cut right through the waves, creating a splendid wake as she travels. The wheelhouse has an extension to its roof, affording passengers shelter both from the rain and the constant buffeting of the winds, and there are lockers for stowing fishing tackle, creels, buoys and other necessary boat kit. She has a cooker, running water and a flush loo, although the flush part is a bit hit and miss, depending on what ghastlies people imagine can fit down that skinny pipe. 'For Natural Waste Only' says the handwritten sign, but it might as well be in Javanese for all the notice anyone takes of it. Alex is forced to spend hours unblocking the narrow pipes and scouring the floors after floods. Or he gets his crew to do it. But that is later on. For now it is just Alex, every day, all day, out there showing visitors the magic of the islands he is already claiming as 'ours'.

It is on one of the fishing trips that everything changes; from nothing to something in one day; from knowing everything to not knowing anything at all. And there is a thrill and a terror in such a day, a rising of blood pressure, a heightening of the senses and a gasp in the throat.

In the pounding waters off the skerry, with ten fishermen aboard and ten lines down into the boiling soup, with the echo sounder beeping cautionary messages and Alex's eyes locked onto the instruments, and while Nature pushes and pulls at the boat and the wind nudges her ever closer to the razor-sharp edges of the half-hidden rocks, the waters part and a huge black back rises up. A cloud of spray droplets fly into the faces of the men, and, as they watch, the slow body rolls back under the waves and is gone. Aghast, Alex searches the lumpy surface, and sure enough it comes again, rolling over, its back glistening and a gust of salty spray shooting up like steam from a kettle.

This is Whale.

Bring in the lines! he calls to the fishermen, but they will have none of it. This is the best fishing they have had today and they are not stopping for a whale. Pulled back a little from the rocks, the tide has turned and the waters subside enough for Alex to climb onto the short mast for a better look. He is, to be honest, terrified. All he knows of whales is the tale of *Moby Dick* and the old fishermen stories of boats being rammed, of disappearing beneath the waves, of being lured onto the rocks and smashed into match-wood. But this whale is showing no aggressive signs at all; quite the contrary. It spends an hour diving under the boat and up again on the other side. It hangs tail down in the water to watch the fishermen, and it lies alongside the boat quite still, just looking. It flips over on its back to show the white marking of its underbelly, and all the time it never snags a single fishing line, nor touches the hull of the boat. Alex is enchanted. However hard he tries, he cannot close his mouth and his head is spinning. He watches the whale watching him and feels a connection, as though he is chosen by this immense creature, powerful enough to tip this little boat over as a child might with a toy. The gentleness in its eyes is almost tangible, soft and trusting, ancient and wise, and Alex is right, he has been chosen, for some distance away are another two whales. They were travelling together, the three of them, when this one turned towards Alpha Beta and Alex.

While the fishermen josh on, supping beer and laughing at their worldly jokes, Alex is in another place altogether. As the whale swims away, leaving a last puff of rotten cabbagey breath in the air, Alex's mind is working like a beaver under his old woolly hat.

If there are three whales out there, there could be hundreds more. And what sort of whale are they? We know nothing about whales, or types of whale, and nor, it seems, does anyone else on the island. If Alex wants to run trips to see these magnificent creatures in the wild, to let other people experience such a powerful encounter as he has done this day, then he will need to make contact with someone out there who does know. He begins with the marine agencies, one of which sends a biologist to assess the area with a view to educational research on all matters marine, especially whales, dolphins and porpoise.

You'll have to prove there are more than three whales in the area, says the biologist. I suggest you start running whale-watching trips, making no promises. I will supply you with a postgrad student as crew/researcher for the summer, plus a list of the information we will need you to collect and send in for analysis.

And so it begins. The rest of our life on the island starts right here and right now with another sign at the gate.

Come and help us find whales! £5 per day.

Within days, the tourist board are on the line.

We are disgruntled, they say. You cannot hoodwink people this way, with false promises and a disregard for the trade descriptions act.

Oh poof! says Alex and casts off with his first boatload.

And he begins to find them, the whales. He learns how to look for them and how to see their rolling backs even from a great distance away. We learn that it is the minke whale, a small fast-moving baleen whale that doesn't blow clouds of spray into the air, nor lift its tail high as a humpback does, and is therefore much harder to spot in a bumpy grey sea. But Alex is learning a new way to find them, and he calls it the Giz. He develops his skills of reading the sea, the sky and the direction of the wind, the state of the tide, the time of year, the temperature of the sea and the bloom of the plankton just under the surface. He looks for any bird activity, especially in groups over a particular area, but mostly he follows his gut. Alex can find whales when everyone else cannot.

The biologist is convinced Alex is made of the right stuff for this work and between them they put together a programme of benign research which is directly funded by the passengers, who are also required to take part in the work. They take turns to collect data, making notes and above all watching, watching, watching the surface for the break of a big shining back. And, without exception, they love it, this being involved, being a part of something so wild and wonderful – the preservation of the whale.

Here, *you* take this bleeping thing and count the bleeps, and note them here, on the left of the page; and *you*, hold this flapping thing over the side for exactly one minute then pull it in again. Over this side, *you* count the minute wiggling things in this jar of minute wiggling things that we have just hauled from the ocean and then write down the number here on the right.

You, up onto the top deck and don't come down till you see a whale.

And they all nod and bob and count and write and watch and pay for the privilege.

What a day! they say, even if they didn't find a whale. But if they did, they are quiet on the homeward run, lost in their own heads, changed forever.

How can people harpoon such wonderful creatures? they sigh.

Money, grunts Alex. Greed! There is disgust in his voice, contempt, and they nod at him and think how heroic he is, the protector of the whale, the strong wild man of the sea. He learns fast, as he always does, and soon he is known as 'the man who looks after the whales', and his boat is full every day, all day, throughout the season. Students come and stay and work the summer months, until we need more than one, more than two or even three to undertake the fine and complicated research of each day. A software programme is developed to hold and collate all the data collected, and still the visitors keep coming. There are calls from the media, requests for documentaries about our work, requests for comments on whaling, on marine matters, and none of it fazes Alex. He is caught up in the new passion and it is all his thinking. While I grow large with another child and another, Alex seeks out his dream, reeling it in along with all the others. I watch him sparkle and chatter and laugh with his new friends as I make them tea and sandwiches and send them off on another adventure, leaving me with a sudden silence and a table full of washing up.

16

Eagles, Tourists and the Bait Barrel

⌒

Although there is a post office and a wee shop in the village, and although 'the boys' deliver bulk supplies, I still must drive the hilly switchback road into the town now and then, although it is a brave woman who drives anywhere in the summer months, when the tourists are off for a wee donder in their cars, through what must look like a moonscape to them. There are some things only the town stocks, such as Polyfilla or flatulence tablets.

Our village post office is the place for stamps, sweeties in jars and important things like parcel labels and paper clips in two different sizes. The postmistress is a gentle soul with an island lilt and 'the Gaelic'. It's her first language and she will speak it often, confounding the long queue of English waiting for their stamps, and waiting is something we all must do with grace and patience in this particular queue. It is a big mistake to hurry the postmistress. She can sense any hurryings from a good distance and when she does, you might think she had turned to stone for all the moving she does behind her little wooden counter. She will suddenly show a great interest in the affairs of each of the customers as they come to the front of this long snake, now winding out of the door and around the corner. She will pick up threads of threads and fly them like kite strings way up into the sky and back down again. And if someone needs a form we are all doomed.

Ach, the for-ums . . . where can they be? I think they'll be in the house! And off she trots, leaving the cash drawer unlocked, to look for the appropriate for-ums, while some people leave, and others wonder if they've missed a birthday with all this waiting.

The postman, also a crofter, is built of the same blocks, and you don't hurry him either. He will, most obligingly, carry a message to someone who lives up an impossible and bumpy track, bring milk from the shop or the weekly paper if you can't collect it yourself. But if he has stopped, mid-road, to blether about lamb prices or the new laird, and a visitor or incomer revs their engine, he will simply take his time, and settle back in his seat. In his opinion, all folk in a hurry are basically unwell and in need of a good dose of liver salts.

This morning I am headed for the supermarket in the town.

Nothing super about it, grumbles Granny-at-the-Gate, as I collect a list from her, and I know she is thinking Waitrose and the flatlands. When she discovered there was only a Co-op on the island she almost moved back South. When she mentions its name now, it is with a lowered voice and a small 'c'.

As I begin to climb the first hill, the old Landrover pulling steadfastly over the lumps and bumps, my eyes are peeled for holidaymakers. Every car looks the same, has the standard wife in the passenger seat and either a dog or a granny in the back. There is a tartan rug across the back seat and a creature with a bobbing head on the ledge. None of them have reverse gear and they never use their rear-view mirrors.

About halfway into the journey, as we move around the fresh water lochs, where two little dinghies are tethered for the fisherfolk, I can see a buzzard hanging in the sky, like punctuation. The car in front of me, travelling at quite a lick for a nervous visitor, stops dead. I scream to a halt behind it, pumping my brakes and holding out my arm to catch any flying children. The Labrador's nose gets wedged under the dashboard and the shopping basket flips upside down. We sit for a minute or two to recover. The passenger's head disappears for a minute, and then rises again with a set of binoculars fixed to her face. They both get out.

This is too much.

Excuse me! I call out of the window, but they ignore me.

It's an eagle, Jeffrey! says the woman, as if she has just discovered a new country.

It's a buzzard, I say, without moving my lips.

In the end, I have to ask them if they could let me pass. They amble back to their car with a sour glance at me, and in no particular hurry. And they don't let me pass.

Run them over, Mum! squeaks Jake, and his brother

Rhua, now two and already with a broken front tooth, claps his hands together in delight. I am just considering it, when the local bus appears over the brow of the hill, on its way to the village we are still trying to put behind us. The eagle-followers continue past all the passing places and come to a stuttery halt in front of the bus.

I know exactly what will happen next.

Absolutely nothing.

Jimmy the Bus does not go back for tourists. He doesn't much like going back for anyone, but we islanders under-stand this. There are unspoken island rules, to be respected, but this visitor appears to think otherwise, and he is being stubborn, refusing to turn. Jimmy the Bus winks at me over the top of the troublemaker and pulls out his newspaper.

In the Co-op there is no rush either, at least not for the staff. There is a three-mile tailback leading up to the only till in operation. In the queue, no one speaks. What is it with queues and British silence? If this was Milan, you would have to shout to be heard over the jibber-jabber. I always feel chatter rising in me like a spring when I stand in a queue. Soon be winter, chuckles a local painter, his body a tight fit in his spattered overalls. I grin back and tell him his crisps and pop will be well past their sell-by-dates by the time he gets to pay for them.

I buy woodchips for the fish smoker and gas for the boat. I collect parts for the old tractor and a big bag of collie food. There are letters to post and some bits and pieces from the ironmongers and everywhere I go, I meet other folk going about their business. We come together with armfuls of whatever we need to keep our work bobbing along smoothly, we collide around corners laden with useful and necessary products, and we fall apart again to go our separate ways down our own bumpy tracks and back into our lives for another week. I never see any of these people, except here, in the town, and I can hardly tell you any of their names, but I remember their faces and what they tell me about their worlds.

I will remember, next time, that this woman's husband is having root-canal treatment and that her daughter is expecting twins in September. I will ask that builder about his dry-stone wall and laugh with the old boy in his woollen beanie, at his tales of fishing off the outer isles, and then they will hear of my life – in part, for all I speak of are the whales and the children, the lambing and the guests. They will hear all about what Alex is doing, but I will never tell them about me, about how often I wonder what on earth I am doing, and if I am going to be able to keep doing it, without crumbling like the cliffs around the shoreline as the sea breaks over them every day for thousands of years. If I let that lot out, I might just go with it.

Back home, the fish await me. I count two dozen at least and the smoker takes four small fillets at a time. Alex has left them in sea water in the cool of the garage and I begin to fillet and wash them, while the children run amok, wherever they please. While the first fish are being smoked and the air is sharp with the tang of wood smoke, I lift the ones I don't want towards the bait barrel. This idea is a good one and one of Alex's best, although the positioning of it is not ideal, just outside the backyard. Even so, it would still be ok if something hadn't gone horribly wrong with the thing and we can't work out what. Alex layered the fish in the barrel, as he was told, sprinkling rock salt between each layer. It is an old way of preserving fish for hungry times and should work a treat, only it does nothing of the sort. We can never eat the salted fish for fear of dying a slow and painful poisoning of the gut, for it is rotting inside the drum.

We'll use it for the creels, says Alex triumphantly, as if this was his plan all along.

Good idea, I say, although I still feel it is too close to the house. It's almost full now, and seeping slime from underneath, so moving it is impossible. My mouth fills with a whine.

Why did you put it here in the first place? Why not down at the farm or up in the woods or anywhere but right here? After all, there are 1,200 acres to choose from.

But I keep my lips firmly closed, like a good wife. Not a bad wife, a grumbly wife, a selfish wife, with no consideration for my hard-working husband.

Let's not worry about it, says Alex, who never worries about much. He lifts the lid and pulls out a handful of maggoty cadavers which he drops into a bucket. The smell is enough to take out an elephant. I turn away gagging and run for the house. I have to walk by this hateful thing every day on my way to the farm. It buzzes at me angrily but the children love it, and have immense fun ripping off the lid to release hundreds of bluebottles in black swirling clouds. When a child comes up from the village, one who is not yet wise in the feral ways of my children, they will be encouraged to peer inside, just to see.

Just one look! Go on!

And I know, from experience, that their poor mother will never ever remove that terrible smell from their child's clothing, and instead will be reduced to burning it on a bonfire, to watch it crackle and spit, raging blue and green inside the flames until all that is left is a clear decision in her mind to never allow little Johnny up to Tapsalteerie again.

17

A Full Hand

It seems to me, that, all of a sudden, I have five children. How did that happen? I don't mean I don't know how, but it just seems to have happened so fast, without checking if I was ready or not.

Jake, our third-born, is a quiet, insular boy, spending a lot of his time alone with his toys, outside in the garden or, if it's raining, underneath the big kitchen table. If the rain comes suddenly, which it often does, he will carefully bring all his earth-moving equipment into the kitchen, along with all the earth he was moving. Outside, of course, any amount of earth is acceptable. He can roll his caterpillar wheels over it, lift it in endless bucket manoeuvres, dump it over here, or there perhaps, and dig into it with his digging attachment. Even when it rains, and the earth turns quickly to a gloopy black mud, this is not a problem – outside.

But inside is my terrain.

Jake, NO! I yell, when a huge pile of once brightly coloured Tonka machinery appears through the door, dropping muddy gobbets as it lists dangerously to starboard. I know Jake is under there somewhere. I can see his wellies. He stops dead. Jake is nothing if not obedient. The stopping caused the mud to slop in a cowpat at my feet. I turn him round.

Go wash it all under the outside tap, I tell him, and then come back for inspection.

He twists his mouth in embarrassment at getting it wrong, and slouches away, a comical little hobbit creature in a big yellow hard hat. In a few moments he is back and together we dry off the equipment as best we can with the dog towel.

Butter beans for inside, I tell him, and hand him a big catering bag.

Much better for inside work, I say, as if a mother would have a clue about working with heavy plant, but he takes it ok and accepts my sandwich of peace. He'll be happy for hours underneath the kitchen table.

I look over at where Baby Rhua snoozes in the tea-towel drawer. It's the only safe place to let him sleep, and besides, we never close it when he's in it, which is rarely for more than ten peaceful minutes. Rhua doesn't just wake up; he explodes into consciousness and lives each moment with enthusiasm, maximum decibels and continuous movement. I cannot possibly leave him in a bedroom for these short naps. By the time I remembered him, he could be tightrope walking along the roof ledge, or redecorating the guest bedroom walls with his little box of crayons. Besides, he is quite used to sleeping in drawers; when he was born there was no cradle available, so Matron tipped out the contents of her desk drawer, blew out the spiders, and popped Baby Rhua inside.

Friends from England expressed their concern when I first moved to the island, pregnant.

How do you have babies there? they asked. Is there a hospital?

No, there is no hospital, I told them, but I expect the baby will come the normal route, and there is an old folks' home with doctor and nurses, after all, and a vet in the event of an emergency – although I would rather not labour in the cow byre, to be honest. There is also a lifeboat and a helicopter should anything go wrong, which of course it won't. Alex and I are quite easy about the whole process, although our ease sounds like lunacy to those who would never even consider such a thing so far from a big sensible hospital with its full quota of blood banks, incubators and surgeons.

Although Jake was born on the mainland, when Rhua is due, I choose a home birth, or as much of one as I can orchestrate, so when the contractions begin, I say nothing until the last ferry has left the island.

Contractions are every four minutes, Alex tells the doctor over the phone, and we are told to drive to the old folks' home, where a bed is being prepared for me. Old Mrs MacFlorrie has been moved along the corridor to bunk up with another ancient inmate.

Just for the night, Mrs MacFlorrie dear, coo the nurses, as they bundle her into a chair and scoot her along to where her roommate is already snoring like Percy Pig.

We leave three puzzled sleepy children with Granny-at-the-Gate and head through the glen into a wild December night.

The doctor and the nurse bicker fondly over my swollen belly.

There's no gas, Nurse, says the doctor.

Nothing to do with me, Doctor, the nurse replies sharply. It's your hospital, not mine.

It's not MY hospital, Nurse.

Oh really?

I yell at one sharp contraction.

Would you like an injection, dear? the nurse asks me, softer now.

No drugs! I shriek, biting down on my husband, whose fault all this is anyway.

As the baby is born, I pull myself up by the iron head-board and watch my baby arrive into the world. This is the first time I have been conscious for a delivery and, sadly, the last time, for when Solly is born, in a hospital far away, his birthing is a very different story.

Matron pops the drawer with my new little boy inside it on the bedside table. He is swaddled in cloths and blankets and is sleeping for now.

I now know he was just recovering from the rigours of labour and all that squashing and pushing and heaving. Once recovered, he will spend all his childhood years at full tilt, mouth wide open, all guns blazing, skin tight against his wiry body as though he is always running into the wind.

He is very small, they say, as his life grows longer and he stays the same.

His voice isn't, we tell them.

Perhaps we should try this growth hormone?

I don't think so. Leave him be. When you have this many children, its handy to have one you can just pop in your pocket.

While other boys are growing and talking about how big they are, Rhua squeezes through the gaps. He is as wiry and as fast as Spiderman and just as fond of heights.

Look at me! he shouts, aged two and half from halfway up a twenty-foot cliff face, or from the top of the massive old oak tree, and we all do look, just to keep him quiet and we keep looking, although I must have looked away at least once, as there is another baby on the way.

Oh no, I can't do this! No. Please! I can't even find the children I already have, half the time, or remember their birthdays, or their names, or what to put in their packed lunches. How will I manage?

Just face it, lady, I tell myself, you won't. So you might as well 'not manage' with as much style and grace as you can muster, and, for goodness sake, tie a knot in it.

I don't think it's long enough, but I will ask him.

Don't be ridiculous, says Alex, horrified at the idea of an attack on his manhood.

Sterilisation is a sin, the priest tells me, when I ask him. He cannot condone it.

Poppycock! says the doctor. You'll be a corpse if you have any more. We'll do it after this baby comes along.

Solly, being number five has the dubious honour of being *multigravida*, whatever that means. It seems I have to go to a bigger hospital some distance away, and as he is due mid lambing, I will have to bite down on someone else during labour as Alex must stay on the farm, a situation neither of us likes one bit. I know the baby will come whoever is or isn't there with me, but Alex is my rock and I am shaky without his strength. But at this time of year, we have no choice. Alex is the farmer – just him, and only him – and even if he could find someone to step in, he would never trust them to be as vigilant as he is himself around his beloved animals.

Lambing is work every daylight minute and beyond, and he cannot even go a few hours without checking on the ewes. The hooded crows wheel overhead like vultures, watching the weaklings and pouncing the moment they are born. If the mother is not instantly attentive to her newborn lamb, be sure the crows will be. Holding down the feeble struggler with one strong foot, they will peck out the lamb's eyes and its tongue before you can cross the few yards to stop the horror taking place. Then, given time, they will pull out the entrails and leave the lamb to die a slow death. If a ewe labours too long, she can suffer the same fate, as she has no strength to rise to her feet. Alex turns into a roaring monster around crows, and ravens are worse, if anything can be worse. He rigs up a crow trap, making a sort of giant lobster pot, with a funnel in and no way back out. He catches one crow and clips its wings. Into the trap it goes along with a dead sheep, and there is always a dead sheep at this time of year, to tempt others in for a feed. Then, once some have trapped themselves, Alex goes in and kills them.

There's a bird in a trap on the shore, poor thing! says the earnest-looking walker at the back door. I sigh inwardly. Another animal-rights groupie.

I explain the purpose of the trap, the safety of the little fluffy-wuffy lambs. Most of them get it eventually, although I can see the accusation in their eyes. These remote farmers who think they can get away with cruelty to animals, mutter, mutter.

One did more than mutter at me.

I let it go, he said.

Well done you, I told him. You just did a much crueller thing. It cannot fly or escape. Any weakness in the crow world is unacceptable. All it is now, is lunch.

So off I go, alone in the ambulance, on my due date, and this wasn't a right guess either, for it is ten days and counting and I am going stir crazy in this place. When Solly finally decides to begin pushing his way out, I am whizzed up to the labour ward, hooked up to endless machines that whirr and beep and flash around my hard bed, which I suspect is actually a trolley. Without any explanation, I am filled with drugs and my waters broken. Labour comes on too fast and I cannot keep my head. By the time Solly is born, at 5 a.m., my legs are in spasm, I am delirious and seeing things.

Why is that light spinning round? I sound drunk.

The nurse rolls her eyes. It's not, she says sharply, and the door slams behind her.

The next day, to my delight and astonishment, I am told I have a visitor. Who on earth could be visiting me here, in this big old hospital miles from anyone I know?

The ward nurse, a cheery Australian, tidies me up, plumps up the unplumpable pillows, straightens the sheets. She wears a smile she cannot suppress and her eyes sparkle.

You can come in now, she sings into the air.

When my mother's face peeks around the screens, I burst into tears. I hadn't realised how much I miss her and I can't believe she has made that long journey for me. Well I can believe it, but there is something deeply moving about a gift prepared with such love and such secrecy. I can see in her eyes how concerned she is for me. Sometimes when we talk on the phone she tells me straight.

I don't know why you have to work so hard, she says.

But Mum, you had five children too!

Just five children, she reminds me, oh, and your father of course, but not a hotel, not all those cottages, not dinners to cook every night.

I lie back on my pillows and love the picture in my head. Calling the children in from the garden for a cheese salad in the summer, or a nourishing stew in the colder months, and then bathing them all, brushing their hair by the fire, telling bedtime stories.

Sol snuffles in his sleep, and I am back in the ward.

It's just different, Mum, I say, ending any further discussion of the subject.

For the whole afternoon we talk and laugh and entertain the other inmates and, when she finally has to go, I hear our happy chatter darting around the ward like swallows until the last light is turned off for the night.

I travel back up the road to the island a few days later. My baby is healthy and strong and I am anything but. This is a birthing I would not have wished on my worst enemy. A 'big hospital' birthing, and I am just a number, not a human being. I am labelled and moved according to their convenience, not my own. Give me, every time, the thrill of knowing the last ferry has gone and the icy wind is rising. Let me feel the rushing into the night, with the taste of danger in my mouth and the beating of my strong mother heart as I set about bringing a new life into the world. Let me feel alive with all the hot pain and let the wild shouting be loud in me, so I know the tearing of my skin and the rush of hot tears to my eyes, without gas or drugs as I fight the sheets in Mrs MacFlorrie's still warm bed, to the sound of gentle bickering, and give me a matron's bottom drawer to lay my baby in. Let me cry the tears of joy and see the same in the eyes of my man.

I touch Solly's new face with a feather finger. There is a bond between us now, not just of mother and son, but one of shared survival.

We made it, Baby, I whisper and he snuffles in his sleep.

That summer my mother makes the long journey north again, to visit us on the island, this time bringing my old granny with her. By the time they arrive I am thoroughly over-excited at this welcome invasion of suffragettes, even if they only 'suffragette' to me and in private. They bring with them practical help, entertainment for the children, and plenty of laughter and fun, for both have an enterprising sense of nonsense. My granny will sleep in the big room and my mum in the garret with the rest of us.

One afternoon, my mother suggests I rest while she takes the children for a walk down the pot-holed track. She puts Solly into the big Silver Cross pram and attaches Rhua to the handle, as she did when we were that small. Jake will stalk them from somewhere deep inside the line of rhododendron bushes, and Bryn and Cassie will ride their bikes. The sun is warm when she sets out and the little group is soon joined by the dogs and then the cats, and finally the pet lambs, for there are always pet lambs somewhere in our world. As she bumps and rattles her way down the track, with Sol well clipped down to avoid being catapulted into the sky, she meets some walkers. She tells me their astonished faces were quite something to behold.

Do you always go out walking with such a troupe? they ask her, but before she can reply, Jake bursts through the foliage firing blanks from his pop gun. The dogs erupt in a barking frenzy, sending the cats yowling for cover and the lambs up onto the bank, felling Jake as they scarper for cover. It takes some time to relocate his pop gun.

I think they thought they had walked into a storybook, my mother said later as she sipped a welcome gin.

They did Mum, I reply.

18

Women and Dreams

When the suffragettes leave, as I always knew they must leave, it starts to feel like a different kind of story.

Life has had her hand in the small of my back for as long as I can remember, and it feels like she is edging me on, that I am always late for something. The road of days and weeks and months is moving under my feet, like those travelling floors in airports, and I am always hurrying through everything and stopping to enjoy nothing. When Alex suggests I go with him up the hill to see the wild orchids and hear the seabirds one summer evening after dinner is over, I am angry that he asks me, that he thinks I should drop everything now, just to please him.

You can leave that till later, he says, indicating the overflow of ironing.

I have a thousand words in my mouth.

I swallow them all and I tell him No. I always tell him No, as if in saying it I win somehow, even though I know I lose.

So I am blind to wild orchids and deaf to seabirds and the daily grind that is my life threatens to turn me into a fine powder that might just dissipate in the winds that ever blow around this house and through it too, for no one ever closes any doors.

Five children; a full hand, and no mistake. Once, I had enough of me to go round, but it is not possible to hold five children, to soothe five brows, to answer five questions, to sit five children on my knee and hug them all close to a warm heartbeat. It would be fine if I was needed in rotation, but need doesn't work like that. Need is RIGHT NOW and probably in a group and my growing sense of failure nibbles at the edges of my mind, no matter how often I tell myself, or Alex tells me, what a grand job I am doing. The words bounce off my ears and skitter away into the sky for others to hear and take in. As far as I am concerned, I am expertly preparing five young people for the psychiatrist's couch and myself for aging bewilderment. The image of my breezy hippy family is fading daily from my imagination, and I am beginning to realise that it only ever was real in my head, like a dream. And with that understanding, there is a dying and a death.

I have met many women over the years with the dream dying in them. I know them instantly. They are sensibly clad in stout shoes, their waterproof hats pulled over their ears against the wind and persistent rain. Their hair tufts in all the wrong places, or fits like a helmet, stiff with lacquer. Their arches are fallen, their eyes are dim, their backs bent and they hide behind polite responses and their husband's dietary requirements.

Oh, but they are fulfilled enough . . . We are fulfilled enough, they clamour, hands flapping the air. We have made simnel cakes each Easter and wholesome soups every day for a thousand years. We have ironed and pressed, turned collars and soothed fevered brows. We have lain awake at nights, berating ourselves for any foolish tears and admitted nothing in the daylight. We have risen and dressed early, just to find a bargain in times of need. We have given. We have given everything.

These women stopped turning heads years ago, way back in girlhood perhaps, admitting defeat shortly after they floated up the aisle on a cloud of impossible promises. They packed away their frilly underwear along with their frilly thoughts, their dreams of carefree days, and nights under a warming sun or lover.

I watch them coming back from a shopping spree on the mainland, as they stomp down the ferry ramp, in their buttoned-up mackintoshes, dragging tartan shopping trolleys. Their scrubbed faces shine; their eyes look tired and I am sad. Somewhere inside that mackintosh beats the heart of a wild woman, a living, breathing vibrant creature who has been quietly captive most of her life. Her children and her husband are doing well. Yes, they are all very successful.

And her? Oh, she is fine, thank you, and full of baking news, her grandchildren, her new fridge, and the turkey for Christmas. Her conversation is domestic, tame. She has given up and given in. When she fell down, she stayed down.

*   *   *

Sometimes she tells me of the old days.

Do you dance, Mary McPhee?

Oh . . . dancing . . . From way beyond her eyes, she is gone, spinning into the arms of some dashing reprobate, tall he is, dark, handsome and full of promise.

You know, once, when I was young . . . she begins, and for a few moments, we are transported into another time, our heads close across the table, the story building its own excitement, until suddenly something jerks her chain. Someone calls to her from the other side of the room, or she remembers she needs a pee, or a bit of her scone drops onto the floor . . . and the flame is snuffed out. Dead. Just like that.

What am I going on about? she says, flustered, accusing. Daft old woman, talking nonsense!

Oh no! I urge her, reaching out my hand. Don't stop now. It's a lovely story.

But I have lost her. I watch her burst to her feet, and pull her old coat protectively around herself.

Och no! she gasps at me, swatting the air for the wasp between us. That's all past now. I must go. Cheerio!

And she is gone, leaving me with the feeling that I have opened up a wound and watched it bleed. Other eyes avoid mine as I leave the café. They know me and my red rebel streak. I am a disease they wouldn't dare catch.

I meet her husband in the pub a few days later. His eyes are rolling about like tangerines in his skull and are about the same colour. He grins lecherously.

Hallo Gorgeous! he slurs to my breasts, and I am showered with spittle. He looks eight months pregnant.

I remember Mary McPhee with her grey moustache, her careworn face and her tall dancing partner. I remember the girl in her eyes and I push past him, silently wishing him terminal droop.

As the children grow strong and healthy, I can feel myself shrinking. When they were little people, I knew where I was with them, for it was I who chose their meal times, their clothes each day, their bedtimes. Nowadays I need a map to find them, a foghorn to attract their attention, and I have lost control. Alex and I have one of our in-depth discussions. I explain my concerns.

Stop worrying, he says, they're fine – and is gone. I realise I must make my own plan.

The next time they dive for the door, I haul them back and make them listen.

Now children, remember this rule . . . (I sound like Mrs Rabbit for goodness sake) . . . You can go anywhere on the estate as long as you can always see the house.

Ok! they chime and in a flash they are away, whooping through the trees with fearsome-looking home-fashioned weapons with which they will, no doubt, go marauding and pillaging, only returning when they are tired.

Tired? laughs Alex. Warriors are never tired. And just for the record, they could go eight miles in any direction, including out to sea and still be able to see the house!

Oh, dear. I believe he's right.

19

Gobbler

~

After a few winters with only Thursday baths, we finally persuade the bank to give us a loan and we buy ourselves a huge wood burner. There is a wealth of woodland on the estate and a lot of fallen timber just asking to be moved along to create room for new trees to be planted.

We need to regenerate. That's what Alex says.

What I say is that we all need to bathe more often. I no longer set my machine for Whites, as we have nothing white left. There is grime on the grime and my fingers are raw with cold scrubbing. There is grease on everything and no amount of elbow work will lift it. What I need is hot water.

Blow regeneration. I am cold, sick of being cold, cold right down to my bones. I am old before my time and weary beyond belief and even lonelier than in the days when I stared at yellow roses on walls and listened to *Abbey Road* on a loop.

*　　*　　*

The lorry has to come up the track whatever the driver might have to say on the matter. He can hardly pop a two-ton wood burner in Granny's garage, even supposing he could survive a gravel reversal. The boiler is lifted off the flatbed of the truck with a fancy red crane. As it lands on the concrete of the yard, there is a loud crack. I pray it doesn't disappear into the bowels of the earth, falling, falling, like Alice into Wonderland; not after all this cold and grubby waiting.

Right, let's get it inside, says Alex, revving up his old digger which he has managed to navigate into the yard, much to my amazement. We have to squeeze past it to get in or out.

The boiler is too wide to go through the doorway, a small detail we've overlooked. But Alex is always there with a second thought.

We'll take out the window, he says, yanking at it and finding it suddenly in his hands, frame and all. He fixes a huge hook and chain around the belly of the boiler and begins to take the strain on the digger bucket. Gingerly he moves the boiler towards the hole that once was a window and may never be again. It begins to swing, and then more, and at this rate it will take down the side wall and we could have left the window where it was.

What if it swings too far? I squeak, back pressed against the outhouse wall.

You stop it, he yells over the roar of the engine and the shriek of metal slipping on metal. With great skill he lowers it, still swinging, onto the floor. Now we must finagle it across the room to line up with the chimney flue, and for this grade of finagling, we will need help.

After two hours of puffing and grunting and hot men all shouting directions to each other, the boiler is in place and glued up to the pipe. We have to wait a few days for the glue to set, and then we can make fire.

The inside of the burner is large enough to host the village hall AGM, but we are not fazed by this. We have acres of timber just waiting to be gathered in and we can hardly wait to find out what it feels like to have hot water on tap all the winter long.

We name her Gobbler. She is a She, because to Alex all things under his command and care are female. He hauls down some lengths of timber, too heavy for me to lift, lays himself a fire and strikes the match.

To begin with, as you might expect, there is a lot of wheezing and blowing back of smoke and coughing from those standing too close, but very soon she is proving herself to be truly remarkable at her job. She could launch the next Apollo spacecraft all by herself with the intensity of that belly fire and we can now bathe every day and more than once if we fancied, which most of us do not. Sometimes, if her flaps have not been correctly positioned, she will go on heating up until the water boils in the pipes, making them jump and rattle against their fixings on the walls and issuing tiny puffs of steam that make me tell the children to run right past and not to stop for anything. All hot taps must be turned on full and right now, to drain off the danger. Alex soaks blankets with the hose and clamps them around Gobbler's mouth to cut off her breathing. Now all we can do is wait. I don't mind too much if this happens in the winters when we are home alone, but in the summer months I must dash about explaining to puzzled guests that this lunatic waste of the hot water is for their own safety and that it isn't smoke billowing along the landing, but steam, which is excellent for the complexion.

Keep away from the water pipes, I tell them, and please don't touch the hot water as it runs away or you'll go home skinned.

I am sure they will all write letters of complaint to the tourist board.

Jolly good show! chortles the Commander, a regular guest, his feet tapping to the rhythmic clattering of the pipes. Suddenly there is gunshot from along the landing. A basin has cracked.

Ho ho! Mildred, did you hear that, old girl? Pass me my rifle!

Mildred rolls her eyes at me and shakes her head.

All this energy requires wood. Alex decides we will all go a-wooding.

Why me? I ask.

He sighs patiently. You need to drive the other tractor and trailer.

Right. Of course. Only I've never driven a tractor before.

My husband grins. Off we go, kids. Load up, let's go!

With faltering pedal work and my heart in my mouth, I lurch after Alex on the little red Ferguson, while he sways along like a happy elephant on the digger. Jake, Rhua and Solly are all in the bucket, way out front. Cassie is with me. The seat on my tractor is just a damp piece of foam balanced

147

on a lump of rust, and I can see the ground easily through all the holes around my feet. We head for the big beech tree that fell down in last winter's gale. This one is comparatively easy to access, not like some of them that crash to their deaths down vertical hillsides or into deep clarty bogs.

Bring the trailer down and stop on that level! Alex yells to me, while slowly lowering the small boys to the ground.

Do what? There is no level. It's all slope.

You can do it, lass!

No, I say, from where I stand, on the brink. *You* can do it.

While Alex saws and hauls, the rest of us lug and stack what we can lift in the trailers, till my arms are twice as long as at breakfast. All the while the boys play their imaginary games. They are lumberjacks in Canada, just like their father once was, and it is minus 45° and falling. They are bear trappers, and there are bears lurking everywhere among the trees, big angry bears with teeth and claws and a taste for small boys. Now they're nomadic Indians, on the run from wicked land-owners who want to send them to Siberia to be eaten by wolves. When we burn the scrub, they are Cree warriors around a camp fire. They flap at the smoke with leafy branches, sending out who-knows-what sort of inflamma-tory messages into the sky. I tell them I hope no Choctaw are looking this way, or we might all find ourselves in serious poo.

They snort at me.

There aren't any Choctaw on the island, they sneer.

Everyone knows that.

*　　*　　*

Sometimes our old Suffolk Punch Duchess works in the woods, hauling out timbers even Alex cannot get to in his digger. He fixes her trace and hooks her up to a huge trunk. With a click of his tongue, she begins to pull her heavy load through the gaps in the trees and out onto the track. Sometimes Alex must lay tracks of wood to ease the trunk over the rough ground. Every time she is stopped, to free the load or ease its passage, she must square up and start again once the order comes to move. I can see her shoulders straining against this one, but even so, her every movement is slow and calm no matter how hard the work and she never stops until we do.

Good girl! I rub her down with straw and feed her nuts before she goes back to her grazing. She watches me for a few moments, and then bows her great and graceful neck down to the last remaining blades of this year's grass.

The water supply to the house comes from way up the hill, travelling its distance down miles of blue alkathene piping. All the cottages are supplied with spring water and it is the maintenance of a steady flow for all of us that falls to Alex. In the winter, he will drain the tanks in all the properties to avoid burst pipes and internal damage, but for us he must climb the hill every morning to haul the pipes from where they follow the burn, onto open ground to catch whatever warmth the winter sun might offer. Often the pipes have frozen overnight and we have no cold water running. No cold water running means no water at all; for to empty the hot tank without the sureness of it being refilled could be a Gobbler disaster. Sometimes Alex takes a blowtorch to the pipes, but there are miles of them and he has animals to feed and water, not once, but twice in the short hours of daylight. Water becomes our story, our headline news. Will we have water today, or not?

With my heart in my mouth, I twist on the cold tap. Nothing; a wheeze of cold air and a clatter of ice pellets land in the basin.

No water! I yell over my shoulder. No flushing!

Alex shuts Gobbler down and heads up the hill in search of sunshine.

Sometimes I wonder, he grumbles into his toast and marmalade.

What, Alex? What do you wonder? Why we ever came here, perhaps? Or do you wonder if you should get us hooked up to the mains? Not that the 'mains' would consider travelling this far. Or is it that you have to eat brown bread today as I forgot to make white? What, Alex? What? Talk to me.

Better go, he says.

Leave me the Landrover, I say, feeling pushed away again. It's a school day.

Ok, he says distractedly. Come on dogs!

As I watch the Landrover disappear up the hill, I feel an almighty scream rising from my cold toes, but before it gets to my mouth, I stop it dead.

20

First Rites

⌒

Sometimes a child will visit from the village. If it is a first time for them, there now follows a rite of passage. Granted, there are no fast cars to dodge or crocodile-infested rivers to swim, but my children are canny and mischievous and have inherited their mother's imagination. If anyone thought being tipped into the bait barrel was bad, they are living in La-La Land.

The first possibility is the Open Sewer that rests in the field down below the house. It is an old-fashioned sort of waste disposal, and a far cry from the septic tanks of the future, and yet a real cut above the village sewage disposal system, which is basically a fat pipe into the sea-loch, where swimming is not encouraged, but where the mussels clinging to the rocks are both abundant and delicious.

Once in the Open Sewer, it is hard to disguise the fact that this is where you have been at some point during the day, so the boys are slow to suggest this as the very first rite. The

Death Slide is the main choice, to be honest. Rigged between two tall trees, the pulley system works with a block and a hook, to which a child is fastened, either by their belt or by the hook of their jeans. One boy fixes the visitor in position with exuberant descriptions of the fun he or she is about to have as they fly through the air to land safely in that tree over there.

Can you see it, look?

They see it.

Off you go! The visitor is shoved off the branch and begins to hurtle towards his destination, imagining, I presume, that he will begin to slow as he would on a fair-ground ride. But this is not a fairground ride, and he will slam into the solid oak trunk, with all the puff snatched out of him, his eyes looping the loop and his brain turning to scrambled eggs in his head.

Another rite is Man Overboard drill, involving a rounded polystyrene coracle, which washed up on the shore last winter. Alex has tied a long rope to it and fixed the end securely to a huge iron loop embedded into the rocks by the old pier.

They don their life jackets, grab paddles and head down to the shore.

We're off to sea! they call over their shoulders. I grin. They're quite safe, all jacketed up and fixed to the land.

You think?

One of the boys paddles like stink, and the tide is ebbing, so it's double stink, almost flying along.

Whaaaaang! The rope runs out and the visitor, sitting in the best place at the bows, is lobbed, like a football, into the briny.

Doubled up with the laughter at their own brilliance, the

boys haul him out, coughing and spluttering and fighting back the tears.

I am furious, and march the poor child upstairs to dry him off and to dress him in borrowed clothes.

There will be NO bread, milk or blackberries for tea today! I tell the criminals.

But he's a skellie-eyed wimp! they wail.

I know he is, I say. Some people are. It doesn't mean you can drown them.

As in-comers – and everyone who failed to be born on the island qualifies for that appellation – we are intriguing. Or so it seems, as Alex and I have regular invitations to other's homes, to meet other islanders.

Around this time we get our first invitation to the castle on the hill.

Come on Saturday! says the plummy English voice on the phone.

I am very over-excited at the thought. Alex loves going out for dinner. Neither of us have done so for years.

What's the dress code? I ask.

Oh, wear anything!

That's no help at all. How do I know my 'anything' is the same as yours? Yours might be a Grecian gown, when mine is dungarees and a cardy, and we won't match at all if those two meet. It will be all lookings up and down and polite dismay. You will think I am weird and I will know you are, although I am beginning to realise that there are more eccentric folk living in this small area of rock in the ocean than I ever encountered in the South.

What shall we wear to dine at the fairy castle? I ask Alex, who only ever wears threadbare jeans and shirts with tatty collars, turned regularly by his mummy.

Warm underwear? he says helpfully, as he pulls on a pair of red corduroys and an olive green shirt, which I really ought to iron.

It takes extreme dedication to find a babysitter. This is probably due to the fact that our house is notoriously cold and draughty and rocking with ghosts, our children number five, and we live two long bumpy pot-holey miles from the village.

It'll cost you! grins Old Rona, and when she arrives, she clutches a bottle of juice, a bag of chewing gum and *The People's Friend*.

I change while she reads them various unsuitable stories.

Pulling on a long skirt to hide the hairy legs, boots, a shirt that can stretch over my six belly rolls, I finish off with a drapey poncho thing that could well be the wrong way up, as Granny's knitting is getting more dubious these days. If she is rudely interrupted mid-pattern, and can't quite remember where she got to, some very interesting shapes result. I brush my hair and steel myself to look in the mirror. I look like a fisher-lassie, ballooning with warm layers from the neck down. Above it there sits my sharply chiselled face, pale skinned with, somewhere under that slap, a few girlish freckles. I grin as I remember sunny childhood days, out in the garden with my bare skin and long plaits and the hum of bees all around.

Well, the plaits are gone, with the help of Granny's pinking shears. One. Gone. Two. Gone. After I had done the deed, I made tea and sandwiches for Alex and Bruce, who was helping him cut the grass for silage. Bruce grinned nervously as he saw me coming, a naughty Raggedy Ann. Alex just looked at me, his face hard and set, like plaster. It was weeks before he would relax with me, stop saying how he hated it, pushing me away in bed. But I had made my first stand.

My   first   stand.

And it felt delicious.

I love the light-headedness of me now, as if I had severed the chains that bound me – or at least made a start. And I like the feather touch of a breeze on the back of my neck. I have a fine neck – kissable, Alex said once, although I know he would rather find it under my chestnut tresses. I fix some beads around it and turn away. I am really looking forward to this outing, to eating someone else's food and to sharing adult conversation, which is not something Alex and I do much of. Our conversations are a series of questions and answers. Life is so demanding, for both of us. We are beginning to forget each other.

Did you collect the thingy I ordered?

Yes.

Good.

Or . . .

No, I forgot.

Can you get it tomorrow?

Yes.

Good.

Conversation over.

*   *   *

On the way to the dinner party, Alex turns left into the forestry.

Oh no! Alex!

There are seven gates to open and close, a track that makes ours look like a runway, and it is now raining stair rods.

By the fifth gate, with my insides now lodged between my ears, and the very real threat of my wetting my pants, I am very grumpy. There is also a bull in the way.

There's a bull in the way, I tell Alex, holding the door tightly closed as if he might hop in beside me. He is massive, with horns like tree trunks and shoulders wide as a table. He eyes me through his ginger fringe. I just know that one false move by me and he will charge with a mighty roar, and stick me through with a horn or two and my lovely dinner will all go to waste.

Just shoo him away, says Alex irritably.

Don't be ridiculous! The matadors that do that at bull-fights are chased around the ring at high speed. I am trussed up here in a soaking skirt that now weighs 20lb and girlie boots and I would disappear completely into that swamp of mud he has churned up with his big feet.

Alex opens his window and lifts an arm in the bull's direction.

Oi! Shoo! he shouts, and the bull ambles peacefully away.

Ok, ok, so not all bulls are the same.

At dinner, conversation is sprightly and I am tiddly with excitement. Being out for the evening, away from the children, the humdrum, the daily round, is truly a wonderful treat. I do all the talking, as there is so much I haven't been able to say for so many years now, and I just cannot stem the flow, but no one seems to mind – except Alex, who always minds, so it doesn't count. The others seem to find me very entertaining and lots of fun, especially when I reach around the centrepiece of flowers and flick my cigarette ash into the pretty silver butter dish with curlicues at each end and a lot of butter in the middle.

I am horrified.

Please don't worry! smiles my hostess, as she gracefully swings the butter dish away, and floats through the door for more. I watch her slim elegance and feel even more like a suet pudding. Her children are older than mine, I remind myself. Perhaps given time I will become a swan too.

Who else have you met on the island? asks our host, from inside his careful assemblage of smart casual.

I tell him of our visit, a month or so earlier, to a lovely old couple who used to run a large estate themselves.

The evening is still warm, I begin, although there is a frisson of autumn on the breeze. The table falls quiet.

We arrive, I continue, at the big house, and pull on the old-fashioned brass bell pull, embedded for the rest of time in the granite door frame.

Silence. Nothing but the twittering of outside birds and the distant yapping of a small dog. I yank again, and hear it bong loudly inside the house. Again, nothing. Alex checks his watch.

What time are we to arrive? he asks.

Now, I tell him. 7.30.

Did we get the right day?

This 'we' bit tickles me. He never has the slightest clue about social engagements beyond initially giving consent, which probably happened days or even weeks ago, and it only takes half an hour for his mind to be completely wiped clean.

Yes, it is the right day, I say. I am going to look round the back.

Hallo! I call in that stupid singsong way we all adopt, leaning over myself and peering into the shrubbery.

Nothing. No one. Silence.

Along the path, past the greenhouse heaving with juicy red tomatoes, a soft pink mallow shrub gives way to open grass, and there is our hostess, looking just as adorable in her big straw hat and billowy flowered skirt at seventy-odd as she would have done at twenty. She has an empty flower basket hooked on her arm.

We greet each other with genuine pleasure.

How lovely to see you! she says, opening her arms and just missing my face with her secateurs.

You too! I smile. How are you, Eliza?

Oh very well, dear, very well. And you?

I am beginning to realise she has absolutely no idea why I have appeared in her garden.

Oh, and Alex too! She beams as he joins us.

Now I am certain.

We are here for dinner? I ask it as a question. Makes it less definite, open to contradiction.

Are you dears? she says. How lovely.

And she turns back to her flower picking, humming a

little hum to herself. She selects some blooms and lays them carefully in the basket.

Now what? I ask Alex with my eyes. He shrugs.

Suddenly, her husband appears, stomping across the grass. He is a dapper good-looking man with a military correctness about him and a splendid moustache.

Gins? he asks, his arms open.

They've come for dinner Gilbert! Isn't that lovely?

Splendid! says Gilbert. Haven't had dinner for ages. Come on Eliza old girl, let's get cracking.

I think we will be extremely drunk by the time we get to eat.

While we sip our way through many gins, others arrive and with each one there is an air of surprise and wonderment in the welcoming eyes of our hosts. We sit down to smoked salmon and baby tomatoes from the greenhouse, although it could be anything now that my taste buds are pickled. Next comes venison, and I must admit to being very impressed with such a spread considering our hosts were obviously anticipating a plate of eggs in front of the telly.

Gilbert carves and serves us all a platter.

Where are the potatoes, Eliza dear?

Eliza pops back for the potatoes which weren't quite ready. We all watch our gravy solidify.

We'll have them later, we all agree after ten minutes have elapsed, and by the time they arrive, we are all talking mince and more than ready for some carbohydrate.

Suddenly, Eliza's head snaps up. It's the fastest I have ever seen her move and I fear for her equilibrium.

The red cabbage! she gasps, rising from the table and Gilbert joins the scurry from the room.

Thirty minutes pass pleasantly enough, although the wine is running low.

What are they doing? asks a woman across from me, as if I would know such a thing. I decide to go and look. I cannot believe the kitchen is that far away, nor the red cabbage that hard to find in it. I try one door; broom cupboard. Ah, maybe this one.

Eliza is sitting on a kitchen chair, sipping something hot and milky from a mug. She has slippers on her feet and a silky green dressing gown over a pink frilly full-length nightie.

Hallo dear, she smiles, turning towards me. How nice to see you!

Gilbert is nowhere to be seen and nor is the red cabbage.

I make my goodbyes and return to the dining room to explain. As we all drive away, well fed and quite squiffy on wine, I wonder what our hosts will think when they wander into the dining room the following morning. Secretly I hope I will be as delightfully fey when I am long in years and as happy with the slow tick-tock of island time.

My hosts are most entertained with this tale, for they know the couple well. By the time we bounce back home through the forestry, an early frost has fallen, and the bull's roan back is a dazzling white, as is his long fringe, which is now a line of icicles.

The night is still and silent, and the moon through the frosted tree limbs lights up the Landrover with a fairytale glow.

We should do this more often, lass, Alex says.

I nod and try to smile, knowing we won't.

21

Holidays

The year turns once more. October comes around again and the summer season is all but over. Sailboats still decorate the seascape, their sails full, their noses rising and disappearing into the sharply chiselled waves of autumn.

For us, it is almost time to take the cottages apart for the winter, but before we begin battening down the hatches, draining water tanks and clearing out all fabrics and soft furnishings, ideal for building nests by chilly mice, we take a holiday.

Where are we going? the children ask excitedly.

Shore Cottage! says their father, triumphantly, as if it was another land.

Which Shore Cottage? asks Jake, who is a stickler for the details.

I would like to answer 'the one on the Isle of Crete'.

Ours, I say, and the word feels sticky on my tongue.

Oh! Cool!

Yes, children, it will be. There is no electricity, no heating and no running water, not that any of you will give a rip about any of that. We are going on a Great Big Adventure all of 400 yards down the track, us and the dogs and our imaginations and we will light fires, fish for our supper, cook outside and share beds as we are too many.

There will be no bathing for a whole week.

Hurrah! they chorus and their father's eyes twinkle in a face that only ever gets washed in a rain shower.

No one is allowed to go back home for anything, making it a proper holiday! I tell them all, especially Alex, who might be quite happy to escape, but who isn't going to be allowed to.

On the morning before we set off, I tell the children to pack. Not their clothes, of course, which will be my job, except for Cassie, who is quite able to pack for herself, being a girl. Boys have no clue about packing and most certainly can not be trusted to include clean pants or socks, or wash things.

Choose whatever toys and books you need and pack them in your bags, and, remember: there is no coming back, so think it through carefully.

I said most of that to an empty room. I think they left just after 'toys and books'.

A lot later, I hear a rumbling along the landing.

What's going on? I ask in my suspicious voice.

Nothing! they chime.

Rounding the corner to the kitchen after thumping and clumping down the back stairs come three small boys and the toy cupboard. Well, not the actual toy cupboard, but everything from inside it, including the broken dumper truck, the wooden garage with two petrol pumps missing, the Tonka heavy plant, the Camberwick green fire engine and the team excluding Barney McGrew who got flushed down the loo a while back and never returned for duty.

What's this?

They slump down around the toy mountain and roll their eyes at each other.

Aar toys of course! says Solly, folding his arms, or trying to. They are a bit short for folding.

You don't want all of these, not the broken ones, surely? I pick up a soft toy that's spewing stuffing from a big hole in its bottom.

Well, says Jake, rising crossly to his feet. You can take them all back then. We are worn out!

Following his lead, the small boys pick up their choice of toys and stalk off in disgust.

While they are packing the Landrover, I grab dustbin bags and fill them with broken toys, old eyeballs, bits of plastic and some battered old rusty cars that look surprisingly like the ones I meet on the island roads.

Shore Cottage used to be the home of an old fisherman, who had a few sheep on his little croft. The story goes that each spring he would load his sheep into his rowing dinghy and take them through the waves to the little islands, where the puffins nest and the grass grows lush and strong. Having been out there with a big boat beneath my feet and a warm chugging engine pushing us along, I marvel at the thought of this man rowing such a long distance, just to pasture his little flock. He will have landed beneath the towering rock face, alive with rising, falling birds, their raucous voices cutting through the wind, while the suck and slap of the waves against the rocks threatened to tip the sheep into the swirling, muttering water, as grey as gunmetal and as deep as dreams. It must have been a lonely life down here on the shoreline with only paraffin lighting and the paltry warmth of a damp driftwood fire. It's well over two miles to the village and a friendly face, or a jar of fuel for the darkness; two miles for help or a song and a wee swallow of liquid gold. I don't suppose he bothered much about pot-holes. Pot-holes don't matter when you're walking.

I walk myself down here sometimes, when there is a moment or two for me. I sit on the rocks and sing my heart out. There is a wonderful echo, great acoustics for a solo voice lifting into the clear, clean air. There is no one to hear, no one to comment, unless the fishermen cleaning their creels in the harbour across the narrows catch a drift of song on the breeze, and look up and wonder if it's a selkie. I learn old sea songs, usually mournful ones that women sang when their men were missing in tiny boats on a broad wild ocean. Once I sat till dark and beyond. The tide had turned a while back and the gulls still cried their eerie sounds overhead. When I got up, stiff and cold from the hard rock, the land had turned to seaweed. I was frightened at first, as there were no lights to guide me across the new stretch of floodtide, and then suddenly my song came back to me and together we half swam, half waded through the freezing water and back to the shore. As we dripped home, I could swear the gulls were laughing.

Now there is no sense of this loneliness for our noisy seven-piece band, all squashed into two bedrooms and a sitting room that would fit nicely into a rabbit hutch. Luckily, none of the family ever wants to do very much as a group, so the lumpy sofa, the only soft furnishing in the room, is rarely fought over.

Alex lights the fire and this is another reason why the sofa is often empty. Billows of smoke pump into the tiny room and send us all coughing through the front door and onto the shore. No amount of blowing and re-laying of sticks or flapping of newspaper sheets makes a jot of difference. The chimney just will not draw and probably never did. No matter, for we are an outside family and a camp fire is a much more attractive proposition. We can toast bread and cook tatties in the embers and I can sing 'Kumbaya', although I know I will be flattened shortly after the end of the first line. But I am happy enough. Camping is an adventure after all and there will be no washing machine for a week, not much cooking to speak of, no beds to make or rules to follow and no one will have to sit up straight or worry about table manners. A week of freedom and wild places and us all together as we rarely are at home.

We collect our water daily from the well, and it tastes delicious, fresh and cold from a deep spring that bubbles up yards from the cottage. We wake in the mornings to the sound of wheeling gulls and the whoosh of the sea against the rocks. At night we sleep to the moaning of the wind as it circles the old stone cottage, lifts the corner of the corrugated iron roof and makes it squeak and crack, before moving on who knows where. The beds are damp and lumpy and the front door, constructed from old ship's timbers and heavy lead strips, has a 3-inch raggedy gap at the bottom, as though chewed at by big teeth. On the outside of the door, I can trace the ravages of weather and time with my finger. Blattering rains, punishing gales, blistering sunshine: all signatures are written here across the old wood, and there is a quiet beauty in the rough healing of such old wounds.

At the back of the cottage stands the chemical loo, enclosed, but only just, in a little wooden hut. Visits to the loo are made in secret, if possible. It is bad enough to sit a vulnerable behind upon the bucket affair filled with bright blue liquid, to peer nervously through the gaps in the wooden slats, to be trapped underneath the nests of a whole red spider colony, without inviting pranksters in as well. This is my family, remember; my children, with their vivid imaginations, water pistols and a wicked sense of timing.

Supper is cooked on the outside fire, unless it is raining so much that no makeshift shelter will stand against the attack. The children mix dough in basins and wind lengths of it around sticks to cook in the embers. These 'dough boys' are teeth-breakers, so we must pay attention. Too long in the cooking and they become missiles, as hard as marbles, and perfect ammunition for our home-made catapults. We toast marshmallows and bake potatoes in silver foil. We are all filthy, smoke-blackened and happy as hippos in mud. I wash the small boys with cold water from the well and they sleep soundly in their grubby sleeping-bags, exhausted with all the games. During the days they spend hours fishing for crabs off the old pier, while the dogs lie in the seaweed, their heads on their paws, watching every move. Occasionally one of the collies leaps into life and snaps at a rising crab, only to release it with a yelp as a pincer fixes onto an upper lip. The skill is to get the crab all the way up to the top of the pier. Not easy, as they know only too well something is up when they leave the water behind and begin to fly like birds through the air. They release the rind and flop back into the sea, only to be caught again in the same way. Crabs are not known for their intelligence.

It's the same crab, you know, Bryn tells them. As a much bigger boy, he knows this sort of thing. Poor sod must have vertigo by now!

His small brothers look at him in disgust.

It is NOT! they all speak at once.

This one's eyes are a different colour, says Jake most definitely.

Oh, yeah! So they are! laughs Bryn. Silly me!

There is no phone here, no hum of electrics or electronics, no television – although we don't have one at home either, so this is no big loss. There is nothing to heavy our days or irritate our heads and keep them buzzing when we should be asleep. Here we have the curlews calling. We don't need the weather forecast; we can decide what to do according to the salt in the wind, and the changes in the wide open sky. Here there are stories around a night fire, stars for light, easy laughter and minds fizzing with adventure.

I wonder why we need anything more.

One year, we decide to try the mainland. Our friend George has agreed to look after the farm. It feels like a trip to the moon and we will have to be much more organised for such a journey.

Just take what you need, nothing extra.

That's what I tell them, although I don't think anyone takes much notice. As Alex, Cassie and I climb into the front seats, we can see no boys at all, just a high mound of kit, floor to ceiling, with a big teddy and two puzzled collies on the summit.

Are we all in? I ask the mound of kit.

Yes, it tells me, and off we go.

Before we have even reached the end of the pot-holes they are at each other's throats, although who is at whose I cannot tell, as I still have no visual. Cassie looks at me and we both sigh and shake our heads. She pulls her finger from her mouth with a pop. It is pink from sucking.

Pay no attention, she whispers. Even at ten, she is already a wise woman of the world.

What if they fall out? I whisper back. Or suffocate?

Good, she says, and puts her finger back in.

On the ferry, they demand sweeties and chips and fizzy drinks and all the other junk food disallowed at home. I never had this challenge at Shore Cottage, or any of the other ones we've holidayed in. In those places, there are no come-hither displays of tooth-rotting, mind-altering poisons, and I could send my children to seventh heaven with one toffee a week. But not here in the outside world.

It's a holiday, urges Alex, already reaching out for something crinkly wrapped and full of colour and promise.

For me too! I reply, but this argument never wins. So, wired with sugars and rainbows in their bloodstreams, they romp around the boat till a man announces we are arriving on the mainland and thanks us for travelling with him.

What a nice man! I say and Bryn looks at me as he might a character in a fairy story.

It's the only ferry, Mum, he says. Perhaps boarding school is teaching him something after all. I watch him as he plays with his little brothers, so distant a child, so different from the rest. When he was taken from me at the age of eight, and deposited in a boys-only school, miles from the island, my heart broke for the first time. It breaks again at the start of every term and after every half-term. I ask him if he is happy, looking into his eyes and he says yes, but what comes out of his mouth is not what I see in his face. In these short years of separation, he has grown away, into himself and I have no idea how to find my way in.

He is fine! says Alex, say his parents, says anyone I speak to. It's good for him.

Perhaps. Yet I'm glad we have no money to send the others.

For a moment I am sunk, remembering the letters from the bank, the ones that threaten all manner of unpleasantness. The ones which have started to arrive with numbing regularity.

A guilty thought occurs to me. If we *had* to take him out of school; had to bring him home . . .

Bryn catches me watching him and looks away from me, back into his secret self.

Suddenly Alex and I are alone and the decks are clearing.

Already tense from trying to keep my sweetie-riddled children calm, I am in no mood for this.

Where the hell are they?

Stop flapping! says Alex, making me flap all the more. They'll be on the car deck.

And they are, having rushed down the steps while our attention strayed, to burrow back into the chaos of the Landrover. Rhua is standing on the roof pretending to be a pop star, and asking his father if he can stay there for the rest of the journey.

See? Alex grins smugly as he hauls Shakin' Stevens off the roof and hefts him into the back. They are all safe, worry guts!

If I had a shotgun I'd blow that smugness to kingdom come.

Instead, I smile through gritted teeth. Ok, ok. Let's do the holiday.

The mainland! Oh the mainland! Everything exciting happens on the mainland. First off, there are traffic lights, something the small boys have never seen before.

Go back Dad, go back! Make them change . . . Again Dad, again! . . .

And roundabouts.

Go round again Dad, again! Oh just once more . . . pllll-lllease . . . Now the other way!

For goodness sake! I say, my stomach turning. The police will be after us if we keep this up. Or we'll run out of fuel.

Police? Oh yeah Dad, make them come, make them neenaw neenaw and flash their blue lights, Dad. Plllllease!

From the mound of dogs and kit, they marvel at everything, and in their marvelling I can taste the freshness of seeing things for the first time, the elation and sparkle in that seeing, like having lemonade in your veins and butterflies in your head.

There are no seat belts in the back of the Landrover, and no law to put them there, so the children bounce and whoop and flip like monkeys, free as air as the car rocks like a boat in a storm.

Suddenly my head is bursting.

Enough! I roar, causing everyone to freeze mid-flip and Alex to swerve. He is not pleased.

Why are you shouting? he asks with a frown across his face, deep as the Limpopo River.

I don't bother to respond, enjoying the sudden silence. Instead I turn to fluff up a very flat collie and to settle my sons the right way up.

What are you going to spend your pocket money on? I beam at them.

Jake is buying a Lego set, one of those big ones with enough tiny pieces to block the vacuum every week.

Rhua wants an Action Man. Well, that figures.

And Solly? Well, Solly wants a gun and chorus.

A gun and chorus?

Yeah! Gun and chorus, like Duncan's at crayboop.

He is getting upset as he always does when we have no idea what language he speaks.

Okay, okay Sol, that's grand. We'll find one.

Cassie, seeing my predicament, pulls out her finger.

It's a dinosaur with flashing eyes. Duncan's got one and he brought it to playgroup. It's called a Gunnacaurus.

She says all this in a monotone, staring straight ahead, like a code breaker in a spy movie.

I wonder what we would all do without her translation skills.

I bend my head down to hers. Where do we get one? I ask.

She looks at me in puzzlement. A dinosaur shop, she says.

Of course. Silly me.

22

Cracks Appearing

~

After the holiday we return to close the cottages down for the winter months against the long wet, cold, windy weather that is no respecter of stone walls, however thick they may be. All the water is drained from all the inside pipes, and the blue plastic tubing that snakes away up the hill to the natural springs. We heft heaps of mattresses, anywhere up to twenty, into the only house we can really keep dry, the big wooden chalet at the mouth of the sea inlet. We hitch up de-humidifiers, and oil heaters, and blow heaters sensitive to the bite of a frost. We always hope this care and attention will keep away the black bitter-smelling mould or the sharp teeth of hungry rodents, but we never quite win the battle. The spring will see Granny-at-the-Gate and me with our upholstery needles and our extra-strong thread, squatting beside a rent mattress in our fingerless mittens, ready to push back the chewed stuffing and to close the hole with large, determined stitches.

All curtains are washed, dried, repaired and ironed before being tied in labelled bundles, in case I forget which ones go where. With seven properties, all with very different windows, any puzzlement over which curtains hang where would cost valuable time. Each property has to be reached by vehicle, so it is not as if I can dither and pop back to check. Dithering and popping could take all morning. The fifty-odd duvets and blankets must be taken to the launderette for washing. I can see nothing but bedding in my rear view. I can only see what lies ahead, I realise, and it is always a long winding road.

We lay rodent bait everywhere and I apologise in advance, for this is a cruel winter murder. Just as they think, 'Oh great, here's a nice warm cottage with no one at home; let's munch on this nice dish of blue wheat!' the bleeding has begun and it will take some time for life to step away from each little body. I wonder, sometimes, what happens when a lactating mother takes the bait. All her babies, eyes shut, mewling for her, starving slowly.

Of course, no one else thinks like this, so I keep it to myself and blink away any sudden salty tears. I scrub out fridges with bleach and prop the doors open. The fires are cleared out and washed till the water is no longer sooty black. Rugs are bashed to within an inch of falling apart completely, and those that cannot hold themselves together are taken as Gobbler food. All ornaments and lamps and other bits of furniture are cleaned, repaired and the windows are left open just a smidgeon, for free flow of air. Doors are locked, if there is a lock, which mostly there is not, and we turn back into our own winter lives.

* * *

Now is the time for cosy fires, for warm soups and stews and home-made bread, for scratchy vests and woolly socks and a robust supply of waterproof clothing. It's time to gather hazelnuts, sloes for making gin, rowan-berries for jelly to go with the venison – not that anyone likes it much. The sheep must be dosed for worms and the stock moved to lower, more sheltered grasslands. Every day from now through to March or April, they will all be fed dried nuts, straw and silage, made from the grass during the summer and fermenting merrily in a deep pit halfway up the hill. The temperature inside the pit can reach boiling and the stink of the stuff, once ready for the feast, is enough to sever all marriage ties with one sniff.

Alex is quite happy to pop in for coffee in-between silage deliveries, waterproofed and coated in green slime. It takes me many flaps of my towel to move the putrid gasses along, but it takes me some courage to ask him to stand outside in the sleet to drink his coffee.

Can you take off your oilies before coming in? I ask him, as a compromise.

He is astonished.

No, love, he says, sounding patronising. It would waste too much of my time.

This is the time of year when everything is absolutely clear, including the fact that I am not coping. The air is thinner, and so am I. The light is whiter and from the shoreline the little islands look near enough to touch. Bracken turns to copper gold under an autumn sun and falls over to form a lacy carpet that stretches for miles across the hills. The shore is brilliant with sea pinks and other rocky plants holding on to the last little bit of a fast ebbing warmth. Geese fly overhead, honking us all to the windows to wonder again where they go and how they manage to fly in such a fine formation. As I watch, the leader falls back into the vee and immediately a new goose takes up its position. There is no bickering, no jostling to be first. I marvel at their synergy. Humans could never manage it. We wouldn't even agree on how to take off, never mind fly thousands of miles together, honking encouragement. I keep watching after the others have moved away, and there is a longing in me.

If I could only go with them.

Instead, I make an appointment with the doctor.

I think you should try some antidepressants, he says, kindly; and despite my initial feeling of failure, I collect the packet from the chemist, with relief.

The rut will begin soon, and the hills will echo to the eerie sound of moaning stags, announcing and defending their territory, their harem. Sometimes, on a still evening, I can hear the whack of antlers coming together in mortal combat and I shiver at the sheer power behind the sound. I picture the winner, proud and bloodied, turning to his hinds, and I see the loser – old perhaps, past his best – wounded and broken and limping away to a lonely end.

As the year moves towards its close, the nights are cold and crisp, the stars like diamonds in the night skies. If we are really lucky, we will be able to watch the Northern Lights flicker and spin across the canopy in a wild dance of yellows, reds, greens and purples, like flames from a heavenly bonfire.

In the daylight Alex goes stalking, for we must eat this winter. This is the time that his day begins when it is still the night before. In full camouflage gear, with a terrifying rifle slung over his shoulder and a thermos of coffee in one of his many pockets, Alex sets off into the coldest hour of the darkness. He must be well and truly on the hill and downwind of the herd by first light, or he will stand no chance of catching them unawares. The meat will fill our bellies during the cold days and provide next season's guests with some tasty venison stews or a succulent roast haunch with rowan jelly and alcoholic gravy. The kill is not something Alex enjoys at all. To him, the sheer wild beauty of these magnificent and proud creatures is something to be watched and enjoyed, to lift his heart to, not his gun, but he has chosen to beget five children, all of whom are growing fast, and besides, the strength of the herd lies in careful culling. We can eat the weak ones and be thankful for their gift to our table, but for them to breed will bring that weakness to the next generation and this is not good management. Years ago, cruel winters did the culling, but not now. Although it may seem cold to us, it is not deadly for the wild things, and so the good farmer must do the job himself.

After the kill, Alex and Bryn take off on their quad bikes to drag the animal back to the farmsteadings. This used to be a task for a hill pony, but we have no hill pony and the fallen beast is miles away over very rough terrain, only accessible by the quads.

The other children gather to ogle. They are silent as they take in the bloodied stag, its fine legs dangling, its nose of soft velvet and its wide cloudy eyes.

We HATE venison! they chant, clamping their hands over their noses and turning away.

No worries, I tell them, already feeling stronger, more able to laugh at life.

When I stew it, we'll call it beef.

Once gutted and skinned, the beast is slung from high hooks in the barn, by its hind legs. It takes two good men with pulleys and blocks and many mouthfuls of cursing to get it up there. It has to hang high to keep the rats away.

Rats?

Yes, I am afraid so. Please don't tell the guests.

Alex threads a plastic lemonade bottle onto the rope between the rafter and the hind legs of the deer, but it doesn't always work. The rats are hungry and often will find a way around the problem, by leaping from the beam. It's a one-way journey.

Once they do that, they're trapped! chuckles Bryn. The younger boys all look up at him as they might a super-hero.

Yeeuch! Cassie shivers. She obviously has the same picture in her mind as I do and is probably, like me, considering a vegetarian diet.

So how do they get down? asks Solly, his eyes wide as he peers up at the stag.

Oh no problem, says Alex. Rats bounce.

*   *   *

When I go to milk Blossom, singing a little song to myself as I walk to the byre, I look up at the corpse and can still see him, full of life and standing high and proud on the hillside, his snout scanning the breeze, his antlers wide and strong. He turns his head quickly, his eyes wide. Then I see the running of him, effortlessly leaping over walls and fences, over the burn and on till the woods fold over him and I am left alone, holding my breath at the sheer glorious beauty of him. Blossom flaps her tail into my face, and I realise I am pulling mindlessly on an empty teat.

Tag says he'll make sausages. Tag is the village butcher.

From this to sausages, I think to myself. What a fall from grace.

However, Tag's idea is a fine one and releases me from endless stock boilings of all the bits useful for nothing else at all, the fatty bits, the offcuts, the gristle. I will keep some for stock, for soups and casseroles, but I always seem to have enough stock in my life to fill a small swimming pool, and, to be honest, it is not for long that my family will tolerate the unmistakeable flavour and aroma of stag in their thick warming soups, however brilliantly I may try to muffle with onions.

As the weather cools further, the deer move down to the low ground for the last of the grazing and for shelter in the woods, although the trees are bare now, skinny without their fulsome summer skirts. We find deer suddenly now, and all of us are startled as we meet around a corner or in the middle of a huddle of trees. The hinds will bark, a comical

high-pitched indignant sound and stamp their front feet as if
to frighten us away. We feel like intruders.

One morning I watch a hind run down to the shore, a way
behind the others who are already moving up into the trees.
She is a young hind, perhaps a year old, and the playfulness
of a child is strong in her still. She noses through the kelp,
pulling up mouthfuls and chewing them, her head up, alert
for any danger. She moves among the rocks, further and
further into the brackish water until it covers her knees. I
wonder if she will swim and I keep watching, for her behaviour is unusual, as is her choice to be there on her own. She
lifts her head to the wind and tosses it. Then, with a little
jump of exuberance, she runs along parallel to the shore,
churning up the water and letting spray fly out behind her.
Six greylag geese fly over the buff and land beside her. For a
moment she is startled by all this commotion and stands
quite still while they settle into the water. So intent are they
on their own fussings around each other they seem oblivious
to her presence, or indifferent at least. She stares at them for
a little, and then takes a small step towards them, extending
her nose to the tail feathers of the nearest goose. He swings
round, startling her, and she pulls her head back. A moment
passes and the hind reaches forward a second time as he
raises his beak up to her. I don't know if they actually
touched, or how long I stood rooted to the spot.

Suddenly, as if she hears the thud of my heart, the hind
jerks up her head and looks straight at me, right in the eyes,
and holds me captive.

Has she only just seen me? I wonder. Or did she know I
was here all along and is now asking, Did you *see* that?

I look right back at her.

Yes, I did see, I tell her. I really did see.

Slowly, she turns and wanders back into the wind-bowed hazel woods above the high water mark.

And is gone.

23

Christmas at Tapsalteerie

ᴗᴗ

All through December, excitement is on the rise. I know that most people are thoroughly over-excited well before then, having had Christmas shoved down their throats since Easter Monday, but with no television – in fact, no reception in this remote and wild place we call home – we are, more or less, able to keep Santa under wraps for most of the autumn months. Catalogues do arrive, however, from time to time and are quickly snatched away by small hands and pored over for hours by torch-light under bed coverings. Fat highlighters are employed to bring just a little closer the prospect of being granted a heart's desire.

Think big, we tell our children. Whatever you believe, you can achieve. Your dreams are always reachable if you give them legs and walk them without giving up, not for one moment, not ever. However, lines are drawn through big dreams when Christmas is on the horizon, and not with a highlighter pen.

Christmas is all about giving, I announce piously across the breakfast table, but no one is listening. It is what they are getting that matters, and blow the giving thing; that's for parents to worry about. What I want is a Tonka digger, a huge Lego set, a mountain bike, rollerblades, a full stocking, sweets and treats. And this is five times over. As they study the catalogues that keep coming, whatever I might do or say to stem the flow, I warn the children that the real thing is nothing like the picture. Jake imagines a whole fire station complete with trucks, slippery poles, firemen and engines with water in their bellies and big dingly bells. What he will get is a small box containing two firemen, a wee plastic dingle-less engine and two weedy transfers. The Lightsabers Rhua craves will stop working altogether once he has whacked two Darksiders through the kitchen window, and this is presuming we remember to buy the batteries in the first place. Solly's Batman cape will be a napkin-sized bit of plastic with a squint logo and only one shoulder tie that will break before he even feels it across his back. In the bin there will be enough packaging to make a two-man toboggan, all of it shouting warnings of certain death to small children, should they be moved to eat any of it.

I make the same mistake myself, so I am not so clever after all. The dress on the model looks really classy. The material falls in soft folds around her slim body and the colours are fresh and tasteful.

When the size 14 version is finally freed from three and a half miles of polythene wrappings it remains as stiff as the bag it was packed in. Where, I wonder are the soft folds? I encourage them out with a couple of sharp flicks. The dress crackles like gunfire. I know, even before I pull it over my head that their idea of a size 14 is not a complete 14, but only in certain places and all the wrong places for my lumpy form. The colours are dull, the stitching wiggly and white like tacking, and when I dash back to the catalogue, sure in the knowledge that the mistake is all theirs, I see my own all too clearly. There she is, that skinny smiling bitch on a warm beach, with her folds soft and her long hair blowing gently in the breeze. It wasn't the dress I wanted. It was transformation.

This year, we have a goose for Christmas dinner, and Sol is deeply upset. He cannot believe we are planning to eat one of the magnificent creatures we all love to watch as they fly overhead on their journey to faraway places.

They fly all the way to the Arctic, I tell him. See how beautiful they are and how they fly in perfect formation, up high where the air is sharp and rarefied and cold? I read him stories of magic geese and golden eggs and then we go and blast one out of the sky to watch it fall lifeless to the ground, its broken body emptied of all that vibrant beauty.

We didn't kill it, I tell him, as if that makes it alright. It flew too high and the ice on its wings made it fall. He looks at me and narrows his eyes, then he picks up a feather and strokes his cheek with it.

Can I have sausages? he asks.

I tie the feet together with string and hang it head down in the outhouse. As it swings to stillness, I feel its eye on me and I am chastened. Geese mate for life, after all.

No decorating in this house till Christmas Eve.

Why the hell not? I want to know. In my family, when I was a child, the house looked like fairyland for at least ten days. My mother was an ace at creating a fairyland.

It is not the way we do it in this house, Alex says, but I can't let it go just yet.

My mother has all her Christmas shopping done by October and the planning for the food too!

Bully for her, he says. What a nightmare. Thank goodness you are different!

I am?

Momentarily, the need to be as different as possible from my mother carries me away and I lose purchase on the argument, if it ever was an argument.

On 22 December, and not a minute before, Alex sets off to the mainland with a car full of excited children. They are Christmas shopping.

Everything will be sold, I warn him, and the shops crowded, people pushing and grumpy as hell. I cannot imagine anyone in their right mind hitting the mainland shops this close to the day, and am happy to be left behind to get things ready.

The Landrover returns around 6 o'clock.

Look what Gran gave us! They thrust a huge box of mince pies into my arms and then dive upstairs with their purchases, long rolls of Christmas paper and labels with golden ties.

Supper anyone? I call to their disappearing backs.

We had egg and chips on the ferry, says Alex. A Christmas treat. He grabs his chainsaw from the kitchen table, where it has been primed and oiled and sharpened, and calls for Bryn. Cassie has elected to help the little boys wrap their gifts.

Off to get the tree now, he grins.

Don't bring the biggest in the wood! I plead, although there really is no point.

I scrub the grease and black dods of oil off the table as they head out into the night.

At midnight I am vacuuming up the trail of pine needles, bits of tinsel and broken glass balls. Half the forest floor came in with this big baby, and it was raining when they cut it down, so there are long streaks of mud running from the back door and right through the house. The tree is a splendid one, too tall to stand unaided in the copper bucket, even with a load of big stones to keep it in place. Alex has tied the top to the curtain rail with orange binder twine. It looks like a washing line looped across the sitting room, but the tree is steady-ish now, although the fairy at the top lists drunkenly to one side. We switch on the lights and step back to admire the tree.

Lovely! I sigh, accepting the glass of brandy Alex offers me.

Christmas Eve finds the children at fever pitch and I am myself in a grand panic about all the things I will surely have forgotten to order, collect, wrap, buy. Now the shops are closed and we are about to celebrate the greatest birthday of all time, not that this will be much in the minds of the children. For them it is all Santa and reindeer, crackers and chocolates and mystery and new toys.

Finally, after many hours, they are all fast asleep.

Do reindeer eat mince pies? I whisper to Alex, as we tiptoe along the landing after tucking them in for what is left of the night.

No, he says, of course not. They eat grass.

So why don't the children leave grass out, then?

Because I don't eat grass, he says, taking a big bite out of one of his mummy's mince pies.

The next morning, after stockings are opened, animals fed and Blossom milked, we drive the alpine road to mass. The little chapel is full to busting and everyone is dressed for the occasion. There is a magical mystery to this day of worship and voices rise in relative harmony to announce the newborn King of Heaven. Children wriggle but nobody minds on this day. I sing with all my heart the well-known words, and when I can find the harmony line I belt it out with gusto.

About an hour after we return home to Tapsalteerie, to the delicious smell of roasting meat, we receive the grandparents and build up the fires. Carols ring out through the house, despite the groans from the children, and the crystal glasses sparkle and chink together as we share this mighty feast, marvelling together at where it all began, so many years ago in a lowly stable.

24

Isobel the Hen

⌒

There is a time in the year, once it has turned, and before
the first snowdrop appears, when it feels like life is on
hold, as if it's waiting for something, and unsure what to say
while it waits. The light is minimal. Children go to school in
the dark and come home in the dark and in the hours between
we all work beneath electric lights, our very souls shivering,
and wondering why it is we feel like old custard. Faces look
skinned and we all clunder around like roly-poly people,
thick with layers and woolly fleeces, our feet plunged into
warm boots as soon as we swing them out of bed. There is a
relentless chill in the air and the winds howl around the
house, pulling at the windows so that they rattle like an old
man's dying. One night, while a gale roars and screams
through the wild darkness, our bedroom window looks like
it is finally beaten. A loud crack shows a new split in the
rotten frame and Alex has to hurtle downstairs, butt naked,
to find something to hold the big picture window in place.

Peeping out from the 75-tog duvet, I watch the glass move like inflating lungs and I wonder if Alex will be in time to prevent an explosion of shattering glass, knocking me to kingdom come. A hole that big in this house, in this gale, could have me lifted, like Dorothy, into the night and spirited away to the Land of Oz. Just as I am beginning to enjoy this fantasy, Alex crashes back into the room pulling an ancient and extremely filthy old door.

Help me! he barks and I am out of bed in a flash. Together we force it against the moving glass, which now looks more like a mainsail. Alex also has the yard broom and wedges it against the door, kicking it firmly into place with his foot. Then he turns back to bed and pulls the covers over his head. He will be asleep in minutes, I know. I stand for a moment looking at the leaves and mud, the grimy door, the splinters of rotten door, and I listen to the wind, deadened a bit now behind all that thick old wood. Outside the animals will be sheltering wherever they can, or they will die defeated, for this is the dying time. Through a tiny crack the wind cries in like a baby.

In the morning I am in no hurry to get out of bed. The wind has dropped to a steady moan, a poor cousin to last night's wild roaring beast. I shake my jeans until they soften enough to pull on. My upper body, however, needs more than a layer of denim to keep it warm. First the vest. I hate wearing a vest. I vowed I never would again once I left behind the liberty bodice of childhood. But, here I am, despite my vows, pulling a brushed cotton semmit over my head, with sleeves if you don't mind, and roses round the neckline, as if that changed everything. Now follows an array of T-shirts, a roll-necked jumper and, finally, a thick padded shirt like something a lumberjack would wear in Alaska. I balloon above the waist as though someone has inflated me with an air pump. I am the fat lady of this circus and am quite unable to make any sudden moves, a point that has not gone un-noticed by my fast children, as they run from my wooden spoon and other sundry threatenings. I haven't seen a flash of skin for weeks and nor has anyone else. Were I to have a sudden appointment with the doctor, I would need to arrive a good hour before time, just to relieve myself of all the layers.

I yell at the kids, for the second time, gather up a pile of washing and make my way down the two flights of stairs to the kitchen. It is warmer here, by comparison, with the constant heat from the Aga and the warm bodies of the dogs. They rush up to greet me, tails wagging, like we haven't seen each other in weeks.

Out you go, I tell them, holding the door ajar, while they peer into the sleet, and dither. Shall we wait just in case summer arrives early, or dash out and risk being frozen to the ground by our vital organs?

I decide for them and boot them through the door.

As I walk back across the tired kitchen lino, laying break-fast plates, finding bowls, cereal, milk, butter and marmalade, a hen taps smartly on the window pane with her beak.

A what? A hen? We don't have any hens.

But there she stands, brown, portly, with a mottled beak, a black-tipped tail and attitude. She taps again, twice, strutting up and down the concrete ledge. I rub my eyes and wonder if the cold hasn't finally denuded me of my senses. Yes, we do have a bird table – well, an old colander tied to a stake with twine – and visitors to it have included a great spotted woodpecker and his family, the usual sparrows, finches, robins and blackbirds, thrushes and yellowhammers, siskins and goldfinches. We have seen crows, gulls and once a buzzard that darkened the window light and startled us all in the kitchen. But we have never had a hen, till now.

As I watch her in amazement, I remind myself that we live two miles from the village, and we have no neighbours and few visitors in the winter months. The hen is a domestic bird; she doesn't just fly in on her way to or from the Arctic Circle, or from Africa with the swallows, nor did she come home with us from the Co-op, as far as I know.

She must be a gift from Heaven.

That's daft, says Alex. You don't get hens from Heaven.

Like he would know.

Mum, there's a hen at the window, says Jake, ramming toast into his mouth. She is now running up and down like a loon at the sight of all this rammed-in toast.

She's hungry, says Cassie, matter-of-factly and opens the window. The hen is in like a bullet, confident as a celebrity. We watch, open-mouthed, as she dives into the floury depths of a bowl of muesli, throwing back her beak to swallow, and pinging bits of nut and raisin across the table. The children laugh delightedly. She dives for Jake's toast, which he graciously shares with her and she marches up to Solly, who is hardly awake, and studies him from behind his cornflakes.

Help yourself, he says, offering her a soggy cornflake, and she does.

When she is done with breakfast, and lightly coated with flour and sprinkles of milk and crumbs, she marches past the jams and the marmalade to slake her thirst in my cooling mug of tea. One of the cats, curious to know what the commotion is all about, jumps onto the table. Without a moment's hesitation, the hen hurls herself at the startled creature, her beak going like an Uzi.

She can stay! Alex chuckles. He hates cats.

So she stays. Not in the house as she might have liked, but in a nice cosy half barrel, lined with hay, in a sheltered part of the garden. We call her Isobel, after a friend whose impersonation of a hen laying a football is legendary.

Every morning, Isobel taps on the window demanding breakfast and a chance to duff up the cats. We place a bowl of warm porridge with creamy milk on the sill outside, and she entertains us all through our own meal. The rest of the day she spends pecking her way around the garden, amusing the summer guests each year with her worm-catching tactics; digging out earth baths and lying in a pool of sunshine, crooning to herself, her eyes almost closed.

When Easter arrives on the back of a soft snow flurry, and the first guests arrive with startled moon faces, we will be hiding chocolate eggs for the annual hunt. We will also be reflecting on the crucifixion of Jesus, and His rising from the dead. Well, some of us will. The rest are in a chocolate frenzy at first light. All during Lent we have fed chocolate to Isobel with her breakfast, encouraging her to lay a chocolate egg on Easter Sunday morning. We know she will. We all have faith.

Alex rises early that day, and sneaks outside to push a foil-covered chocolate egg beneath the warm sleepy hen. After breakfast, we all troop out to witness the miracle, but the nest is empty.

The disappointment around me is palpable.

I know where it is, says Solly.

Oh great, he's found it!

It's still stuck up she's bum! He gives a triumphant flourish.

Let's give her breakfast, I say briskly, grabbing his hand and herding the others back indoors, wondering how I can possibly escape to plant another egg in secret. Isobel follows us to the ledge, but when I put her porridge down, she turns away.

How odd, I think. She is always hungry in the mornings.

Then I see it: a telltale snatch of shiny blue paper winking at me from the corner of her beak.

Isobel shared our family life for some years. She chased the pet lambs and pecked fleas off the dogs as they snoozed in the sun. She flew onto the garage roof and laid eggs we only discovered when they were well past safe eating. One year she shared her barrel with a lamb that couldn't walk, nestling into the warm wool of its back to sleep. When the lamb eventually died, she looked lost for a while, so close had the bond grown between them over their months together.

And we finally found out how she came to be at our window that first February. Some travellers who had lodged

on Tapsalteerie for a summer had kept hens. On their departure, they had caught all but the wily, independent Isobel,
who had flown herself into a tree and refused to come down.
After a chilly month or two of foraging and avoiding death
by polecat or mink, she had found our kitchen window and
joined our family.

When a visiting collie killed her, I was heartbroken. This
comical creature had made me laugh when laughs were
scarce. As I took her down to the sea for burial, I cried like I
was never going to stop. I wrapped her and some heavy
stones in a linen cloth and, as she sank beneath the salty
surface, I thanked her for coming into my life. Perhaps she
was from Heaven, after all.

25

Girl Friday

I tell Alex I don't want to be on medication all summer. I need my wits about me. It's okay, all this daft floating in the winters, but soon I will need to crack on at breakneck speed all over again. Last summer I tried to shove a load of washing into the fridge, and it wasn't a joke. I am already fighting the horrors of losing track of my children from March to September, of being too busy to play, too tired, or too caught up with dinner preparations to read the bedtime stories, or to sing them lullabies, although they are probably quite happy about that bit.

He agrees I need help in the house, but doesn't want to pay a wage.

They get to stay in this lovely place! he argues, as if that would bring anyone in.

And to work hard, I remind him.

It takes a long time to agree a figure.

* * *

We set to, wording an advert for *The Lady* magazine, where nice middle-class families advertise for nice middle-class girls.

'WANTED. Girl Friday for busy family-run hotel on idyllic West Coast island.' We buy a box number and wait for publication day.

The phone rings off the hook. Sorting the good from the not so good is initially done over the phone. Girls who think that lambs are cute, or that an island sounds romantic, that children are sweet, that hills are alive with the sound of music, that this life will be a magical mystery tour, are all as deluded as I once was, and put firmly in the picture. It makes not one jot of difference. They are all drunk on the dream of the good life, and dying to meet the couple who, they are sure, still have regular sex and laugh happily together of an evening, sharing tales of the day over sparkling glasses of home-made elderflower wine. They shrug off my warnings about the daily hardship, the lack of money, the visitors who are too many and who stay too long.

Once the list is a manageable length, we invite the survivors to the island for an interview. This is instant whittling. Out of dozens of applicants, only a handful make the journey. The others disappear, having discovered just how far we are from anywhere else and how much it costs to get here.

A few girls come and then leave again after being snuffled by collies, or frozen to death in their damp, cold beds. One leaves in tears after Rhua flips his gravy-coated sprouts into the open mouth of her handbag during supper and another when Solly asks her, albeit quite politely, why she is so fat. One has dreadful body odour and one stays for a few days, looking more and more frightened each day, and finally leaving after telling me she's pregnant.

And then comes Maddy.

Halloo! Ah've came fer the Gurrl Friday job!

They probably understand her in Glasgow.

She stands in the doorway, a tiny girl with huge hair, red and curly and falling down her back like a waterfall, where it stops just above her very small bottom. Over this, she has pasted a minute leather pelmet. Her shiny black boots dazzle me and I cannot see where they end. She can hardly stand in those heels, leaning against the door frame for support.

Well, have you now, young lady? I say, certain she will be another cross on the ever-dwindling list.

Aye, she says. Can ah come in?

Yes, please do, I manage to say and she bobs down onto a chair, leaving most of the seat visible, and crosses her skinny legs. One boot bounces as we talk. I like her and, despite all my instincts, all my lookings for a sensibly clad, motherly, gentle creature with an even temperament, I am actually considering employing a firecracker in high boots with wild hair and the look of the Irish rogue in her sparkling eyes. This is not an interview. This is the start of a friendship, and we both knew it as soon as our eyes met. The wild crazy in me is waving at the wild crazy in her, at the woman, the girl, at the lonely dark places and ones full of laughter un-laughed. She knows nothing of my life and

I none of hers. She hasn't even seen her bedroom, nor met the kids, and yet we both know she has already moved in, with her fishing rod and her need for adventure, and the temper in her and the wild bright song she sings that sounds so like the one I remember as my own. I can feel it rising back up into my throat and my mouth is ready to be filled with it once more. If she can breeze in through that door, loose limbed and ready to dance, with the freckles still peppering her grown-up nose, then maybe, just maybe, I can find the feet to dance with her.

The pay is crap, I tell her and she flaps me away. So Alex was right.

Okay . . . when can you start?

Our days begin very early – or at least mine do. Maddy has a spot of bother with the whole morning thing, preferring afternoons, if she could choose. I tell her she cannot, and although she takes it well enough, I can see from her face that it's a big blow. Guests just don't want breakfast in the afternoons, I tell her gently, becoming less gentle on the mornings I have to put the breakfast on hold, pop the hypothermic lamb in the tea-towel drawer, tell the children not to touch ANYTHING and hurtle up the two flights of stairs to shake her awake by pouring black coffee down her throat.

Is it my day on? she asks me, dreamily.

It is, I tell her. You were off two days ago, remember? You went fishing and forgot to come back again and I had to drive halfway round the island looking for you.

Oh yeah . . . sorry about that.

One leg creeps out from under the duvet. I haul the rest of her out and have to smile at the over-sized sleepsuit she wears at night, with its yawning bear on the front and its pink paws and little pocket for her night hanky.

By the time she is down, the guests are served and there are dishes to wash.

There's a lamb in the drawer, Maddy says, easing out a tea towel from beneath the sleeping baby. Is it ok?

I pour boiling water on the coffee grounds, fire up the toaster for seconds, and throw my husband his packed lunch. Jake, Rhua and Sol are chasing each other around the big table on pedal tractors making engine noises. Fly has jumped onto the master's chair for safety and is curled up tight as a football. We are already late for school.

Its fine, I say. Just don't shut the drawer.

We have new guests arriving today, so I send Maddy to change over the big bedroom with the turret, the bay window and the bathroom large enough for a ceilidh. There are fresh flowers to pick for the dinner tables, fires to clean out and lay, the downstairs rooms to be vacuumed and dusted, all the tea trays to be refreshed and all bathrooms cleaned. I am only glad it isn't a Saturday, with heaven knows how many cottages to muck out and clean for changeover. There will be a mound of bed linen and towels, napkins and tablecloths to wash and hang out on the drying green, and today it's delivery day for the grocery boys who will, no doubt, already be shaking in their boots as they move ever closer to the small and dangerous Granny-at-the-Gate.

* * *

When the guests arrive, they look like they have just stepped out of a hot wash and a 1600 spin cycle. I divert their attention away from such topics as pot-holes or the threat of rain, and transport them far away into the exciting world of puffins flying in to nest, exciting small islands to visit, eagles so huge they block out the sun, and I finish with a mouth-watering description of the dinner menu.

Just come and see the view from your windows, I tell them, on this glorious spring day, and they follow me up the sweeping staircase with its fancy newel posts and its brilliantly coloured stained glass-window halfway up. By now, they are completely wowed and have quite forgotten the bumpy track and that funny whine coming from the under-skirts of their rather low-slung car.

Somewhere, in the middle of a conversation about the family crest depicted in the stained-glass window, I hear a sound that causes my heart to thud into my boots. I know it well and it should be coming from outside, but it's not. In fact it is quite nearby. I lower my voice, almost to a whisper, and encourage my guests to speak instead. Picking up speed, I steer them hurriedly along the wide landing and into their regal bedroom, where I wave my arms about a bit, showing them this and that and the bathroom and the view, finishing off with the promise of tea and home-made shortbread in the drawing room in twenty minutes. They know they are being suddenly hurried, but I close the door firmly on their puzzled faces. I have no intention of explaining this one to them.

Now I am going hunting.

I find them in the bathroom halfway along the landing. One of them is nibbling at the roll of loo paper and the other has jumped into the bath and is skidding about desperately trying to stay the right way up. I need gumption for the filthy streaks in the tub and something miraculous for the blobs of sloppy excreta all over the carpet and the bath mat.

You little buggers! I hiss at them, and they both erupt in a rush of adoration and calls for mummy.

That's me, and these are my pet lambs – lambs their mothers didn't want and nor do I but I don't get a choice in the matter. I poke my head around the door. All is quiet.

Come on! I whisper and they blaa at me like bagpipes warming up. The three of us hurtle down the stairs and out of the front door, one lamb pausing to pee on the hall carpet and finding my boot up its backside. It takes me a good hour to clean up while the guests, unaware, sip tea in the easy chairs. They can already smell the rosemary and garlic-basted lamb I am roasting for their dinner.

Later on, just after the main course has been served, Alex brings news of a small ewe struggling to deliver of her lamb. I cannot leave my post, so he brings her into the kitchen, spreading newspaper across the floor. I soap up, as Maddy clears dishes and lines up the puddings. The lamb is facing backwards and Alex's hand is too big to turn it around. I can see a small hoof poking out from the swollen vagina, and it's a back hoof. Very carefully, I push the hoof back into the warm dark and concentrate on turning the lamb around inside the womb, eventually finding the head and the two front legs. The mother is sore and exhausted and she whickers softly in her pain. She has no energy to push, so I gently pull on the legs, easing the head into the birth canal with my fingers. With a whoosh, the lamb is born and I wipe off the muck and mucous and clear its mouth, offering it to the mother. She begins to lick it clean, making little grunting sounds of affection and we all smile. Ewes this young, still really lambs themselves, should never become pregnant. This one obviously found herself in the wrong place at the wrong time among the tups last autumn. She could easily reject her lamb once the pain stops, and walk away from its tiny cries for help, leaving her baby to become lunch for a circling crow.

Thanks, beams Alex, lifting the worn out mother and her lamb away to a warm bed of straw for the night.

Compliments to the chef for the pudding, sings Maddy, who has kept everything running smoothly while I played Kitchen Vet. Lady Squeaky Boots wants the recipe if you'll give it. She dumps the bowls at the sink and swings round for coffee cups.

Chocs are in the fridge, I say, and we both step over the bloodied rags and stained newspapers until there is time to clear it all up.

If Visit Scotland could just see this, laughs Maddy.

Coffee delivered, she returns with a smirk on her face and the two silver dishes of chocolates.

What? I ask her, and in reply, she scrunches up an empty chocolate wrapper.

They're all empty, she says.

Empty? Indeed they are. Some clever person has carefully

opened each one, removed the chocolate and reassembled the paper around a pocket of air.

Brilliant! I say.

My children are clearly destined for great things.

26

Men in Uniforms

～

This summer we have more than house and cottage guests. This summer we have the army – not the whole army, you understand, but a battalion or two for four weeks of field training – and they obviously don't arrive as a surprise, knocking at the door, clutching their berets and asking gingerly if we'd mind them putting up their tents.

We had an official call from HQ. They want to camp way out on the hill and be able to use the coastal waters for canoeing and general watery manoeuvres. The prospect is wildly exciting for a pile of kids two days into their long summer break and already bored rigid.

Day one, they go through the entire holiday quota of popcorn, finding my huge jam pan and turning up the heat while they popped out to score a few goals. Gunfire brings me hurtling downstairs, but there are no commandos firing off rounds in the kitchen, no one at all in fact, just a hailstorm of popcorn and a pan with a bottom as black as a witch's hat. I find popcorn in my dustpan for days after.

Day two, changeover day, sees them roller-skating through the cottage we are attempting to clean, firing stolen road mix at each other from their catapults. When my patience and the road mix run out, someone suggests making a pudding.

Yeah!

The others grin and they are gone. Well, at least Old Rona and I can finish our work now, although my head is spinning with the thought of unsupervised pudding making.

When we return to the kitchen, all is calm.

They must have made it and eaten it! grins Rona, although we are both searching for devastation, knowing them as we do.

As I push open the door through into the house a bowl of pink goo lands on my head.

Rona makes the mistake of laughing at me.

Tastes good! she chuckles, wiping a blob off her eyebrow.

The following week the army arrives and I am delighted to see them.

Can we go, can we go! clamour the small boys. Bryn, always quiet when he first comes home, watches his brothers, but says nothing.

No, I tell them. You have homework to do first.

I have my own opinions about the pointlessness of summer homework, which I keep to myself; but this apart, I am pretty certain the army has not arrived here just to amuse small boys. They have come to work on their subterfuge tactics, for manoeuvres in the dark and in the ocean, preparing for an enemy they are unlikely to meet on this remote island off the West Coast.

So the boys make a show of doing their homework, and I make a show of believing them.

Every day we watch the trucks and tanks rattle their way down the hill track and past the kitchen window. If we are outside, we wave like crazy. Actually, I am not sure waving to a load of running soldiers with blackened faces is quite the thing, but my own excitement at being so close to so many fit young men, all in uniform, quite carries me away. It is probably me who does most of the waving, to be honest, and they don't wave back – which is understandable, as they all clasp machine guns to their chests and have no waving arms free. The sound of their feet, in perfect time with each other, sounds like someone eating a whole bowl of dry cornflakes. One or two of them wink at me through the smears of mud. The whites of their eyes flash and I feel a strange turbulence in my belly. I also feel very safe. Nobody is likely to attack Tapsalteerie in the dead of night – not while these muscled young men bounce over hillocks, and canoe around the coastline, their night-vision goggles fixed to their faces.

One afternoon a couple of officers, including the colour sergeant, drop by the house, while Alex is at sea.

Would your kids like to come up to camp? they ask.

Some hours later, after the most peaceful afternoon I have had for years, a bunch of tired boys are safely delivered back home.

* * *

We saw the Honey Monster! squeals Solly, his cheeks on fire with excitement.

Jake, who has worn his combat gear for days now in the hopes of being enlisted, explains.

He's not the real Honey Monster, Mum, he says. He's the cook. He's dug holes in the hill for ovens, and he cooks with huge gas fires like afterburners on a jet!

Sounds like a nightmare to me.

And the shower is a bucket in the tree with holes in it. Someone climbs up steps to pour water in for the guy underneath.

Opportunity for some ghastly pranks, I imagine.

A few days later, the colour sergeant pops in for a cuppa.

Don't you miss a bath? I ask him, and he admits he wouldn't mind one, now and again.

Now I am thinking. Four bathrooms, a hundred or so men . . .

Not everyone, he laughs, seeing my eyes on stalks with the maths. Just the officers. The regulars can freeze under the cold showers. It's good for them.

You'd have to chop wood for Gobbler, I tell him.

Deal done.

The first officer to alight in the woodshed to chop for his bath is built like Captain Universe. I watch him through the fly screens over the larder window, marvelling at his muscles, his taught stomach and his strength, for he chops the timber as if it was cheese, stacking it against the stone wall. I have to strongly resist the urge to ask him if he would like his back scrubbed.

* * *

One night, Alex and I are invited for camp dinner. An armoured car collects us at six. Maddy is babysitting, much to her chagrin.

The camp is impressively immaculate, tidier than any room in our house could ever be if I never slept at all. Of course, up here there are rules.

Did you ever think of joining the army? I ask Alex.

Not for one minute, he says cheerfully.

The next morning the sky opens and torrential rains batter the ground. I have to drive down the village for some supplies and, as I cross the wee bridge and swing around the bend, I notice a small upright tent, like a sentry box, in the middle of a fast-growing puddle. Before the entrance stands a bedraggled young soldier, stood to attention, his rifle over his shoulder. Rivulets of rain run down his face and his boots are almost drowned.

You all right? I ask him, in my best mother voice. He is not much older that Bryn.

Ma'am, he says, staring straight ahead and I realise he is not going to let me take him back for fresh clothes and a cup of tea.

An hour later, when I return, there is even less of the soldier showing above the waterline. What can this manoeuvre be, I wonder? He'll be dead from hypothermia by teatime, and I tell the colour sergeant so when I see him later in the day.

He chuckles. You mean Private Parts, I presume?

Private Parts?

He was sent off at reveille this morning to find a good

spot for a halfway latrine, to erect it and guard it. Tomorrow we'll need it.

But he's in danger of drowning, I say, and besides, that is NOT a good place. All the rain runs down into that gully. It's obvious when you look at the camber of the track.

Precisely, says the colour sergeant. This is why he is still a Private.

Jake is asked if he would like to join a manoeuvre. I remember Private Parts and feel instantly sick.

You don't really want to go, do you Jakey? Why not visit Granny-at-the-Gate instead, and build a Lego castle or something safe and warm and dry and miles away from the cruel soldiers . . . ?

He gives me a look.

They collect him mid-morning and ask him if he has packed supplies. He tells them yes, and I wonder what he found to pack. I have already fussed over a sleeping-bag, warm socks, a change of underwear, his thick pyjamas and so on, and all he did was scoff. This is soldiering, he snorts, tough stuff, not a primary school outing.

When he returns the following afternoon, he can barely walk. His face is filthy and his feet soaked.

Had a great time, didn't we Jake? says the big soldier who now fills the doorway. Jake smiles wanly.

Did you have enough supplies? I ask him once we are alone and he is shoving doorsteps of bread and Bovril into his mouth.

He shakes his head and once he can speak, he says, Pot Noodles.

Not enough Pot Noodles?

No hot water. No cooker. It was a survival manoeuvre.

Did they have food?

He nods.

Did they not share?

Nope, he says. They laughed.

As the summer closes down and the yellow and brown are in the woods and over the hills, rehearsals begin for the local pantomime. This year, Rhua, always the performer, has elected to audition for a part. I am quite certain he is thinking Prince Charming, but he ends up as whipping boy to one of the lesser knights. For three evenings a week, he must spend hours hanging about in the dressing room for his two minutes of glory on stage. Needless to say, he is bored. I suggest that he catch up on his schoolwork while waiting to be called. He is horrified. He needs to concentrate on his part, remain focused at all times.

But you don't have a lot of lines to learn, do you? I ask him.

No, he says.

You just canter across the stage on a wooden horse, whinnying and calling out: Back my liege, in the name of the king!

Yes, he says.

Well, just how much focusing does that require?

He rolls his eyes at me. What would I know about such things?

I tell him that I always played the lead in school plays; that I was asked to play the lead in a Greek drama by an amateur dramatic society as a young woman; that his father's first sighting of me was on stage, singing a bawdy song while stripping off my big petticoats. I get quite carried away with the memories, all that greasepaint and the buzz of the dressing rooms, the whispering tension in the wings. He is looking at me strangely.

That was in the olden days, he says, and I come back into my sagging skin with a whump.

Yes, I say, you are right.

One evening the phone rings. There is an angry stage manager on the other end. It seems that Rhua has set off the fire alarms, requiring a full complement of firemen to leap into their kit, slide down the pole and nee-naw their way to the town hall.

Oh dear! I say, wondering if the hall is now a pile of smouldering embers and the panto cancelled.

There is no fire! she shrieks.

I am tempted to ask her if she would have been less angry had there actually been a fire, but I resist. Alex agrees to come immediately to collect the criminal, even though his regular lift will be leaving with the other whipping boys in just a few minutes time. We are to be punished too, it seems.

I don't know how Alex will deal with this, but I expect he will quietly advise Rhua to keep away from fire alarms in future, and, like me, will swither between relief at the lack of a blaze and the desire to laugh at the sheer naughtiness of the prank. I do know, for sure, that Rhua will be punishing himself already, feeling very small and stupid as disapproving eyes stare him out of the hall.

When he arrives home, he goes straight up to bed without a word.

The next morning, there is a stern rap at the door. Two constables stand on the doorstep dressed for a street riot.

Where's the boy? one asks.

Which boy? I have four.

I think you know which one. Rhua.

Rhua? This isn't about the fire alarm, is it? Surely not?

The incident last night? Yes it is. Call him please.

They can hardly squeeze through the door for all their attachments: truncheons, night sticks, whistles and other menacing black things. Their polished boots squeak.

It's a criminal offence, one of them mutters.

I don't bother to hide my astonishment. He is just a lad, I say. You two look like stormtroopers.

I don't offer them tea.

27

The Man Who Looks After the Whales

Alex finds himself overwhelmed with the demands for places on whale-watching trips. He has crew now throughout the summer months, students usually, whose work is marine matters. Over the seasons, others ask to work with us for we are, after all, the first ever whale-watching business in the country that carries out benign research on these Leviathans in their natural habitat. The software designed to catch and develop all Alex's research is often quoted by the media as fact, even though Alex is the very first to insist we know very little about the whales, that no one does, even if they say they do. Everything affects everything else. We count the birds each year, and over time compare data to make what can only be assumptions. And still the questions roll in. Are whales less likely to 'visit' the boat in the early part of the summer because they are too busy feeding? Are they more sociable when the seas are rich in food? Do the numbers of puffins nesting each year have anything to do with the numbers of whales, and do they both need sand eels to fill their bellies? How do the plankton levels affect all of the above?

The boat heads out each morning and Alex sniffs the wind. Last night, a local fisherman called him to report killer whales up north. He might be able to find them again, but they are fast movers, and will most likely have gone by now. Everything is taken into account before Alex points his nose out to sea. Perhaps the tide is ebbing, or flooding. Perhaps it's mid moon-cycle or at the beginning or end, with clear skies and a skinny luminous fingernail hanging in the night sky. Maybe it's Tuesday, or foggy, or there was a gale last night and the beaches are heaped with colourful flotsam.

Alex will go the way he feels is right, for only he can find whales ninety-nine times out of a hundred and never through logic. After that very first whale, this give-me-the-facts man moved into the realms of the spirit. We can call in the science experts for the research, for all the data collection and its development, but without Alex, his passion and his boat, none of this would be going anywhere, and he is humble with his gift. Although he has no science degree, he reads every bit of literature on whales, on dolphins, porpoise, fish stocks in the Atlantic, the food chain, everything. He learns his subject and he learns it fast. People who really want to see the puffins now have to whale-watch first, landing on Puffin Island for lunch, after the boat has travelled miles this way and that, undertaking all sorts of different scientific studies, all leading towards a greater knowledge of the whales, dolphins and porpoise, who have just found themselves a father protector. Individual whales are identified by the marks on their dorsal fins, and this method of ID, the work of one of our early students, is now used around the world. The wild idea has become a big business, seemingly overnight. I am already seeing folk advertising whale-watching trips in their guest houses and hearts are captured right across the country. Visitors are coming to the island for the sole purpose of finding a whale in the wild.

Do they come to the boat . . . really?

Yes, they really do come to the boat. It is the only way Alex will work with the whales. No invading of their space, no chasing, no close encounter unless the whale chooses. Sometimes he will pull away from a nearby whale if it shows no interest in being watched. There will be a good reason; he knows that, respects that.

Hey, you can go closer! a passenger may say to him. What they are really saying is that they have paid for this and he should provide them with value.

Value to whom? he asks. The whale or you?

A grudging respect grows for the man who looks after the whales. Never a man to be seduced by anything the material world has to offer, Alex shows a fierce dedication to what has now become his life work, and, for all my frustration at his growing absence in my life, I admire him. I realise that he has never really been here with me; not from the very early days. He may have his backside in the kitchen chair every morning and his body in my bed each night, but his mind does not rest with me. It spins away on adventures and into worlds I will only ever hear about. When he talks to the students for hours about research and discoveries and as they share conversation and laughter and beer, while I move in and out of the rooms supplying food and care, I feel like an outsider. And that is what I am. I may be wife, life partner, mother to all his children, but I do not fire him up like they do and perhaps that is how it is in a marriage.

As the business blooms, Alex gathers a whole team behind him, and I warm myself in the reflected glory. We are high profile, or Alex is, his comments in the papers regularly as the anti-whaling lobby fights to save cetaceans across the world. As each new piece of information is collected, it must be added to the information these bodies need in order to convince governments to take action. We attract funding from big organisations wanting to be a part of such innovative research, such sexy research, for this has captured the hearts of the public, and no mistake. We buy underwater camera equipment, hydrophones and other expensive electronic kit. Research divers come to look from beneath and small planes from above. The BBC make films of us, we are recognised in books – both fiction and fact – and the phone keeps on ringing until my head is full of dings and requests, and my freezers of whale poo.

Is this stewing steak? Maddy asks me, flapping a bag of brown under my nose.

Whale poo, I tell her.

So we won't cook it then?

This is the lampoon that is my life. And it's not just whale poo in the freezer alongside the meat and the fish. There is a dead seal pup for autopsy, bags of frozen plankton, a puffin, and one of these days my guests are going to get a surprise, for nobody bothers to label these extras. Although a dead puffin is clearly a dead puffin with its rainbow beak, there are bags of some things that could quite easily be mistaken for another. I toss in my sleep at the very thought of whale poo stew.

The student team lives on site in caravans like gypsies. Every six weeks or so they change over, although some stay the whole season especially if their final dissertation can benefit from working in the field. This gypsy camp booms to the sound of jungle drums and hiphop most nights, although Alex is fierce about hangovers and periods. Neither is allowed.

But girls tend to have them, I explain. It's not a choice.

Well, I don't want them working for me when they do, he grumps. Bad-tempered and scratchy and clutching their bellies and making a big fuss over nothing!

There speaks a man.

I believe he enjoys all this importance, for all he waves it away. He is a big fish now in a pond he dug himself. He is now called The Whale Expert.

Just think, I say to Solly's old teddy one morning, a few years ago he was the first man to cure onions to prolong their life and to turn them into their Spanish lookalikes. He was the first to irrigate potatoes. In a dry summer he made a fortune. He was the first to work heavy horses as a tourist attraction, and now he is the first whale father. Such a glory in it all. So, tell me, Teddy old chap, where is my glory?

Teddy just stares straight ahead.

*   *   *

It seems that the students need a team leader, mainly to get them out of bed in the morning and to finish what they started. Ability to study in a lab or work in a university atmosphere is not what Alex needs out here on the wild seas, with people to help aboard and practical skills to learn and perfect, such as casting off the mooring ropes without getting them wrapped around their legs, or leaping onto a rock without being sucked back by the waves and disappearing into forty fathoms of turbulent wet. It is astonishing how impractical these kids can be. One of them, told to collect the dinghy from its outer mooring before a trip, ran it straight up the rocks, not once, but twice.

She lives in Leamington Spa! I tell Alex as he stamps around cursing her lack of intelligence.

She has never set foot in a dinghy before, or used an outboard. Why did you send her?

I told her once, he grumbles. That should be enough. And how she managed to ram the rocks twice is beyond belief!

It is at this point that I realise Alex has no patience for teaching.

I need a team leader, he says. They can teach.

I know right off I am never going to take to her from the first minute I meet Jenny. She is long and blonde and stunning with more than her fair share of tanned legs and white teeth. She is tousled and independent and wild and that's quite enough about her. She also has no degree in anything, never mind marine biology. I have no idea why Alex is considering her for team leader.

Well, there is something about her . . . he says.

Indeed there is. I take great pleasure in telling her that the caravan she is to live in has no running water.

That's ok, she grins. I drink gin.

Over the days, Jenny teaches me. She shows me how to 'step out' of myself. It seems that for years I have been weighed down with domestic chores, children and the demands of a country life, where money is always in short supply and the subject of many a tense argument, and where everything has to be repaired and never replaced. I have also become PLM, it seems.

What's PLM? I ask her.

Poor Little Me, she says.

I am astonished. Do I sound sorry for myself?

Yep. Have a gin.

So I do, and I learn from her that I am woman first, and not a vessel for carrying things, things like babies, self-pity, hang-ups, fury, envy, piles of washing or other people's worries. She speaks to me and I listen, and I am hungry for it. The doors Maddy led me gently through in the beginning are now thrown wide, and I am hungry for this new learning, this colourful, lipsticked, high-heeled, sassy-ass learning. As each new light flicks on, illuminating each new truth, I know that I know it already, and this is not the fantasy of the young woman who hoped that if she flapped long and hard enough her arms would turn into wings. This is ancient in me, in every woman, wild and forgetting of herself amid the demands of a hungry motherless world.

Suddenly the inevitability of steady decline seems less inevitable. I am not, after all, going to turn into a leathery faced wifey with soup constantly on the hob and Tuesdays set aside for baking. I won't have to join the WRI, nor learn country dancing. The prospect of such a new freedom goes quickly to my head.

She's a bad influence! grumbles Alex, as I swoop down the stairs in a weeny skirt and a crop top.

Way too late for that realisation, my lord and master. Way too late.

28

Winter Peace

～

And so the seasons come and go, and it's time, once again, to put the cottages to bed. I could go myself, to be honest, and probably for the whole winter. Although I long for this time of year, my aching body screams for it, I always sink into a terrible gloom as it barrels in with the first autumn gale. Dying leaves skitter across the kitchen floor every time someone leaves the door open, and someone always does. Fly and the other two young collies are always wet and always faithful, so when Alex comes in and when Alex goes out then so do they, and that can be fifty times a day.

Alex, please can you build a kennel for these dogs?
     Alex, can you take your boots off when you come in?
     Alex, Alex, help me, I'm drowning . . .

I don't say any of that. Even if I did, even if he turned, he would quickly look away, not wanting to see the disappointment in my eyes. Besides, I am too ashamed of such weakness, so I just pop into the surgery for my usual order of antidepressants. Within days, even though I know the black holes are all still there, they are now quite hidden under pretty rugs, so that everyone, including Alex, thinks I am all better now.

Maddy will stay a bit longer to help with the end of season strip down, and Old Rona is always game for some pennies in her pocket and then there's Granny-at-the-Gate to wash and iron. I am a lucky girl for sure, with all this help around. Jenny has flown to foreign parts, to work in a jungle with orang-utans. Jenny always leaves for foreign parts in the winter, for she is single and brilliant and passionate about God's creatures. She hugs me goodbye.

Keep the faith! she says. And drink gin. Life around Alex will never be dull!

I remember the day he told her to row between the rocks at Puffin Island, in a cross sea with a gale rising, and she told him what he could do with such an order. I had yet to find the courage for such a retort.

I watch her go sadly. She and Maddy both help me to lift my nose from the dirty dishwater, and what they teach me sinks deep into my bones, but when they are gone it is easy to fall back into the old shoes.

For Alex, the winter days are all about feeding the stock and gathering wood for Gobbler. We might like to dine out now and again, Alex and I, to spend time alone, to talk about life and love and what we like about each other. Unfortunately, the whole island closes down for its own rest and relaxation. Some lucky ones will holiday abroad, but everyone knows farmers can't do that. You can't put animals on hold.

The children will run where they will, whatever I am doing, learning from the professional how to leave doors open and how to rush indoors with all the mud of the farm stuck to the soles of their boots. At their heels will run the pet lambs perhaps, or my setter Jinx who thinks she is human but with too many legs.

We work from cottage to cottage, checking first to see what has been left behind. Rona is always fearful at this point, in case the last tenants left a dead granny in a cupboard. Someone did leave all their clothes hanging in one once, which puzzled us a lot. There were shirts, trousers, skirts, shoes, everything.

Perhaps we should check the garden for recent burials, says Maddy, and Old Rona squeals and clutches her chest in horror.

Over the years we have found school bags full of home-work, expensive copper-bottomed pans, a bicycle, and many bags and jackets and children's toys. No one ever calls to ask for them to be returned. In the beginning, when I had a zeal long since abandoned, I spent a while sourcing the owner and wrapping parcels for the post.

Oh thanks, but we didn't want that old bit of nonsense anyway! laughs Mrs Thing.

Cheeky bitch, says Rona. She just dumped it on you, like you were a nothing maid servant.

Yeah, right, says Maddy. Want me to do some voodoo on her?

And we laugh at it, as we always do. I watch their faces crease up and feel the healing of their giggles as I join in, and off we fly, leaving Mrs Thing and her baggage way below us.

So, we decide to benefit from the carelessness of our visitors, although one bike isn't much good to a family of five children.

We wash, iron and fold curtains, bed linen, and all the rest. We label bags with the name of each cottage and store them in the wooden house at the sea inlet.

Then the whole family decamps into the guest rooms, one floor down. This is always huge fun, exciting to have all that space, to be able to run along the landing without being shushed and halted by the firm hand of a hotel proprietor. Now we have room for everything, a comfortable bed, and easy hot water, as it only takes minutes for it to rise this high. Even in the summer, when the spring water comes in to the house at a reasonably warm temperature and Gobbler is burning like Rome twenty-four hours a day, the upstairs water still manages to look exhausted as it dribbles into the tub, like it is all out of puff.

I'm having this bed, Jake yells, just because he can. Being quiet is a Summer Thing and we all look forward to shouting our way through the corridors and big airy rooms and at each other to remind our lungs just how full they can be given half a chance.

Jake leans his array of guns along the wall at the foot of the bed. Now he can watch them while he lies in bed, instead of having to get out and go around a corner to check on them. Rhua, who is currently forty feet up in the air, is having this bed, because it bounces really well. Solly is quietly rigging up a complication of trip wires in the room of his choice.

Can I have the blue room, Ma? Cassie asks.

Of course, I say, and look across at my little girl, who is now a beautiful young woman, with huge almond eyes and a sting in her tail. She seems to have grown up overnight. Bryn, still at school, will be home soon for half-term. He is taller than me now and I sometimes feel a great sadness, for while he was growing up I was always hundreds of miles away. Maddy and I wander across to the big window and stand quietly together just looking at the wide open spaces spread out before us; such a change from the poky little squares of glass on the maids' floor. In the garret, way up high, we had to stand on a chair to look out, to climb into the deep window recess and press our noses against the glass to see just a small square of sky, not even big enough to make a pair of sailors' underpants, never mind the whole trouser. I could stand here for days, just watching the sea, the sky, the rolling grass all around me, Alex's beehives, in the crook of the lawn.

Oh Ma, look! Cassie comes over and touches my arm. A young hind noses her way across the grass. Food is growing short now on the hills, and the deer will come to the lower ground to catch the last shoots of summer. As she grazes the lawn, she moves closer to the front door of the hive. Closer, closer she moves and Cassie and I hold our breath.

Suddenly, her head snaps up with a jerk and she jumps backwards, shaking her pretty face which is surrounded by a small black cloud of Alex's bees. She won't come here again.

* * *

225

Now we can enjoy hot deep baths anytime we like instead of having to fit in with guest times, and we are at least a mile closer to the warm pipes. I can 'pop' downstairs, instead of having to set off twenty minutes before I need to get there, and we will light the fire in the small sitting room each evening, all squashing together on the tatty leather chairs, with rugs around out legs for the draughts, to watch something Granny-at-the-Gate has recorded for us on her video, which may or may not be what is written on the label. I will now cook very different fare for my family. There will be no fancy meals for them, as my fancy is on hold till March, along with my enthusiasm for food preparation and my interest in eating it. It is not the same for them, of course. The steady lowering of temperature brings with it an extra hunger and bellies cry out for thick and nourishing soups and stews which I make using all the cheapest cuts of meat that fall to the freezer floor as the summer guests chomp their way through all the choice cuts of venison, beef, lamb and game.

I haul out two scraggy hens, still feathered up and looking as appetising as old pillows. I can pluck them once thawed, batter them into submission, marinade them for a long time and cook them up with an abundance of root vegetables and a good slug of sherry. If its scrag end or tail end or some other delicious-sounding morsel, then I may add a good dollop of blackcurrant jam – first scraping off the layers of mould, of course – some fusty old wine from the cellar, some bruised apples too, or whatever looks like it is about to die in the fridge, and has this one last chance to be glorious. Nothing is wasted; every part of everything has a place somewhere in some dish. I boil up the mutton bones and cool the stock overnight to allow the layer of fat to solidify on the surface. In the old days, this fat was rubbed into chests to ward off coughs and sneezes – amorous husbands too, I've no doubt.

There is always something bubbling, simmering, rising, baking or steaming on my big blue Aga, and it is me who juggles it all. Everyone else is just hungry.

What is this? someone might ask.

Supper, I say. I always say that. I have usually forgotten what I began to cook anyway. Is it stag tonight, or beef or mutton? They all look and taste the same after I have taken them from dangerously tough to really quite chewable and poured on the drink. Sometimes I talk to mothers who, unlike me, do not have so very many children, and who buy cuts of meat that would never break teeth, nor require hours of pummelling and whacking to soften them up. Chops, for example, and cutlets and steaks, lightly dressed half an hour before cooking, popped under the grill, drizzled with a lemon sauce and garnished with parsley.

But we don't have central heating of course, and I must warm my family from the inside.

Mum, Donald's here! sings Solly as he shoots by on his skateboard and only just misses Old Rona and the vacuum.

Donald has come to play. They all do it once.

He has arrived in well-ironed denim jeans and very white trainers, his soft fair hair slicked into an extraordinary quiff at his brow. My children's hair is cut by me and there is not enough on their heads for any such slickery.

Donald has agreed to stay for supper, which is brave of him. It's Shepherd's Pie tonight, as it very often is, for when I cook mince I cook it in vat loads and freeze it. It's also a safe bet for visiting children, as is bangers and mash. By the time supper is called, it is getting dark and there is a chill in the damp air. Donald, in his trendy lightweight jacket, looks perished and his nose is running. He will be in need of the mutton fat this night, I think. He refuses the loan of a large and grubby jumper and sits at the table with chattering teeth. He looks terrified as I spoon out the meal and pass his plateful all the way down to the very end of the big table, where the small boys have chosen to huddle. From where I sit behind this big dish, they look like small dots in the distance. Cassie and her friend join us for two small helpings please.

After a sudden burying of heads and muffled whisperings, Solly speaks out.

Donald wants to know what that is, he says, jabbing a finger in the direction of the slop on Donald's plate.

No I don't! says Donald quickly, blushing a splendid crimson.

My children know never to ask this question, but it is fair dinkum for an unprepared visitor. Nonetheless, all eyes are on me.

Minced whale pie, I say, and there is a gasp and a lot of theatrical gagging around the table. All but Donald tuck in, and I watch him watching them, incredulity on his face. He eats almost nothing, even when I tell him the truth, and when his father arrives to collect him Donald clasps his hand as if he never wants to let go ever again. His trainers, I notice, are spattered with mud and his hair sculpture is quite flattened.

As the boys had disappeared the minute the meal finished, along with their father, professing they all need to find the something that Donald left behind, I ask Cassie if she and her friend will help me. Girls are always easier to coerce, as I know only too well. I run hot water into the basin and toss them a tea towel each.

What's this for? asks the friend after a few moments of obvious puzzlement. I study her face for any sign of a tease, but there is none. Her eyes are wide, her question a genuine one. Cassie stifles an unladylike snort.

Don't you dry dishes at home? I ask her, after demonstrating how to use the rectangle of Irish linen.

No, she replies firmly.

Later I collect grubby boys for bathing. There is a change in the air these days when it comes to bathing. The small boys are suddenly aware of themselves and uncomfortable with it. They used to play together in the big bath with bubbles and ships and teapots and water pistols but not any more. Now a shyness has crept in and they conceal their nakedness with big towels, demanding privacy and solitude, which is really a grand excuse for not washing at all.

Jake, as the biggest, is trusted to wash himself, which may be a mistake as I watch him heading for the bathroom in his wet suit, flippers and mask.

I WILL wash you! I growl at Rhua, who never stands still long enough to be trusted with anything much, and he defends himself by folding his arms across his chest.

Arms down! I say, and then I say it again. Finally, against the might of the mother, he concedes with a muttering of disgust. I begin work at his neck. As I finish his back and flip him around to start on the front, he clamps his hands over his nipples.

Mind my earrings, he says.

Sol is still young enough to spend long minutes squirting water through the backside of his yellow rubber duck. After half a dozen attempts, he manages to hit the far wall.

Do you think Donald will come again? I ask, holding the towel out to him like angel wings.

Nah, he says.

29

Boarding School

~

Some children like boarding school; I read it somewhere. My brother's children did; they loved it, all neatly labelled and packed perfectly, bouncing with sports cups, and with a set of parents who visited them at every possible chance, to cheer them on, to keep them balanced.

Personally, I hated it, although I was desperate to go at first, until the shattering truth dawned on me.

This was not the *Malory Towers* story, nor that of the happy-go-lucky *Chalet Girls*, with their big adventures and midnight feasts; where friendly groups of laughing girls in regulation grey skirts saved the world from all kinds of dastardly dangers. My matron was a wicked old witch with a permanent sneer and a big fat dislike of me at first sight – a far cry from the bosomy warmth I had imagined. The uniform at Malory Towers may have been regulation grey, but no one seemed to mind very much if you tore it to shreds while clambering over Old MacDonald's fence in search of rosy red apples, or for a picnic in his barley field. In fact, some kindly soul offered to mend it for you – probably the bosomy matron.

My trunk – dark navy and gilded with my initials, as though I was off to India with the Foreign Office – was packed with blouses and skirts, vests and jumpers, all carefully labelled. My gym kit, house dresses for evenings, and stockings were folded and layered in maternal order in the lower layer. In the shallow shelf above rested the many pairs of socks: white for gym, blue for weekdays, and for Sundays – to make quite sure all flesh is compliant with the Ten Commandments – long brown thick stockings with seams that must be straight at all times, not wound around your leg like a climbing rose. There were twelve crisp white cotton hankies for the twelve colds I was obviously going to get that first term, and a weird-looking felt hat for Sundays, with the school badge on a blue ribbon around the rim. But I didn't mind any of it. I was off on an awfully big adventure.

The truth dawned slowly.

My regulation grey spread wide and was stiff enough to shelter a whole Japanese family from the rain. On windy days we had to button our coats all the way up to avoid taking off into the blue. It was very hard to imagine any Chalet Girl wearing the enormous scratchy underpants, as we had to on weekdays. It was excruciating to sit for long in warm classrooms, and around 4 p.m. many a girl could be seen wiggling her backside on the seat of her chair, just to relieve the itch. Sundays were better, but only in the pants department.

Although sitting on hard pews was no doubt more comfortable in our Sabbath drawers than it would have been in scratchy greys, we were always aware, as the holy man growled at us and wagged his big red finger over our heads, that somewhere down there, inside those Sunday pants, lay the world's most wicked wickedness, the greatest of them all, and not one of us had the faintest idea what it was.

When Bryn is born, his enlistment for boarding school is a foregone conclusion.

It's a boy!

Great news! I'll call the school.

At the age of eight and hardly able to see over the edge of the table, he is labelled, packed up and dispatched and I cry for weeks. In fact, I never really stop for all the time he is there.

This is inhuman, I say to Alex, to his parents – the ones who have bought this boy's education. This is sick, stupid, wicked.

No, this is good for him, says Alex. And we are lucky to have it all as a gift.

We are?

We don't visit him. It's too far from the school to here, to the island, and we are too busy. We don't even take and collect him. We just pop him into someone's car and wave him off, hearts breaking. Slowly, term by term, he grows further and further away. Instead of shouting his feelings out loud, he turns in. By the time any of us really understand what's going on, he is almost out of sight.

* * *

I was homesick for weeks every single term. If I thought the rules at home were ridiculous, the ones at school were way beyond that. Baths were measured to 6 inches per girl. Matron, who did the measuring, would dawdle if she didn't like you, so that the water was all but cold by the time you got into it. Hot-water bottles were to be filled from the supposedly hot tap before dinner and no refilling later was permitted. Bed coverings were kept to two skinny blankets and should a girl be discovered wearing socks or any extra articles of clothing to avoid frostbite, she was made to stand for an hour in the dark, chilly dorm without speaking. Term after term, despite tearful pleas for clemency and tales of the horrors that went on behind the cloak of respectability, my father was kind but firm, and my mother said it was all good for me. She didn't believe a word I said.

Girls all around me – including the one whose parents always drove me the five-hour journey to and from school – loved it. They positively bounced with boarding school gung-ho and never cried once, or stopped long to see off their parents – parents who popped in, turned up for sports days; parents who had faces and something to say out loud, and not just in a weekly letter. I sobbed into my pillow night after night until it gave up trying to dry. When one prefect got herself pregnant and was bundled out before any awkward questions were asked, I considered doing the same thing, except I didn't quite know where to begin.

When we walked to church every Sunday we wore galoshes, regardless of the weather. Pulled over our stout brown shiny lace-ups, they restricted any fluidity of movement and our calf muscles screamed. It was like walking with a rubber dinghy on each foot, but you had to keep marching beside your partner in strict crocodile formation all the way to church and all the way back again, squeaking like you needed oiling. The village kids lined up to laugh at us, the little madams from the previous century with our long shapeless coats, our daft hats over our eyes and our galoshes. And we mustn't make eye contact. It would be very dangerous to be caught grinning with the hoi polloi and could result in a punishment that would make standing in the chilly dark in the dormitory look like a holiday.

In this sexless and cruel environment, we still managed to bloom, those of us with something to bloom about. The sporty girls got better at sport, the musicians at music, the swats at their chosen subject, for being good at something lifted you above the rest and such an elevation could take you far from the misery of the ordinary girls, trapped down below in their own personal loneliness.

Bryn's home! Bryn's home! The house buzzes with excitement as the car arrives in the driveway. To his sister and his younger brothers he is an enigma, the mystery man who makes everything exciting, everything fun. All our ducks are in line when Bryn is home, but I am not sure it is the same for him. As the eldest he carries a weight the younger ones know nothing of, and never will, and because of his long absences, a distance grows between him and his siblings that no holiday period is ever long enough for them to close.

And Alex is lost around him. This child, our first-born, is still a child. Around Alex you would think he was a challenge to the throne.

Go to your room! he says in his dangerous voice. We are in the middle of supper and Bryn is trying out his newfound manhood by refusing to pass something along the table, refusing to acknowledge his father at all, in fact.

No one speaks. No one dares. The air tastes of bitter metal in my mouth.

Please . . . I begin.

But Bryn rises to his feet and leaves the room.

There are times like this every holiday and I cannot see why we don't blow apart, all of us in a bloody ripped mess of broken hearts. I become devious, secretive, and protective in a thousand ways. I begin to grow away, to go inside myself, to choose which side I am on, not that this was ever in question.

Later on I take a plate of food to Bryn in his room.

I'm sorry, I say, and reach for him, but he pulls away.

It's fine, Mum, he says, and eats nothing.

What I want him to do is yell at me, lash out, something. I want him to say to me: How can you send me away, leave me there and never visit or see my paintings on the walls in the art room, watch me run, or take me out for cake on Saturdays? How could it happen that it took Matron to see all my shoes were two sizes too small? Are you my mother or what?

But he doesn't invite me in, and if Bryn doesn't invite you in, you stay firmly outside.

*   *   *

One year I am to take him back to school myself. Well, not all the way, but as far as I can with the time available to me, putting him on a train for the last few hours. I am determined to go, and no one is going to change my mind. This time the wimp is on the rise and she is stepping out and stepping up and it's about bloody time. I think it was the small shoe thing that galvanised me into action, the sheer and dreadful shame of it.

We go by train as I have no car, and even if I did, all I would do is go round roundabouts for days on end as I freaked out at the traffic mayhem around me.

We arrive with my own beloved granny that afternoon, planning to spend the night with her. Tomorrow afternoon I will take Bryn to the station, where he will join others going the same way. It's not a chatty evening. Bryn is white and nervous and everything in me wants to tell him he can just come home again, but I am beginning to realise that this young teenager is wiser than I. He knows who rules the roost in our world and it certainly isn't me.

We all fear a breach in the family; lines drawn that cannot be undrawn. So I say nothing.

Please don't make me go back! Bryn sobs as the train begins to pull out of the station. He holds fast to the sleeve of my coat and I run along with him until the platform dips away, where I must shake him off, stand there in the dirt with the breathing fast in me and a sound like ice cracking in my ears. I wave through the tears but his blonde head has long since pulled in and it is just me, flapping my arms at a leaving train.

* * *

When I get back to Granny, I am a mess. She pours me a gin and sits down to listen. The phone rings.

Mum? I'm not going back, he says, and hangs up.

Outside it's dark. I can't believe this is happening.

Call the police, says Granny, more calmly than she feels.

After some seriously personal questions, the policeman tells me Bryn will call again.

When he does, ask him where he is and reassure him he can stay with you tonight, he says.

Bryn promises to stay put.

Would you like to come with us to pick him up? asks the policeman.

In the car, he takes me past housing estates where children younger than Bryn are caught in the headlights. It is way past midnight, on a school night.

Where are their parents? I ask, in amazement.

In the pub, he says.

When we collect Bryn and bring him back, the policeman takes me on one side.

Listen to him, he says and then repeats it, looking me smack in the eyeballs.

Listen to him.

I call Alex who is as lost as I was. Now I am not lost. I'm doing what the policeman says and listening to Bryn; I already know what he wants.

Don't make me go back, he said.

Easy. Done.

Well, not that easy.

He should go back in order to leave in the right way, says Alex.

He has a point. This is my upbringing after all. You don't run away. You just don't.

Ok, I say. And he can leave at half-term?

We are agreed on it.

It is the longest and hardest journey I have ever made. Bryn hardly speaks, eats nothing, and arrives as a sliver of the boy I know is in there somewhere.

The school send him home before half-term in a car with two boys whose mother has been killed in a car accident. He arrives with no trunk, no belongings, nothing but what he stands up in.

We never get his things back. I'm not even sure we got him back.

30

Duchess

I love the springtime. Even the sound of its name is full of hope. I can almost hear the collapse of the cold wall of winter. In my eyes, there's a new looking over new lands and the chance to run again without the weight of cumbersome layers. But spring takes her time in coming fully through. First the short green stalks of snowdrops and crocuses, standing for some time now, give way to brave petals, rich in colour and form; in the morning air, there is a shift in the song of birds, new notes and phrases, more conversation between them, reminding me how quiet they have been for months. Butterflies skitter and twirl on the still cold winds, warming their backs for a little in the newborn sunlight. At this time snow can fall, and catch us all unawares. Lambs born in yesterday's warm breeze can die today in the jaws of a spiteful ice-wind. And there is one around our ankles this Easter day.

I am reminded, as I swing us all around the endless corners, of another Easter drive to church, when the children were small and we were giving a nun a lift.

Does anyone know what happened that very first Easter? I foolishly asked the rumple of sleepy young in the back of the Landrover.

I do! Cassie piped up.

Go on, Cassie. I was hopeful. She should know, after all. The nun and I share a smile of anticipation.

It's when they rolled Jesus down the hill! says Cassie triumphantly and all the boys clap.

Granny held her own Sunday school at the gatehouse on Saturdays, which I suppose still counts, although I am not sure she got her message across.

Travelling to Mass nowadays is not so straightforward. Hormonal children do not favour Sunday worship, and tend to disappear or feign a sleep from which they cannot be wakened, as they hear my footfall on the stairs. Sometimes it's just me by myself and, to be honest, there are times I wish my conscience was as easily quietened.

I have known hot sunshine at Easter, on the island, but not this time. It's cold enough to fix you solid if you stop too long to chat.

A blizzard grows overnight, and is still screaming the next morning. Alex goes to check the horses down on the shore, Duchess and the old mare Maggie, her companion. The wind is so strong down here, it's hard for Alex to remain upright and he can see nothing with the sting of snow in his eyes. He finds the old mare hunched against the dry-stone wall, although the shelter it offers is poor. Neither of the horses should be down here in this. Duchess is nowhere. And then he sees her, belly deep in a bog, her big head falling to one side unable to move out of the freezing blast. Her breathing is harsh and short, and she grunts in obvious pain. She must have been here all night in the lonely bitter cold while I pulled the covers up and wondered if I would ever be warm again. The new grass, seduced into popping above ground by a gentle yesterday, called her into this sinking land.

We cannot pull her out without machinery, winches, ropes, men to help. They come, as they always come when someone needs them, with warm jackets and willing backs and their word that they will stay till it is over. They build a windbreak of straw bales around her to stay the battering of the sleet-heavy wind and throw warm blanket layers over her frozen back. Although she may not last the night, we cannot move her without a sled and the dark is coming even now. Soon it will be black around her, and she will be alone again, out here, buried alive on this wild shore, while the seas smash against the rocks and the winds shrill about her mean shelter, drowning out her soft whispers of pain.

The men set to building a reinforced sled and assemble the tackle and ropes they will need. At first light they move towards the shore in a sad silent march. If she is dead, they will feel relief and grief, but if she lives the dying will still be her song, for it is too long the cold ground has held her fast, draining her legs of life, and twisting her gut into knots that no one can see to undo.

She is barely alive as they carefully pull her from the

clutching mud, her limbs torn and stretched as she grunts in pain. Onto the sled they lift her, and cover her with blankets. I watch her glide by behind the tractor, the men walking heads bowed, as I have seen them many a time following a coffin to the graveyard, and my heart is breaking as I join them, touching her big old head with my warm fingers. I look into her eyes, and she, despite the agony, looks back at me, her eyes soft velvet.

I'm sorry Duchess! I whisper. Forgive us.

She takes three days to die. Her legs have died already, and she cannot stand to ease the chaos inside her. Gasses build up in her gut, and the pain must be unbearable. Alex rigs ropes over the beams so that we can turn her every few hours, dosing her with morphine to ease the pain. One morning I wake at five, ready for my shift at her side. Alex lies beside me.

I am out of bed in a flash; perhaps I am late. Why didn't he wake me?

She's gone, he says. I gave her the injection. It was all too much for her.

I knew nothing of the injection. The vet must have left it with him to administer when he knew it was all over.

I run to the steadings, my throat choked with grief and remorse, and fall on her, calling out her name over and over again, my heart bursting with the agony of regret and self-blame. I should have remembered she was down there and reminded Alex. We both forgot. We are both guilty. And worst of all, that gentle, loyal, trusting ton of workhorse would have patiently faced that storm, her brown eyes looking up hopefully at every new sound.

But we never came.

We never came.

When Duncan, the shepherd comes to work at eight, he finds me still there, exhausted and cried out, hollow and forever changed, sprawled across her empty body.

Come on lass, he soothes. You have the living to think about.

The next day Alex takes the digger and two men to make a deep pit to lay her in.

Not on the shore, Alex? It is almost a question.

No, he says, his voice soft and reassuring. Not on the shore, but in a good spot with a view of the little islands, and with plenty of warm sunshine.

They are gone all morning, for this horse is a big one and the land here is pitted with sudden rocks like hidden glaciers beneath the grassy earth. It has taken a few attempts to find enough depth for a grave. As she is lowered in, we all stand alone in our thoughts. I remember her gentle nose nudging the pocket of my jeans for treats, and the way she lifted her head and answered me when I called her over. I remember her befriending old John the bull and Blossom the milk cow with whichever calf she had following on. I remember piling up the small children on her back and letting her sway them along home again after hauling tree trunks onto the open green, or riding her myself, legs stretched wide over her broad back, swaying through a gentle afternoon, letting her choose the way. Lowering my head under summer trees, their fresh smell in my nose, I would tell her things no one else would ever hear. I'd smell her breath, feel its warm punch on my face, and bury my head in her neck while she nibbled at my jersey.

Duchess. Gentle regal lady. Patient and steady, trusted and trusting.

It will be a long time coming: forgiveness for myself, from me.

In the spring, the farmers burn their heather to encourage fresh new tasty shoots for the sheep to eat. When the wind is in the right direction, the heather dry, and adequate fire breaks are erected to contain the burn, the match is struck and the farmer stands well back. For days after a moor burn dies down, smoke fills the air and eyes, and we taste it in our mouths.

This is presuming it does die down, of course.

Millie calls around 4 o'clock.

Is Alex there? she asks. Bo needs some help.

Bo and Millie are neighbours, living a few short miles from Tapsalteerie, and our main instructors on hill farming. Their farm is huge and spread out almost all the way between the town and our little village. It flanks the only road for miles.

The heather burn, it seems, has leapt out of control and is fast moving towards the forestry acres on one side and houses on the other. Alex grabs blankets for dousing flames and is gone into what now looks like a massive firework display in the black sky. Another estate across the valley has had the same mishap and the two fires blaze, rivalling each other for flame height and intensity. I can feel the heat from outside the big house and yet I am miles away from the blaze. The fires are devouring hundreds of trees in their raging, despite the work of many islanders, local firefighters and the fire engines and crew brought across in the ferry from the mainland. Flames rise higher and higher into the stars and the noise is deafening. Trees fall like tin soldiers, crashing to the ground, screaming in their death throes as the sap hisses out of them and their needles turn to dust. The heat is so great that no man can get anywhere near the heart of the fire, now a wild creature drunk on the excitement of destruction and greedily moving on faster and faster, careless of who or what lies in its path.

I stand outside for a while, watching the sky pulse red and black, the sparks rising into the darkness, and I listen to the sound of a whole forest burning alive.

Where are the wild creatures now? What of the roosting birds, the insects, the hibernating wood animals, with their stores of old nuts and their sleepy waking into a broiling night with nowhere to go. Not even a hare can out-run a fire of this intensity, with the wind as an ally, and the dry ground spread wide and ready for the taking.

All night Alex is out, fighting back one of the fires with just two other men. They bash with fire brooms until their arms give up and they can fight no more. At last the rage is out of the beast and the dying begins. No houses are threatened, and the road is just enough of a break to hold back the flames that are now weak and faltering.

When he crawls beneath the sheets, around 3 a.m., he is black as my old gollywog and smelling like a bonfire. I hold him close, vowing not to comment ever again on his membership of the great unwashed, for he is here with me now, and safe.

As he fills me, the urgency is strong in us both and we rock together holding fast, until the fearful storm dies away with the first notes of early birdsong.

Anyone hurt? I ask. People, stock, houses?

He shakes his weary head and is asleep.

You've got visitors! calls Alex, looking like a chimney boy with his eyes a flash through the grime. He could go for weeks like that unless I steer him before a mirror.

I have visitors?

Well, you make them too welcome, he says, and stands before me making lame excuses for his immediate departure that the visitors swallow like a sweetie. Although it can infuriate me, I do envy him his tactics. Whenever he finds himself trapped between a visitor and an escape route, he only has to announce that he has some work he needs to complete and he is instantly off the hook. It is only to be expected that someone as important as Alex will always have work to complete.

We talk of the fire and Alex's heroism and his arriving back exhausted and blackened and crawling into bed fully clothed.

Did the smell come out then? asks my guest, Jeannie, ever the sensible housewife. She would probably have marched poor old Bob straight back downstairs, stripped him of his offensive apparel and hosed him down in the yard before ever allowing him back into the marriage bed.

I haven't stripped the bed yet, I tell her, ignoring her little intake of breath, but, no, it will never come out. The kids have bagged the sheets for dinghy sails.

One less thing to iron! says Jeannie triumphantly, as though she just lightened my workload all by herself.

Oh I don't iron sheets, Jeannie. I hardly iron anything.

She tells me she does. Everything, including Bob's pyjamas – a revelation Bob finds rather uncomfortable.

Alex doesn't wear pyjamas, I say. Alex doesn't wear anything.

Jeannie's hand leaps to her mouth. Oh! she gasps. I don't think that's very nice!

Bob, behind her is grinning.

Oh I do, I say, feeling deliciously wicked.

They leave shortly after, Jeannie refusing their usual second cup.

31

Catering and the Co-op

⌒

Warm days and frilly frocks, beaches and picnics, ice cream and adventures, that's summer, they tell me, and I can see the sparkle of it in their eyes. My eyes, on the other hand, are scanning to-do lists, or designing recipes and, in my annual rise from the sink of medication, my head is busy wondering if this tear in the patch on the curtain for the second bedroom of cottage number five can be mended with another patch, or if the whole rail will collapse under the weight of endless patchings. Is the rail plastic or metal and are there rawlplugs holding it up or just old plaster and glue? I try to picture it, but having had a whole winter off, my inner order thinks it's on holiday.

When we moved here and I said, Ok, Alex, let's run this as a hotel, I hadn't realised that it would be with an empty bank account, nor that all of the inside jobs would be mine. I can see that my husband, the Whale Man, has quite enough on his plate without doing my work as well, but that doesn't stop me feeling like Cinderella when the rest of the world seems to be playing outside.

I keep in mind, as best I can, the teachings of my angels, the girls like Jenny and Maddy, who talk of being a woman first – although it's easy for them, being single and sassy. If they don't like something, they just say so. I breathe it back in, to keep the peace. But, I am learning, bit by little bit, to speak my mind, and sometimes when I do, Alex looks at me in a different way and I like it.

The problem with being willing to turn your hand to anything, is that you very soon find yourself turning your hand to everything.

Over time, and making many frightful mistakes, I eventually turn myself into a very fine cook. And even in this task I find the opportunity for the sort of sharp humour that I inherited from my mother and her mother before her – along with their sheer bloody-minded determination.

Fancy names hide private jokes.

Lemon Mountaincake is a lemon cheesecake that flies out of my hands as I collect it from the fridge. It lands face down beside the dogs' bed, startling Jinx who leaps up in fright and lands in the middle of it. I patch it up, fill the holes, grate dark chocolate over the top and the guests love it, as does Jinx who spends a long time licking her paws.

Or Venison Jumble. This is stinking old stag that reveals its unpleasant odour too late for me to thaw a sweeter cut. I cook it slowly for hours with sweet root vegetables and a whole bottle of . . .

Bring some port from the cellar, Maddy, will you? Not the Dow's, or the master will upset himself.

I add bitter apricots and half a jar of runny raspberry jam mixed with lemon juice. I top it with a savoury crumble.

And so it goes on. Meals are daily miracles and, even more surprising – considering the process of preparation and the sudden changes required for success – is my high rating among the guests. They leave happy, fat and ever so slightly drunk.

Delicious, my dear! they beam. How do you do it?

Lady, I have no idea.

We have nothing to decorate the fish, I sigh to Rona who is working on Maddy's day off. She stands on the other side of the kitchen counter, a small woman with a large brain.

She looks at the pale and colourless mess.

Looks like puke, she says helpfully.

Decoration? I remind her.

Oh yeah. And off she toddles in her gumboots, although the evening is warm and dry, returning with a handful of petals, which she expertly arranges on the plates.

Best not eat these, I tell the guests, as I lay down each serving.

Shopping is another on the list of women's work. And I hate it. Not for a summer dress, or perfume or shoes, or any of those girlie things I haven't seen hide nor hair of for well over a hundred years, but for food supplies. Finding nowhere to park near the shops, I march the kids along the street, preparing myself for the ordeal ahead. I pass other women holding pretty baskets. Inside them, I just know it, will be a piece of French cheese and a pot of olives in garlic for lunch; and for supper, two fillet steaks and the ingredients for a nice green salad. I can feel the frazzle rising up as my feet pound the pavement and I field off grubby boys, all clamouring for comics and crisps and scarlet drinks.

The trolley behind me snaps at my heels like a metal terrier.

Sorry love, the young woman says. She is trying to pull chewing gum off her tights, and is knee-deep in sticky children. Ahead lies about three-quarters of a mile of women, most of the island in fact, and all of us with better things to do with ourselves. Not one of us is here because she is pursuing her dream, but we all know this about each other and we all make great effort to make each other smile.

You look well! I lie to one fraught-faced, badly dyed blonde who smells faintly of sick. Her pre-school darlings are practising their fighter-pilot techniques in loud and imaginary jets, swooping and looping and finally tailspinning, arms wide, into the tower of chocolate-coated Swiss rolls, reduced to half price. The cakes spin across the floor, their cellophane coverings crackling like sparklers on bonfire night.

That's them reduced a bit more, eh? chuckles someone near the tinned veg. At this point two of the till girls smile sympathetically at the chaos and head off for lunch, and I realise with a deep inner sigh that most of us in here will be lucky if we manage a swig of coke and a puff on a Regal before school is out and our men folk are swinging home asking, brightly, What's for tea?

*   *   *

My boys are under very strict orders to behave, not that very strict orders have ever meant anything much to them to date.

There will be no catcalling, I warn them, and no looking up ladies' skirts. No racing up or down the aisles on trolleys, no undressing and no removing of marmalade lids. This is someone else's shop, not yours, and, if you behave, there will be ice cream at the end of it all.

Clear?

They grin and nod.

As we move down the rows of stacked foods, I watch them like a hawk. Bonios, tinned tomatoes, cornflakes, natural yoghurt, pasta, dried fruit. I stop here and there to exchange some chat with friendly faces.

How's Jimmy's knee? Did he? Oh my goodness!

And so on. I should have thought of this ice cream bribe before, saving myself all the usual embarrassment over spitting competitions two aisles over, or price labels stuck to old ladies' backs.

Just remembered coffee. Stay right there, I tell them and dive around the corner and back again. Nearly done now. Like a very old snake, the queue moves past the hair dyes, the wines, the loo paper and round towards light bulbs and Toilet Duck.

Next!

I move forward and begin to unload my trolley, my heart in my mouth. Although I tried to add up as I went through the shop, I can easily run out of fingers or be distracted by a small boy or two, so that this feeling of dread and shame always hits me about now. I watch the girl punch in the numbers and the total rise and rise and rise again. I know what I have in my purse and there is no going overdrawn for me. To overdraw is for other folk, folk who know they can put it right one day.

The boys hate this part. Rhua begins to whistle something through his gaps and Jake has his hands firmly inside his pockets.

That's too much! I whisper, the red shame rising into my face. I will need to put something back. The till girl sighs and rolls her eyes. The queue grumbles as I lift out this and that, and maybe that too?

Now we have it. Exactly right. Empty purse. Back to the Landrover boys!

No ice cream, then? asks Solly, although it's more a statement of fact.

32

Blue Days

⌒

Some days I feel really blue. Not blue like the sky, but a miserable blue which is quite different. Blue is the colour I wake up in, and it fills both me and the room like an invisible cloud, although clouds aren't blue, as everyone knows, and not invisible at all, except on blue sky days, which today most definitely is not. Today is grey, with a yellow wind flattening the flowers and flinging their petals, red, pink, purple and yellow onto the grass. There is little point in thinking today, for thinking could be dangerous; it might take me into the world of wishes and no one can change their life that way. Somewhere, deep down, I know that this is the right life, that only Alex and I can possibly live it, for nobody else in their sane mind would give it a second glance, and there's a pride in there somewhere and a subtle lifting of the heart. And for all the fairy tales inside my head, I am a practical woman. I know how to bat away the swarms of locusts to find the honey, and that to turn a grimace into a smile

255

requires a handstand. And it is impossible to do one of those without laughing.

Blue sky days are very different. These are the days when I am comfortable in my own skin, and it's thrilling and empowering and I want to stay there forever. Everything goes according to plan, everything works, everything fits, and these days are gifts, which is why people write songs about them and rapturous poetry.

The niggles are still there, of course; even on days like these. First and foremost there are the mounting money worries, which rise like bile every morning as we waken.

We should talk about, I tell Alex, but where would we begin?

Every day brings new urgent demands and we must keep moving, moving, moving, and besides, it is hard to notice such menace when there is such brilliant light and such glorious music playing all around. Live this day minute by minute, I tell myself, because heaven knows when you'll get another one; and I do, my eyes wide open, my heart filled with thanks. Everything seems lighter, breezier, although the circumstances are just the same as they were yesterday. I have no explanation for this gift of a day; nor do I need one. A gift is just that – a gift – and only needs to be thankfully received, to be treasured and valued. For I have learned to dance when I have the feet. Nothing planned ever happens and everything unplanned does. Best to just put on my dancing shoes and make life swing, and, if I am light-footed, spinning in space, with my throat full of laughter and the music wild in my head, then maybe, just maybe, I won't notice the dust and the chaos, or hear the old clock eating away at the minutes of my life.

It's not easy on yellow or grey days.

On blue sky days I don't care. Do your worst, I tell the doors, the phone, the CB radio, for now it is I who want to fling my wellies off the pier, as my children did, just to watch them sink, and I who will eat cake just before lunch so I have no appetite, and I who will drive out to the Point, leaving puzzled school children to walk home. And, dinner will not be prepared, because I have chosen to stand alone while the sun sets behind the black rocks and the oystercatchers pipe to each other over the wild hiss of spume against the ancient shore.

At least that's what happens in my head.

One lovely day, the thistles burst open and the sky fills with down. As I walk along the track to the farm and on through the woods and down to the sea, the spores nudge against my face, soft as cobwebs. Some land on my jersey, hovering there for a moment or two, and are tugged away by the breeze to float silently over the water. Now thistles will grow everywhere and Granny-at-the-Gate will have a thing or two to say about that, I can tell you. The sheep will munch around their crimson purple crowns all summer long and in the autumn, and the goldfinches will twitter with delight as they balance on sturdy stems, picking away at the seeds. The council mower will come at the summer's end and cut them all off at the knees, but it won't stop them. Thistles are not the emblem of Scotland for nothing. Thistles are Bravehearts. They cry freedom from every bit of ground, claiming it as their own, and refusing, in the face of all the enemies, to die back or to be wiped out. Inside the house, down is everywhere, clinging to the carpet and the furniture, caught in the webs of the house spiders.

Alex tells me his passengers were enchanted. Today he took the boys out with him, as he always tries to do during the long summer holidays. Bryn is off with his mates in someone's car for a spin, probably literally, and Cass has work in the local hotel.

Yet even scattered to the winds, none of us can ignore the thistledown.

It arrived on the breeze, miles out to sea, over a flat calm. Like a low cloud, it moved over the water towards the boat. A cloud of thistledown, a wonder of nature, and we have just one day a year to see it.

When Jenny came back, her blonde curls were full of it. She said they had to eat their sandwiches covertly, to avoid breathing it in.

Clipping next week, if the weather holds, says Alex after breakfast one morning. I am well acquainted with the whole clipping performance by now, but I smile to myself as I recall my first.

I had to call Millie, of course. Millie is my guru in matters of farming wives. She has learned the ropes at her mother's knee so she breezed into the whole wifely thing with hardly a backwards glance, and she does it all with confidence and aplomb – two things I have yet to develop in myself.

What is my part in the clipping day? I ask her over a cuppa in her busy kitchen. I have escaped from Tapsalteerie for the sake of my ears, to be honest. Jake is currently learning to play the drums, and does so, often and loudly.

Rhua is learning the cello, and if the instrument survives intact I will be astonished, and Solly has chosen the clarinet, but refuses point blank to learn any musical score. The secondary school has a big music department and the promise of stardom is wild in their hearts. Whenever I remind them they should be practising for at least half an hour a day, the temperature in the room rises high enough to set jam.

Half an hour? they squeal, as if I had said half a year.

I know they all expected to be masters of their instruments by the end of the first week, and we do encourage them to aim high, but I fear they are all beginning to realise that it might be ten years before they play in the school band, never mind at a Royal Command Performance. I can feel the passion waning.

Solly, I say gently, as I listen to him squark and parp his way through what should be a delicate little melody by Debussy.

I don't recognise that tune from this score.

He smiles up at me, as if I were a few strips of ivory short of a keyboard.

Mum, he says, I don't play the notes I don't like.

Millie is baking. She is always baking.

The most important thing, she tells me, is that you feed them. The clippers.

What . . . sandwiches? I ask, wondering why their own wives can't rustle them up something.

Not just sandwiches, she says, you give them a meal after it's done.

Oh great! So that's five kids, one Alex, twelve guests for dinner and now a raggle-tag of sheep-smelling clippers filling up my kitchen.

Ok, I say, with more confidence than I feel. What do I feed them? I don't suppose they would enjoy Mackerel Crumble with Marsh Apple Coulis?

A stew is good, she chuckles, and loads of tatties, but not vegetables. They're not good at vegetables, but they might pick at carrots. Oh, and a big pudding, something filling, with ice cream . . . and whisky too, of course.

Huh. Their mummies obviously weren't as strict as I am. No vegetables equals no pudding at my table!

They arrive at ten and the whisky bottle appears by eleven. By the time I take the sandwiches down at midday, there is a right ceilidh going on and the smell of sheep urine is abominable. Everywhere I look there is muck and slosh and the concrete floor is as lethal as an ice rink. Each man is smeared with varying shades of brown and dark green and not one of them is getting near my kitchen table without completely stripping down.

You coming to the turkey shoot? asks Bo, Millie's husband, a strong handsome man who tells a good tale and has a wicked sense of humour. I turn from where I stand at the sink with a hanky pressed against my nose.

Turkeys? I am horrified. You shoot turkeys? I cannot believe you men. They're domestic birds . . . they can't even fly!

Bo's face is a picture. It looks like there is a ferret in there trying to escape. Someone snorts further down the table.

Alex touches my arm. It's a clay pigeon shoot, he says gently. The first prize is a turkey.

The next morning, after I have almost washed the stink out of the house and scrubbed the muck from the lino, there is a call from one of the wives who lent us her husband for the clipping.

Is Dougie there? she asks, trying to sound nonchalant.

We find him fast asleep beside the lily pond, his tractor slewed across the track. Luckily the night had been a warm one. When we wake him, he stretches, grins guiltily and climbs aboard his old Ferguson. He cranks her into life, and trundles home with a cheery backward wave.

33

Alex's Accident

～～

Thistledown in the wind means the holiday season is coming to a close. Every year the Landrover needs a thorough service, and this year is no exception. It is a tireless workhorse and things that shouldn't rattle quite so loudly are beginning to cause us concern. Cassie and I follow behind in the little runabout car to bring Alex home, for it will be a few days before the work is done. A late summer fog chills the air and it is quite hard to see far down the road. No matter; we have plenty of time today. As we move past the gates of the primary school I can see the Landrover has stopped at a strange angle. Alex has ploughed into a metal hawser that was stretched across the road from a digger to a tree, all but invisible in the fog. In seconds the Landover is cut open like a tin of sardines and there is no sign of Alex at first. Then we see him, rising up from where his seat collapsed against the strain of the hawser, covered in blood, his face white with shock. Cassie rushes into the school to call for help, while I try to persuade Alex he does not need to walk back home. Soon Cassie is back, as is the driver of the digger, whose mouth is wide open in horror at the damage. He holds out his shaking hand to reveal shards of teeth, picked up from the road. Shock has made them crazy, these men. And me too, but I am on autopilot. I have a job to do, and there is no room in it for my feelings. My eyes are dry. Perhaps I am all cried out.

Drive him to the old folks' home, says Cassie. The doctor will meet us there.

It takes two of the medics hours to pull the tiny shards of glass out of Alex's poor battered face, for the side windows imploded on impact. Most of his teeth are either broken or missing, but he is still alive with his head on his shoulders, which, by all accounts, is a miracle.

I whisper many prayers that day, genuine thanks from my heart. I remember the times I wished I had never met Alex, and the guilt burns hot in my face.

For days he can only take liquids. He cannot suck through a straw and needs to be fed like a baby. He is bashed and bruised, but not beaten. The children watch him from a distance, curious but not wanting to come too near, for he looks at best strange, at worst grotesque.

From the beginning, he has the attitude that he is truly blest to be alive. He never thinks of what might have been, and when people shake their heads and drop their jaws at the scars on his face, he brushes them off like flies. He adopts an air of jaunty cheerfulness and has no problem with his sunken empty mouth, although he finds it difficult to speak. Beside him, I am torn. On the one hand, I am full of admiration for his positive attitude; and on the other, deeply embarrassed at the look and the sound of a man, my own husband, with no teeth and not in the least bothered about it.

How could I feel that way? I can make no sense of it.

If we could just talk about it, if he would ask me how I felt when it happened, if we could go back through it together, find a new way forward. But for Alex it is over, done, behind him; and no matter how much I might want to talk, it takes two to make a conversation.

At home, he is not an easy patient. Alex is not an easy anything, to be honest. Once the series of infections caused by the minute splinters of glass have all died down, he is fitted with a set of pearlies that are at first painful and then uncomfortable. But Alex accepts this as he did the accident. He is quite happy to remove his teeth in order to enjoy a meal, and I fight to keep my appetite as I studiously ignore the bulge in the top pocket of his shirt, knowing I should be feeling only relief and a renewed adoration for this man who escaped death.

But that is not the truth, and it is hard not to let these feelings show.

Slowly, at a snail's pace, I learn to overcome them. I laugh with him when he sneezes and the whole set of dentures shoot across the floor. I smile as he burrows down the bed in the morning to find them, or pulls them out of the dog's bed and pops them right back into his mouth. I even laugh when he loses them overboard and thinks it's the funniest thing, but my laughter sounds hollow.

They just don't fit, I tell him, again. Let's go back to the dentist.

No, he replies.

You should make him go, his mother says, and for her it makes perfect sense. If her husband had gone through this, she would have organised the whole repair programme and informed him of it as a fait accompli.

Alex doesn't do what I tell him, I say.

Granny looks at me as if I'm to blame for that.

34

The Recording Studio

⌒

In the early years on the island, our winters are for the family, for recovering, for spending time together and for me to collect my medication. In the summers, I am too busy to think, to wallow, to create a monster within; but as the days shorten, the guests leave and the daily round is no longer a circle, I founder. Some lucky island folk who worked all summer will holiday now in far-flung places where the sun shines on their faces and another country takes their hard-earned cash. But we have no cash. As much as we work, just Alex and me with a handful of loyal helpers, we cannot rise out of debt and the debt just keeps on growing. I suppose if we had come to Tapsalteerie with extra money, lots of it, and had been able to repair all the holes that make the draughts that demand more heat that comes from fuel that needs to be found, and dried, and cut, over and over again, things might be different. But we didn't, and there's an end to it.

So, what shall we do?

I know! says Alex. We'll take in stalkers. I know how to find the deer and you know how to cook and look after folk. It's perfect!

Perfect?

But I agree, as I always do, eventually. It makes sense, after all. We are unable to keep the bank from the door. Looking across at him, at Alex, my husband, I feel like a frightened rabbit peering out of its hole in the ground. There is no escaping this, I know it, but behind those rabbit eyes I am running on a prayer and nothing else.

Now the big cauldron can come into play. This boiling pot will have a good fire burning underneath, be filled with water to boil the meat off the heads, and it will be placed . . .

At the steadings? I suggest, quickly.

Certainly not. That's far too far away. It can sit right here, just outside the backyard.

Oh. What fun.

The butcher, Tag, is enlisted as head stalker. He knows about meat, alive or dead, and has walked these hills for years, as if they were his own back garden – which in a sense they are, for Tapsalteerie belongs, in truth, to the village. I often meet folk gathering fir cones for their winter fires, or sticks for kindling, hazelnuts and berries for their larders, and occasionally someone fishing for the salmon in the narrows. Village folk trundle out to the Point to fill their sacks with whelks, and these sacks can fetch a tidy sum to help out at Christmas.

Tag's task will be to guide the guests to the right place and the right stag and to make sure the shot is true and the beast killed quickly.

The first guests arrive. Germans. Blustery gentlemen with big guns and very little command of English, but that doesn't bother Tag at all, for he doesn't speak much English either and all he has to say can be done with a bit of handwaving and a shake or two of his head.

They leave happy enough, with their trophy heads and antlers, and I wonder how on earth they will get them on the plane home. Boiled until the meat drops off and the eyeballs float like ping-pong balls across the scummy surface of the water, the skulls look nothing like the fine strong and proud heads that arrived here a day or so ago. Bloodied and broken, their carcasses hang in the byre awaiting Tag's sharp knife.

I wrap the dried skulls in layers of paper for each guest to take home, but in my mind I see the proud rise of his antlered head on a hilltop, lifted to the wind, eyes of velvet and a wild freedom all about him.

Don't go near the cauldron, I tell the children, but I should know that a big boiling pot, large enough to hold a brace of missionaries, would offer boundless opportunities to enterprising teenagers. Every night after school, while their peers hang around telephone boxes and watch videos in their rooms, my deprived young spend hours dancing round a cauldron, cackling like witches and stirring up body parts into an evil-looking soup. Every night they come in for supper reeking of gamey old stag. Even when the meat is cut and frozen at the lowest temperatures, I can still smell the boiling pot and no matter how many bundles of herbs or bottles of port I cook the meat in, it always tastes of that memory.

During that winter, my parents make the long journey north to visit us. I know by the fact that neither of them can move easily that they wear all their jumpers at once. My father is a vet, once a vet much like that one on the TV series, and the stories they tell make me chuckle.

If an emergency came through while your father was up the glen in the snows, my mother recounts, I had to call the postmistress who lived halfway up the glen to ask her to hang her husband's white shirt out of the window, so that your father would know to pop in to call me.

Sounds like life on the island, I tell her.

That night, in a freezing hailstorm, Blossom begins to calve. Her timing is brilliant, for the vet is on hand and he has calved a few in his time. My mother is unsure.

It's too cold, she says, and he is not young anymore!

My father, warmed with a peaty nip or two, flaps her away and heads out to the barn with Alex. After a while, mum, me and the kids tog up and join them. It's black as pitch, this night, and cold as ice.

In the barn my father, stripped to the waist and sweating heavily, is at one end of a calving rope. Blossom is wailing like a banshee and her eyeballs are white and rolling in their sockets. What is on the other end of the rope is yet to be revealed. With the next big contraction, my dad's face contorts and his muscles tense as he pulls the rope with all his strength. We can see the nose and the two front feet poking out, and then with a whoosh the calf appears and the men lower it gently down to the straw. Blossom spins round like a top and begins grunting a welcome, her long rasping tongue cajoling her calf into life.

Hallo Rosie! says my father, with what is left of his puff.

We leave them, watered and freshly strawed, until the morning, although it won't be an early one for the medical team.

One winter is enough to tell us that the stalking idea will never pay, so Alex comes up with a new idea, one it seems he has been ruminating over for a while. And it is inspired by me.

We could open a recording studio, he says, one morning. To record your voice.

My voice? Me? I look to see if he is joking, but he isn't. A 'but' rises to my lips, but I keep them shut. The fact that he knows diddly squat about being a recording engineer has nothing to do with anything. He is self-taught in everything he has ever taken on, and, I might add, highly successful. For a moment I am stunned, but only for a moment, for I have heard him say he wants my voice and it's very different from wanting my hands for work, or my body for making love to.

Alex begins to source distance-training programmes and all the electronic equipment we will need to begin. Meanwhile I hardly notice the arduous demands of the summer days, as I work on my voice techniques at every opportunity. This is a spoonful of sugar, if ever there was one, and somehow even multiple Saturday changeovers seem lighter and easier, as if they no longer define my life.

As soon as the last guests leave, we strip the dining room of furniture and create sound booths from eggboxes glued onto hardboard screens. Alex has ordered microphones and stands, a synthesiser, an 8-track mixing desk and three hundred miles of wiring that snakes across the wooden floor, linking it all together.

The word goes out that our first recording, the one during which Alex will hone his recently learned skills, will be open to all the island musicians, and they are keen as mustard. They arrive with their instruments, their voices, their drums and pipes, their musical quirks, their egos, their hopes and dreams, and with all their faith in Alex. Night after night and well into the depths of each one, Alex has learned how to make music sound wonderful, and now he has to prove it. With his innate love of good, well-balanced musicality as his guiding force, he learns how to push forward a sound, or pull it back, and how to gently persuade a musician of the best way to make the best sound. He cannot play an instrument, but he can hear every layer of a piece, build it up, or take it apart, with a skill I never knew he had. Neither, I suspect, did he.

We advertise the studio to outside agents, companies, bands, and we wait for the first knock on the door. Some bands come from far away to work on an album in peace and quiet, some come for a day or a weekend, and they all need feeding. Unlike the summer guests, who ask me when meals are served, members of the music world just tell me. These artistic creatures are at the mercy of their creative flow, and food is the last thing on their minds. I am thankful they work mostly at night, for it is almost impossible to keep the house quiet in the daylight hours. Children, dogs, visitors, telephones, all must be silenced while a sensitive acoustic recording is in progress, and one single yap can render a whole track useless, writing off many hours of work. Of course, in my initial excitement at being asked to sing my own words into a microphone, to harmonise with a lead singer, I had not considered this keeping-the-house-quiet thing. Nor had I thought through mealtimes.

One year, the up-and-coming Scottish band Capercaillie book in for a ten-day stay. They are working on their new album, *Delirium*.

We won't finish till after midnight, Alex says. Can you leave some food out?

I leave a casserole warming on the Aga, the table laid, and the drinks on the sideboard. The next morning, when I come into the kitchen, it's all cleared away and the dishes washed.

I hadn't thought of that, either – of people actually considering me enough to work for me while I sleep.

The band joins the family. There are no seams visible, as if they always lived with us. They help me too, with the cooking, and the washing up and even the ironing. They befriend the children and join in their games, and sometimes we walk together around Tapsalteerie as they create their songs, their arrangement, their own unique signature. I sing with them – not on the album of course, but around the kitchen table or down at the local pub, when their work is done for the night, and there is still music in them. It's an exciting time for all of us and a successful one for them. Alex is now a talented mixer of music. When they leave, they bring me a gift. Silver drop earrings in the shape of a treble clef.

All through those recording days, I make sandwiches and hundreds of hot drinks; although, to be honest, musicians tend to start on the beer shortly after toast and marmalade. I don't know how they can perform with all that booze inside them, but they do, and with Alex at the controls, any off-piste twangs or yodels are artfully dampened and lost in the overall sound.

With all this music around them, the children have endless opportunities to develop their own musicality – not, as before, with such dull instruments as cellos and clarinets, but with electric guitars and synthesisers able to produce any sound imaginable; with percussion, clackers, ting-a-ling tubes; with pluckings and pingings and thuds and crashes. Jake works hard on his drumming skills, learning the ropes on wooden blocks with car tyre inners stretched across them. Any visiting drummer is always inveigled into giving a lesson or two. Rhua spends hours with huge headphones clamped to his ears, designing a complex piece on the synthesiser, and I learn backing tracks, harmonies and how to breathe while singing. In short, we all have a lot of fun living the celebrity dream, albeit mostly with people no one has ever heard of – yet.

Children from the village are keen to come up and play, now that there is a studio in which to do it, and Alex is happy for them to move in once a band has finished a session, to make whatever noises they like on the various in-house instruments. Sometimes he records them and they cluster round the desk, eyes wide, listening for themselves in the bizarre cacophony of sound that is children at play.

Soon, demand for the studio becomes more than a winter can manage and Alex moves the studio into the garret so that he can record at times in the summer months. Maddy happily stretches her Girl Friday role into secretary for the studio business, and the hours are much more her thing, to be honest.

I watch my children develop an American edge to their language and their choice of clothing. They say, 'Hey man, it's cool!' through their squeaky, breaking voices and slick their fringes into what looks like fencing. Personal hygiene is now of key importance, but as everything that comes out of my mouth is highly embarrassing, I must make no comment on this dramatic change. Nowadays they appear downstairs with a swagger to their gait, and a lot of shrugging if home-work is mentioned.

What's all the fuss about, man? Chill!

Tonkas and dens disappear, and they lean against door frames choosing words I only ever heard before in movies.

This band is from a wee village on the mainland, I tell them. Not L.A.

But it makes no difference to them. They have the taste of stardom in their mouths and there is no longer excitement over ice cream bribes or drowning wimps in the sewers and all memory of their childhood to date is as though it has never been. When a very famous member of a chart-topping band visits with his wife, an old school friend of mine, and tells them he never had a music lesson in his life, they sit around the tea table with their mouths open and a daft look on their faces.

And I can taste it too, this thrill, and I love it. I join a local band as their singer and learn to play the bodhrán, the Irish folk drum, and the spoons. I join the folk club, although I can see this is not my way to enjoy music, for there is a lot of droning on about ancient battles and lost opportunities, ships and virginity, and most of it – it seems to me – is the fault of the bloody English, although I can usually cheer the whole miserable story up no end with my booming drum.

The local pub employs our little band one evening a week in the summer months, and I cannot remember when I last felt this happy, this full of energetic life. I love the attention, the evenings of practice when we work at new music, new songs, and new ways to play old tunes, when we smile and joke and create our own sound. Sometimes a tune goes so well that it lifts us all up and away, out of the room, out of ourselves and into a spinning crazy fiery dance, faster and faster until someone runs out of puff and we all collapse in happy laughter.

I love the pub nights, the eyes on me, the flirting. I love to hear my own voice silence a room, fill it with a single sound, taking everyone captive until I am done. Here I am a million miles away from the washing line, the domestic round, the grey drudge of cleaning and cooking and ironing dinner napkins; away from having to be nice to people all the time, when there is murder in my mind. This is me, being me, and

I become the music, the song; I let the rhythms pulse through my body and my mind, and my poor torn-about heart has time to mend a little.

But Alex is unsure. It seems he is unhappy with the sparkle in my eyes, the clothes I wear, and the way I flirt with the band members. He loves that I sing, but would prefer it was here, at home where he is, in the studio he made for me, and not in a public house under the lustful gaze of merry men.

He asks that I be home at 11 p.m., so that I don't disturb his sleep when I return full of light and energy and unable to settle my racing heart into rest; when I want to talk to him, to tell him stories, to laugh with him over the events of the night. But Alex has another long day at sea ahead of him and not much night left to gather sleep.

His asking is not really a request, and it heralds my death knoll, or at least my removal from the band, for who would want a singer with a curfew? 11 p.m. is when it all really kicks off, but I can see he is tired, worn out with the Tapsalteerie fight for survival. I have a choice; and yet, in my heart, I know I don't.

They are kindly, the band, but with regret they ask me to leave.

I may have said farewell to the pub, but not to the music; nor to the songs in me.

35

Exams and Teenagers

◡

Around thistledown time come the exam results, and it's hard to breathe with all this tension and down filling the air, both inside and out. School has never been a big thing to any of my family, including me and Alex in the olden days. Exams are vicious cruel predators that lie silent all year so that you forget all about them. That's when they appear on your timetable. It's way beyond sneaky.

Cassie, at fifteen, tried boarding school and lasted half a term. The choice was her own, for she was unhappy here at the island school. With no cash whatsoever for such things, we managed to gain her a full bursary, and she was welcomed with open arms by the headmistress. But it seemed her head was full of the Chalet School, just like mine was – or, at least, its modern equivalent – because life became intolerable for her after a few short weeks. She could not believe the small-minded rich girls she encountered down every corridor. Each gel's daddy seemed to own half a county and they all had ponies and swimming pools.

It was awful! she says to me, as we collect her. The headmistress never even came to say goodbye. Only one teacher, a kindly nun, wished Cassie well as we dragged her trunk into the car.

You know, Mum . . . I really thought it would be good for me . . . but the stupid rules and the fact that you're wrong until proven right, and it's impossible to ever be *that* . . .

I know Cass, I know.

Some of their dads are in government . . . ruling us, for goodness sake!

Well, some of us, Cassie my dear. Not this family, though.

We don't mind, Alex and me, about high grades or prefect badges, as long as the children learn something. Tapsalteerie can do the rest, can teach them all the practical lessons, like how to live on their wits and not much else; how to crog a sheep, milk a cow; how to cook inventively, service a chainsaw, mend endless tears and paper over a million cracks; how to build death slides and how to hoodwink people into situations they least expect; and how to fold napkins.

Passing exams doesn't make you a successful person, says Alex, who never took one himself.

And look at me! I tell them brightly. I passed all of mine, including Latin, and now look at me starching tablecloths and sewing on buttons, like Mrs Tiggy-Winkle!

Alex chuckles and I glower at him, stabbing the needle into my finger by mistake.

Whatever we might say, the pressure builds as exam dates loom, and the reason is a simple one.

No one has done any work all term.

Is that my fault? I ask, as Jake flings a history textbook at the wall. Rhua is firing spectacular insults at his physics project and the offending teacher, while the scream of Def Leppard leaks from his headphones.

Could you go to your rooms? I suggest bravely, pulling back one of Rhua's black cones so he can hear my request.

He shakes me off with a threatening hiss; none of the others even bother to respond.

Then, before we know it, the exams are over and we are all exhausted. Alex and I have mopped tears, encouraged, repaired wall-damaged textbooks and listened to mile after mile of recited dates and formulas – and all the night before the first exam.

Now that Bryn is back in the local secondary school, he must take his O-grades, like everyone else. When the big brown envelope arrives, he just shrugs and sticks it in his pocket, folding it twice first. He disappears for hours and comes in looking dishevelled with grass in his hair.

Don't worry, I soothe. Just tell me.

Tell you what? He is genuinely puzzled. I remind him of the envelope.

Oh, that! Fine!

And tells me nothing.

The following year, when Cassie gets her results, she takes herself up to her bedroom, refusing all encouragements to come down and talk. She only appears to make big mugs of tea and to watch her favourite soap on video. She takes baths in the middle of the night, making the old pipes clank and ping like a steel band warming up and I hear her wailing loudly from time to time, shouting things no nice girl should ever shout, and still we don't know her results, although we can guess it isn't six passes.

All of a sudden she pulls herself together, turning intense grief into an outraged indignation, which manifests itself in a battledress of tight black jeans and many layers of mascara on her lashes. In a boiling fury, and with unshakeable focus and determination, she shoots past a startled interview panel and straight on into college to study Tourism Management.

We've never taken on anyone so young before! the head of department squeaks.

I smile. That's Cassie.

The tourists, chuckles Alex, will be managed now, whether they like it or not.

The next exams she faces, she is well-prepared for. This time, she knows precisely where she is going and no one is going to piss on her parade. When she graduates, it is with an A-coloured degree.

Jake, at fifteen, is now waiting for his envelope, while Rhua sniggers from behind his trendy shades. It will be his turn next year, but for now he is looking forward to a laugh at his brother's expense. He hovers around Jake as the results are revealed. He has passed every one.

See what you can achieve next year, oh you with the trendy shades? If you do your homework, that is.

Homework? No thanks!

Solly doesn't plan to take any exams at all. He'll skip, if that's ok. I tell him it's not an option.

Anyway, it's much fairer these days, Sol, I tell him. You get assessed as you go along, and you don't have one huge paper at the end of it all. In my day we had absolutely nothing until all of a sudden we are sitting at desks, half a mile apart, and some horrifying questions smirking on the other side of the white sheet of A4.

Solly rolls his eyes. He has heard about the rigours of the olden days all too often.

And what's more, I continue, we had to write with messy old fountain pens, filled from our personal inkwells. All that scratching of nibs on paper made the room sound like it was filled with itchy baboons.

What I could never understand is why kids with hormones raging have to take exams at all? Someone at high level should think it through properly, for teenagers have enough bother just being teenagers.

You were never allowed to be teenagers, my mother reminds me.

I remember, Mum. I remember.

I remember feeling no interest at all in my own exam results. My teenage mood swings were most inconvenient and never really allowed out in public. So I try, with my kids, to be patient and understanding, even if I do feel I am living in a war zone.

Just leave them alone, snaps Alex, as I persist in wheedling angry Rhua into explaining his inner turmoil. Actually, it's more yelling than wheedling, as he refuses to turn down the sound on his Walkman. Someone is screaming about destruction and the metallic fury of it fills the air all around us. I

281

might have guessed Alex would snap at me. He finds teenagers and hormones very alarming.

I mutter something insulting.

He gives me that 'Oh, grumpy now are we?' look.

I take a big glass of wine and myself upstairs to sort out the boys' rooms. I have no idea why, unless it is to do something with my hands, other than attack my husband for another example of his complete lack of sensitivity. If a girl took her sense of self from such times, she could quite easily be looking for her reflection in the mirror and seeing no one there at all.

In Jake's room, devastation peaks. In order to open the window, to save the room from spontaneous combustion, I have to negotiate a range of hills, one I know of old to be dangerous. What looks like a nice soft jeans-and-sweatshirts hill is, in fact, a drawing-pin trap, one of which sinks into my bare foot. As I step backwards onto the desert rat camouflage jacket, one of the pockets hisses at me. The other thirty-four are, no doubt, asleep. A scattering of manuals offer me instructions on *Night Loading*, *Slap and Funk on Base Guitars* and *How to Skin a Porcupine*. There are emergency rations, crampons, a tyre lever and a road sign warning of a Blind Summit. I decide not to change the sheets, as I can't see the bed anyway.

Next door in Rhua's room, it smells like Yarmouth Quay. The current fad in his life is fishing for green crabs, which will, he assures me, turn him and his best friend Tam into overnight millionaires. Kissing him goodnight, if I am allowed to, is like kissing a mackerel, three days dead. I brave myself to gather up his laundry and am buzzed at by a plethora of angry bluebottles.

I don't know what you're all so cross about, I tell them, swatting them away. Replacements will arrive later this evening.

If clothes don't answer back, I take them to the cupboard, although here I must be very careful. As I pull open the door, checking first for bowls of liquid overhead, I peer into the depths for any signs of danger. Rhua could quite easily have shoved in his mountain bike which would overbalance and pin me to the floor, where I could lie for hours whimpering and calling out and nobody would give a damn.

In Solly's room, I bat to one side his Samurai sword, which swings from the ceiling. He has rigged up a network of strings and pulleys that allow him to winch his clothes from the cupboard direct to his bed, a distance of about three feet. His cupboard is open plan now, as he saw fit one day to saw off the doors when they got in the way of his pulley system. Vacuuming his room requires me to work on my knees and wearing a hard hat on my head. Once I made the mistake of yanking some clutter out from under the lower bunk only to find the stinking carcass of a chicken, a dirty blue goo in a pint beer glass and a drawing of a wicked looking witch with 'My Muther is a Cow' written underneath.

The next day when I collect the boys from school, there is something very wrong with Jake. He is fighting tears, and has green shit all over his face. For a while he will tell me nothing.

Sam made him eat shit, says Solly, who is still young enough to communicate.

I slam on the brakes, giving everyone a head rush.

What you doing, Mum? they ask, righting themselves and sounding nervous.

I say nothing. All my fury gathers inside me and the heat is boiling. I have watched all my children bullied and done nothing but talk about it to teachers who also do nothing. Not this time.

I see Sam cutting through the gap behind the pub and I am out of the car and running like the wind in hot pursuit. Righteous Indignation courses through my veins and I am almost flying. He will not escape me. I catch him, plum in the middle of the wee burn that runs through the village, and I bring him, this big lad, to his knees. In front of a gathering crowd of children and passers-by, I flip Sam over and push him down into the water, which is only 2 inches deep. I straddle his chest, sitting down hard and slick water all over his face.

Don't you EVER do that again! I roar at him, with all the red hot anger in me and all the air in my lungs. Not to my boys! Not to ANY boys! Not ever! Do you understand?

He is white with fear, his eyes huge and staring. Mothers are respected like gods on the island. Even small ones like me.

Okay, he whispers.

The awe in the Landrover is tangible. I am exhilarated, soaked and filthy and I couldn't give a toss. I look at Jake in the rear-view and he smiles at me, admiration written all over his grubby face.

I'm not grumpy now, Alex, I whisper. Not grumpy at all.

36

Through the Narrows

～

As my children grow strong and supple, I feel more and more reduced. Oh, they don't reduce me – far from it – but it's the glowing skin on their faces and the bright flame of hope in their eyes that makes me realise I have never really been a young woman at all. It's as though I skipped that part and went from little girl to housewife overnight. I see it most in the lines around my own eyes and the sagging of my own skin so that boundaries become undefined and gravity rules. Although there never was any chance of me on a catwalk or playing beach badminton in my bikini, I grieve for the life in my body, the fire in my veins, the tight muscles of my belly. I am not fat by any means, but even my non-fat sags in places, not in a jelly roll, but more like the dough that slips over the edge of my proving bowl. No matter how much I exercise, this will always be with me, to some degree or other, and I find myself wishing I had really loved my body when I was young and able to go naked, or semi-naked, without causing alarm. I never looked at my breasts and liked them, or my bottom, or my face, for there was always something wrong. Too wobbly a bottom, lopsided breasts with wonky nipples, freckles and pale skin on a face that never really got acquainted with itself, nor matched itself up to the rest of the body. Now it feels like it's too late, somehow.

I love your body, says Alex. Why won't you let me see it?

I am pulling the towel high around me, right up to my ears.

Because it is hideous. Stop staring at it. At me.

Alex sighs. He cannot understand me at all.

One afternoon, after pushing paper around the desk and not quite getting down to the weekly housekeeping tally, I decide to let the restlessness I feel these days take me away. Everyone is somewhere else and the air is alive with sunshine and a soft-fingered breeze. I breathe it in and head for the shore. There's a canoe there somebody 'found', and I plan a wee spin along the coast, just for an hour or two, underneath those wheeling gulls, with the lilt of a sea song in my mouth and the salt sting on my skin.

I may never have done such a thing before, but Jenny is always at me to 'brave up'. It's alright for her to say those words, she who has led whale-watching expeditions off Iceland and camped under the stars in a jungle in Borneo. Nevertheless, such encouragement rings in my ears as I look from the canoe to the cool inviting water. And besides, we have a cook this summer to give me a break, and the children, who are hardly children any more, are somewhere else with their friends. My time is just a little more my own.

The dogs bound after me down the shore road, as always, and Jinx is with them. She is daft, soft-tempered, and has fixed her love on me alone. The sheep lift their heads as we pass and the lambs, strong now and grazing with their mothers, skitter away from where we walk, calling out like children in the playground. In another field the bull raises his huge head and watches us with slow eyes. The insects hum around our heads and the afternoon is empty of anyone but me and the animals.

Stay! I tell the dogs, as I launch myself into the water. It takes me a moment or two to stabilise, to settle with the paddle, and when I look back at the shore it is further away than I would choose it to be, and lined with dogs, heads on paws, watching me go.

This is the life, I smile, with the sun on my face and the swish of the water in my ears. Gathering speed, I move along the shoreline and the dogs skitter across the rocks with their sure feet, light as air.

Suddenly Jinx, who has separation issues, leaps into the water with a yelp, and begins to swim towards me. As she gets nearer, I can hear her frightened squeaks, see her powerful long legs going like pistons. I pull in the paddle and watch her, wondering, with some apprehension, what she might do once she arrives.

Hardly pausing at all, she tries to climb in beside me. This is a canoe, I tell her, a one-man canoe, and you have the legs of a deer. There is only one ending to this.

By now, we have drifted into the fast flow of the ebbing tide and I can see us landing up on some beach on the little isles if I don't do something quick. There is blind panic in the dog's eyes, as her claws scratch away at the nose of the canoe and she begins to tire.

There is only one thing I can do. Grabbing her by the scruff of her neck, I haul her aboard, and to my amazement we remain upright, although I can see nothing now but large wet dog, and I cannot paddle with her on my knees. Thankfully, she sits still and upright, so with some left-handed flapping of the paddle, using my other arm as an oar, I manage, inch by inch, to bring us into the shore, albeit a way from where we first began. The collies leap around us, yapping their greetings, tails high, while Jinx sits erect as a queen on her throne.

Later that evening, there is a call. A whale has stranded on a peninsular not far from Tapsalteerie, a humpback whale, and it still breathes.

Every time I see a whale there is a lump in my throat. That seeing of such majesty, alive and free, is quite overwhelming. No one speaks on the boat, and we hardly move, holding the moment in a caught breath. The whale may float alongside, may dive under the boat, may lift its great head and fix us with a watching eye, and when it slides away back into the expanse of ocean we turn to each other blurry eyed, our hearts pounding, silenced and in awe.

So to hear of one in trouble, suffering, frightened and in pain is almost unbearable.

What's the story? I ask Alex, almost not wanting to know.

Someone saw it from the rocks, he says. There were three of them and this one turned into the beach, swam right up it. It knew what it was doing.

Leave it alone, I hear him tell someone on the phone. It has chosen to die, in the way of whales. It's an ancient way.

But nobody can. Someone always has to interfere and it makes Alex furious. Ropes and winches, boats and man-power, dragging, yanking, tearing at the dying body and for what purpose . . . to watch it turn back to the same place, the same choice, only this time bloodied and terrified?

But a huge humpback on a small beach is never going to be left alone.

The army is called in to blow it up, after it has finally breathed its last. Having tried first to pull it back into the sea, only for the carcass to find its way back with the tides, gunpowder is employed and the charge is set.

Bits of whale fly in all directions and for miles. It peppers gardens, washing lines, playgrounds and streets, it sticks to vehicles and buildings and it smells appalling and all this in the hottest summer for years.

Our seasonal whale students work for six weeks or so at a time, and around them I can forget my self-pitying visits to the mirror. Jenny is back from her exciting foreign travels, and, by this time, she and I are firm friends, even if she does have far more time with Alex than he ever gives to me. They talk about whales and research and plankton and weather patterns, and I realise that my conversation is likely to be dull by comparison. We go out together, laugh a lot, and both of us work hard. Alex is a lucky man.

Every year the CVs fill the letterbox, for the chance to work with Alex is indeed a sexy way to spend the summer holidays. Alex develops protocols for everything so that the students can learn quickly and remind themselves, when they forget, just by grabbing a protocol and mugging up on the rules. They wear sweatshirts with the boat logo emblazoned on the front and gradually the business grows and thrives and becomes a leader in the world of whale-watching – the first in the UK. We attract funding for expensive equipment, and scientists renowned in matters of whales and other cetaceans come knocking at the door. It's exciting and energising, this melee of vibrant young students, and I make many friends. It's a new lift to my life. Throughout the summers I worry less about my aging body and spend more time having fun, with visits to the pub of an evening and sometimes going out on the boat – not because I love being at sea, but because the students are fun to be around, stimulating and interesting, individual and independent and with exciting lives behind and before them. I was short on all of that till now. Sometimes when we walk back from the pub and I tiptoe in beside Alex with beery breath and my head full of happy chatter, I realise that we are living our lives in a different order. These students are moving towards being sensible whereas I am doing exactly the opposite, for my exposure to these carefree youngsters has lifted a new wild confidence in me, inch by inch, up from my boots, and I hardly feel the guilt at all. It's not defiance, or it doesn't feel like it. It's more that Alex has less say on the subject of my independence, if that's not too big a word for this new state of things. Maybe it's all down to the likes of Jenny and Maddy, for whom he has an undisguised respect, although he wouldn't want either of them for a wife.

*   *   *

The following February there is a call about a whale in a little loch on the Island of Lewis. Alex always gets these calls now, as he has become the Whale Man and his advice and wisdom is called upon whenever a situation like this one arises.

It seems the whale, a minke, just swam in one day and stayed. The problem lies in a couple of places. The first is that the whale is trapped.

Alex rolls his eyes at that one.

The second is that there is a fish farm in the loch and the owner is jumpy.

We plan to drive the whale out, says the coastguard, but will you come and check its health first?

We fly out on an icy day with snow clouds overhead, taking with us a crew of specialists, Jenny included. We have a hydrophone to listen underwater, cameras for filming and all the bits and bobs we need to monitor this whale's state of wellbeing. Every day Jenny and I stand on a freezing hillside timing the blows and the dives of the whale, while the men folk do their thing down below us. Every evening we compare notes around the little kitchen table in the holiday cottage on the shore. The whale is well; there is no doubt.

Someone reported seeing it swim out of the loch this morning early, says Jenny, and then back in again. There's no way it's trapped.

Alex reports to the coastguard.

Do nothing, he says. The whale will not touch the fish farm.

It might damage the cages with its bulk, the coastguard says.

Alex describes his encounters with whales; the way a whale will swim for an hour beneath a boat and between eight monofilament fishing lines, snagging not one; the whale that came into the harbour when a yacht race was on and there was no room for a goldfish to swim through, let alone a whale, and no boat, nor dinghy was touched; the way a whale swam up the River Clyde, through the narrow channel alongside big coasters and touched nothing.

Leave the whale alone, he says again. It will go when it is ready.

And it does. On the way to school, a child watches from the rocks as it rises, once, twice, and then dives deep into the wide mouth of the Atlantic Ocean.

37

Leaving Tapsalteerie

~~~

Although we fight the good fight with all of our might, the debts are mightier. We have probably known this for some time now, Alex and I, that we can no longer hold on to the estate and survive. We have worked it as hard as anyone possibly could, on a shoestring and with minimal help, and it is not enough. We have sold off some of the cottages, racked up the whale-watching business, pushed the recording studio under every music agent's nose, made calls, designed advertisements, written press releases and none of it is enough to save Tapsalteerie. Not for us, anyway. The cost of running an estate is too great, however big our dream may be, for an estate is a bottomless pit, a wide open mouth – greedy, and big enough to swallow us all.

We talk to the bank, who tell us what we already know. If we don't find the courage to take this decision now, there will be nothing left to build ourselves another home, which cannot be small – not yet. All the children still live at home, although Bryn, who is studying at a crammer school for his physics O-grade, one he needs to join the Merchant Navy, he still needs a room to come home to.

When we tell the children, they don't believe us. It's just not possible. How will they live without Tapsalteerie? Who will move in? Will they love it – the running and the games and nobody to complain about noise pollution? Who will watch the deer on the lawn, or ride their bikes over the dirt tracks, and what about the tree house?

What about the tree house, Jake? You can't even fit inside it now!

That is not the point, it seems. This is not a practical argument, but one from deep inside the heart.

Their questions hurt, and they are supposed to. We are, in effect, throwing away their childhood, all that they know as well as they know themselves, for they have never lived any other life.

I call my parents, while Alex drives down to tell his, although they already knew. Alex has had coffee with them every morning for almost fifteen years and I don't suppose the talk was about baking, or plumbago tweaking.

Oh goodness! says my mother. Does that mean you are coming back here?

No, I say very firmly. Never that; not after Tapsalteerie.

My father asks more questions, such as How do you feel? and Will you be alright?

I tell him I will always be alright. It's how you made me, both of you.

* * *

295

We begin the sad process of organising the sale. Photographs are taken for the brochure and we sort through what is to keep and what is to go, for we must live in caravans for a while until a new house is built, a smaller house, one with floors and walls that fit together and windows that keep out the weather; one with no bat-friendly cellar, no open sewer, no wrap-around sea. Although that might sound like a neat description, all tidy and simple, it is very far from that.

I cannot lie about the fact that I am relieved, now we have made the decision, for Tapsalteerie has had the best of me and I am not sure how much is left. And Alex has taught me well, over the years, to move smartly on to the next thing, no looking back, when the thing before collapses.

Giving up on Tapsalteerie is not the same for Alex and the children, although Alex shows none of what he really feels. Perhaps he thinks we should work harder, try for longer; perhaps not. Either way, there is – as always – no time for in-depth conversations on such a topic, or any topic for that matter, beyond the list of tasks for the day. We must keep moving moving moving, or we might run out of time. I do feel sad for the children but, perhaps because I can usually find a positive, I spin them dreams of a new life, and it seems to work on a moment-by-moment basis.

But deep in their young hearts, I know they feel cheated. They are leaving the greatest place on the earth, one that should be always theirs, not sold to someone else. Each childhood has been an adventure, a wild, free and exciting one, and now it is all being taken from them. This place of death slides and dams is where the stories were thought up, and really lived, where all the laughter grows and blooms, where mysteries are mysteries and lunch is anytime between ten and three. This is the land of peace and of soft rain, of tides and moons and selkies crooning on the rocks; where the wind brings ancient songs of lives lost and found again and where the washing always dries eventually on the high green above the house. What about the bees and the old milk cow and the bull with slow eyes and huge balls, or the blind ewe . . . ?

Will the new people do the same as us? Solly asks me.

I doubt it, Sol. Not if they have any sense.

There is no danger for children here; no bogie men, no hazards to threaten young bodies, to grow them up too quickly, to make deep scars that no one can ever see. In their time here they have been fashioned into strong young people, healthy in body and mind, clear on the most primary rules of life and of death and clear in their thinking, in their knowledge of right and of wrong. And they have a good eye for any opportunity, a rollicking sense of fun and adventure and they are clever, and I don't mean school clever. Their reports are full of the usual nonsense about pulling up socks and applying themselves and not answering back in class, and other things we have all heard before so many times and paid little attention to. They are feisty and funny, wild and interesting, and if I feel like I am a bit short of blood, it has all been worth it to see them grow as they have all grown.

* * *

How much d'ya want? asks a rotund balding man with spark-ling dentures. He has heard the estate is for sale and thought he might chance his luck. His wife shuffles nervously on the doorstep, clutching her designer handbag. He thrusts a fat wad of notes under my nose. Got plenty more! he chortles and I bristle with indignation.

This is an estate, I say primly. You should contact the sell-ers in the city.

He doesn't, of course.

For weeks we collect and throw out, gather together and sell off all the things we don't need any longer. The new owners want none of it for themselves, not even the stock and we must send them all on trucks to the mainland. Blossom gives me a black look as she stumbles up the ramp, her old legs wobbling with the climb. There's no way to sit her down and explain the situation, and the guilt is sharp as needles. I can hardly bear to watch her go as the truck turns around and begins its journey down the bumpy track. I can hear her call-ing back to me through the air flaps.

Thank you for all the milk, the cream and the butter, I whisper. For making us laugh, for kicking over the full buck-ets of milk, for suckling all those calves, for your soft velvet eyes and the way you crooned softly when we scratched your back.

I remember icy fields on winter mornings, pulling her to her feet for milking and seeing her warm shape in the flat-tened grass, and I can feel her nudging my back to move me quicker to the byre, and the hay, and the warm stall. I see her resting close to old Duchess and John the Bull, and I remember a night of rising gales, when they didn't lie under the old elm tree, as they always did, and the clutch of fear in my belly, seeing it broke-backed and fallen in the early light. My heart in my mouth, I searched for bloodied and broken limbs or worse, wounds beneath a ton of dying tree. Then I saw them, wandering over from the other side of the field and calling out for breakfast, their heads swinging with each waltzing step.

As the day for leaving comes closer, I collect helpers from the village, an army of goodly women who work beside me scrubbing and cleaning, dusting, repainting and repairing what we can. These women know work like this, and have helped each other for centuries, side by side, fingers reddening with water and soap, tongues always ready for humour, for a good story, a kindly word, their mouths full of easy laughter. They have weathered big storms in their lives, all of them, with enviable grace and fortitude. They have birthed the young and laid out the dead. They have made repairs, amends, sandwiches, pots of tea and welcoming homes for their loved ones, as did their mothers before them, their grandmothers too. They work until the job is done, and there is no clocking off for them. Their arms are always open and their doors unlocked and, most of all, they really know what it is like to be a woman, living a woman's life, feeling all the joys and all the pain and ready at any time of the day or night to support each other, and since I came to Tapsalteerie, that includes me too. They saw how things were for me; for Alex and me. It was the same for some of them.

You fancy a bloke and he fancies you . . .

We are sharing a cuppa mid morning.

And he makes a move . . .

Old Rona snorts through her nose and then chokes on her cigarette.

And then the bugger marries you, because his mother throws him out and then . . .

He tells you, you can't wear that dress again as it's cut too low . . .

Or you can't have the car because he needs it . . .

And to wipe that muck off your eyes right now . . .

And so, your only choice is to do all of the above when he isn't around!

I laugh with them, amazed at how similar our situations are, but however much we joke, there's a backdrop of sadness and disappointment, and I can feel it in the room. Perhaps their honesty, hidden inside those words of fun, helps to lift the loneliness from my heart.

We work our way from room to room, broom after broom, using hundreds of cloths and endless tree trunks to keep the water hot. Our fingers crack, our backs ache, but we keep going, keep calling out to each other, joking our way through it all, while outside Alex and the men folk lumber up and down the track, shifting heavy machinery, furniture and farm equipment from dawn till dusk.

When it is all done and the house is hollow and empty as it was when we arrived thirteen years before, we wait for the new owners to arrive. There is tea to welcome them, milk, sugar and shortbread. I wander through the empty rooms, hearing echoes of laughter and chatter, of music and stories shared, of tears and dancing, games and parties, and my heart swells with gratitude. This house has protected us and helped us grow a family. Inside its thick strong walls, ideas have been turned into businesses, into a life that has touched on hundreds of others, changed them and made them better. It has been filled with happy guests and chattering children and our story is deep in the stones now, along with all the stories that were and those yet to come. Although I am ready to say farewell to these stones, I will never forget that we lived together, them and us, for a while, and shared a time that can never come again.

Alex finds us two big caravans and they are secured near the gate of Tapsalteerie on a piece of land not included in the sale. It's a hill where he used to feed some cattle when the grass was scarce. It was also supposed to have a magic stone circle, although I never found it. An old village tale, perhaps. The land is flattened around the caravans, the drive marked out, and a connecting walkway fitted between two of the vans. This is where the collies will live, and the boots and jackets and roller skates and all other kit that might be part of a big family's collection. Alex, me, Rhua and Solly will be in one van; Jake, Bryn and Cassie in the other. It seemed like a really good idea to separate the teenagers from the rest of us, leaving them free to play loud music and swear and watch daytime television, for now we have television and it's the first time in their lives.

We are much nearer to Granny-at-the-Gate now, so that she can wander up for a cup of coffee and the youngsters can drop in to see her and Granddad on their way back from the village. Being closer to the village is a big advantage. Friends are nearer, the bus stop is nearer, and most days I hear the whoops and crashes of games being played out in the woods around the vans, and I have no guests to look after, no cottages to clean, no dinners to prepare. And this is the moment when what it means to leave Tapsalteerie hits me like a truck. I was somebody there. Now I have no idea who I am.

In short, I am redundant. Although I have longed for this for years and was certain I would love it, I don't. I have stopped, and I feel as though I have run for years without stopping and been suddenly switched off at the wall.

Silence.

Nothing.

I tell Alex, but he is still busy, so how can he understand?

After the initial excitement at the prospect of being hill gypsies while our new house is built, the caravans feel cramped and the gas fire gives me a headache. The dogs have no sheep to round up and they look balefully up at me, expecting walks and action countless times a day. They look switched off too, and the two cats have encountered village opposition of a night. One is terrified and never goes out again and the other picks endless noisy fights so that Alex has to bang on the flimsy tin sides to yell for silence. Worst of all, it has not stopped raining since we moved out of the big house.

On a cheery note, the whale-watching business is flourishing, Jenny and the students are in their own caravans just beyond the bog, and Maddy is now full-time secretary in a

Portakabin all of her own. It takes me one hour, two at most, to clean our caravan and then I go for a walk in the rain.

This gets me up to eleven o'clock.

The rest of the day stretches out before me – not like a ribbon, but like a leash.

38

Dissolving

⌒

I wonder what on earth I am going to do with all this time and with all this freedom. For years I have longed for it, cried salty tears for it, watched it surround other women like a warm glow, envied them. Now I have it for myself, I have no idea what to do with it. My days are long and unaccounted for. I have become pointless. I search my mind for ideas. Once I was needed; now I am not, and, apart from the daily feeding of a hungry family, there is only a stretch of slow hours and endless, endless rain.

From somewhere I find an idea. I will sign up for a distance writing course. After all, hasn't Alex always told me I can write? One day I send for an Open College of the Arts brochure and pick my course. Although a part of me is excited about this new idea, the rest of me flops in a cynical heap. What's the point of this course, hmmmm? You going to be a journalist, an author now? It's a hard world you know, and besides, what makes you think that you will succeed where countless others fail?

To shut my head up, I begin to paint tiles for our new kitchen wall, the one that will stand solidly behind the cherry red Aga. I have no idea what I'm doing. Acrylic paints, with a varnish on top, I decide, and every tile different.

You can paint some if you like, I tell the children, and they all paint at least one, all jumpered up against the cold and stabbing at the hard surface with primary colours and little understanding of composition. Rhua paints a lot of fast-moving lines and not just on the tile. Jake arranges a careful row of weaponry and Solly paints a purple vacuum cleaner with a long silver pipe.

A vacuum cleaner, Sol? I query.

It's a Dalek! he says contemptuously.

Oh, so it is! Silly old me.

I ask the editors of the local paper if they would let me begin a column about family life, and they are delighted. It is good practice for my writing course, although journalese is a very different language to that required for, say, a short story or a novel, and I know that, if I know anything at all about the world of wordsmithing. But it keeps me writing every day and focusing on something instead of nothing. I walk for hours in the cold and wet, through the woods and across the bog, trying to find the ancient path that won't sink me forever. And still the sadness grows in me, more and more, for I am a lost child in a strange country, and I can see no recognisable landmarks.

Alex is now completely embroiled in his role as the Whale Man, and has nothing else to talk about. I watch him energised and animated in conversation with his students, or with a visiting scientist, discussing new equipment for studying the whales and other cetaceans that frequent our island waters. He talks long into the night with everyone but me and I feel stupid and unnecessary. My children grow independent of me, popping in for meals or to change their clothes, all washed and dried by me, and disappearing again. It seems I am no more than a domestic hand for any of the people most precious to me, and that sense of utter failure leads me to a wine bottle, where I find a short-term peace.

I never really had what they call a relationship with alcohol before now. When I first met Alex, I might have enjoyed a single glass of wine at dinner, which is surprising when I remember back to all the raucous parties my parents used to throw, with champagne and wine and Pimms flowing the whole night long.

But this isn't enjoying a drink. This is a conscious attempt to float into a dreamworld, to escape the empty life that stretches so cruelly before me.

Gradually, over the days and weeks and months, I forget my pain in part as I totter further down the track to Wonderland. But there is a sting in the tail of it for when I wake each morning, with no memory of the day before, of what I may have said or done, I fill the blank spaces with a whole gamut of hideous possibilities. Did anyone notice my eyes were wild, bloodshot and slow to focus? Did I cook supper last night at all? Does anyone know that I buy two bottles, hide one and keep the one in view looking barely touched? I cannot fall asleep, although I am tired all the time, and when I do, the dark demons haunt my dreams. I long for the cocktail hour, and spend it not in effervescent conversation with Alex, but alone, and cold and ashamed. If the phone rings and I answer it, I know it to be a mistake. I pace my responses and choose my words carefully, avoiding combinations of letters that might give this game away. I don't want to be caught out, and yet it is the one thing I do want. The crazy thing about a drunk is that they think they are sober. I honestly believed myself to be coherent and in control, and no one said a word, not Alex, not anyone. And through it all, my self-loathing grows like a beast inside me. I am used up; I am purposeless; I am ugly.

And there's another summer looming.

I apply for a chambermaid job in a local hotel.

You are over qualified for this, says the kindly owner, but I tell him I have been a chambermaid for years now and he takes me on. I also take on the job of cleaning the lodge for our package holiday guests.

The morning work, the fact that I am busy again, and needed and – more importantly – part of something again, helps a little. At least it's a reason to be sober and I am a good cleaner. I put my all into it, fresh-faced, bright eyed, chipper as can be with my mop and bucket and eco-friendly detergents. It gives me a chance to chat with the visitors, the students, the film crew – for there is nearly always a film crew. These are wild strangers, with big lenses and the smell of the outdoors in their hair. And they have seen everything above and everything beneath the waters – not just of the Atlantic, but the Pacific, the Sea of Cortes, the Dead Sea, the

Mediterranean; seas I know only from the television. But when they tell me of the Spinner Dolphins, or the giant Leviathans half a mile long, I can taste the words. And they all want action shots – of Alex, the boat, the whale, the bird 'hurries', when birds gather to indicate a shoal of young fish – and Alex will do everything he can to make their day perfect. When they are gone with whoops and lenses and a big packed lunch, I clean their rooms. It feels – just – that I am doing my part towards the development of this great adventure that is Alex's life, and there is some peace in that, even if my part is all over by coffee time.

And still I drink on, although never during the day. All I have to deal with are varying degrees of hangover. By now, I am thin and gaunt and I rather like it. I can wear leggings without a long top and my breasts are almost flat. My cropped hair is kept that way until I take the notion to shave it off completely. I spend hours staring into space after cleaning and working on whatever piece I am halfway through for my next writing assignment. I avoid going anywhere in the evening where I know there won't be wine on offer and, bit by bit, I see people growing quiet around me. Not the visitors, for they must imagine I always looked this way, and besides, I can still entertain as I always did, make people laugh, cheer them up.

At the other end of the scale is Granny-at-the-Gate. She doesn't talk to me straight. She has always been known as the mistress of the stage whisper and I hear it often while I quietly go into her kitchen to top up my gin.

She's getting herself another drink, you know! she might say to Alex or Jenny or Maddy or whoever had come to visit with me, and there would be a murmur in response. These days I always make sure to have company when Granny visits. It takes away any chance of a direct barb; besides, I am a walking body of shame, weakened, feeding my sense of failure daily. Even my Granny armour has dissolved.

I begin to suspect that all around are frightened of what they see, of the slow crumbling of a person who has been so strong, so alive, so absolutely there, and who has obviously flipped. I wonder if Alex will notice, will turn to me now, lift me from this greedy despair? I write poetry filled with angst and pain, and tear it all up like so much sentimental clap-trap, and during the long sleepless hours, beside Alex and yet miles away from him, I dream of desert islands, of wild places, of kisses and sunshine and laughter.

I often thought myself in love, although I never said a word. Our summers were pulsing with young male students, postgrads, film crew, outsiders who didn't know me and whose exciting lives held me in their thrall. They laughed with me, flirted and joked; for them it was summer fun, but not for me. For me it was a chance to escape from the cold and the dark, to be myself, whoever that may be. I really can't remember if I ever knew in the first place. But I can write now, it's official, and paint – well tiles for now, but who knows? I can sing and play the bodhrán, I can dance and cook and clean and patch wounds, soothe fevers, ease burdens. Surely the world is my oyster? All I need is a man to spirit me away, one like Alex used to be, with the daredevil in his eyes and fire in his heart and a completely consuming passion for me.

* * *

When we first met, Alex asked me out to dinner, and told me to pack an overnight bag. I spent most of the afternoon putting clothes on and taking them off again, fixing my long hair just the way he liked it, way too excited to eat lunch. After we had been on the road for an hour, travelling through lands I didn't recognise at all, I asked him where we were going.

London, he said. To an Italian restaurant.

We arrived at eight to a reserved table in the corner, the only one empty in the busy warm dining room with its red gingham tablecloths and the smell of garlic thick in the air. Wine glasses glinted in the candlelight and we had to speak up to be heard.

We talked for hours in that little corner. Then we walked through the night streets, still alive with life and colour until we arrived at his friend's luxury flat. Only it wasn't hers, she was just looking after it, and had told Alex we could stay in one of the grand bedrooms with a private bathroom.

Drink? she asked, as if we needed more.

We nodded and she turned to push a concealed button beside a Picasso original. The Picasso began to rise until it revealed a gleaming drinks cabinet hidden in the wall. Another button kicked the bar into life and it slid almost silently along curved tracks, coming to a halt as the semi-circle completed, presenting our friend as the barmaid. She shook martinis, found olives and cherries and ice and lemon wedges and I kicked off my shoes and settled in for the night.

What seemed moments later, Alex shook me awake.

Come on, he whispered, breakfast!

Not hungry, I groaned, but he was having none of that nonsense. Bleary eyed, I followed him down the still dark streets, calling for my warm soft bed.

Suddenly, he was gone. There was almost nobody about apart from the odd shadowy lurker, and I was momentarily afraid.

There! he said, leaping down from a high wall beside me, a bunch of stolen roses in his hand. For you!

His hands were bleeding and scratched. Thank you, I said. You are bonkers, you know that? There might have been a guard dog.

Was, he said. We made friends.

At the door of the Dorchester Hotel, we stopped and he led me up the steps.

What are we doing? I was not a little alarmed.

A cleaner was washing the marble on her hands and knees.

Good morning! Alex said cheerfully and pushed me through the revolving doors, through the grand hall, and towards the dining room. He had obviously been here before.

Table for two, sir? asked the immaculately dressed maître d'. Alex smiled, and nodded, and we were shown to a table by the window.

I ate what I could in amazement, certain we would be discovered and thrown out on the street. Fresh fruits of all kinds, a butter sculpture with water trickling down it, every kind of bread and cake filled the centre table. Waiters and waitresses glided silently around the room and conversation was like the hum of contented bees in a summer garden.

Is this to go on your room, sir? asked the head waiter.

Not this time, said Alex, as if considering his options. I will settle the bill with cash.

Very good, sir. Have a good day, madam; sir.

And we left, trying to hold in the grins.

39

Sail and Return

⌒

Alex and I have lost each other. Somewhere in between our wild beginnings and now, all the colour has drained away. I know we have five fine children, a new home growing from the rocks on the hillside, a successful business, but we have no life. We may be together as husband and wife, but we no longer speak the same language and we have both changed into team leaders, but on opposing teams. We have let go of each other's hands.

One morning I wake knowing I can't do this anymore. In a dream, I take my children to school, with their school bags ready, their lunches packed, and I keep driving. On down the glen road, on through the little villages, and right up to the ferry as its huge metal mouth opens wide to spit out the arrivals and to swallow the leavers whole. All the way over to the mainland, I stare out the window over my cup of brown liquid that called itself coffee on the sign. I never once ask myself what I am doing, or what Alex and the children will feel once they know I am gone. There is no logic or sense in my head, not one jot of it. I am leaving and that is all I know. They are better off without me, anyway. All those winter days of looking out through drugged eyeballs, all those tears, all that guilt and remorse and all that girlish longing. They deserve better, I tell myself, and with me gone, they will find it.

I buy a one-way ticket to Glasgow and board the train.

Hallo, says a voice I recognise. A woman who lives on the other side of the village, one I hardly know but already like, invites me to join her. She isn't scared of my shaved head, my go-away black leather, my pale sad face. She indicates the seat opposite her, across the table and, grateful for the friendship, I sit myself down, my small bag beside me. On the journey we talk, mostly about me. I find myself opening up to her, a comparative stranger, and she listens quietly, watching me with her gentle eyes.

Would you like me to read your medicine cards? she asks me.

Why not?

She lays them out higgledy-piggledly across the pale grey surface and tells me to choose one, pulling it towards me to reveal the animal picture underneath. It's a porcupine, upside down.

What does that mean? I ask her.

Porcupine, she tells me, symbolises innocence. Playfulness, faith and trust. Your task is to find the pathway that is most beneficial to you, and that uses your greatest talents. A porcupine has quills, but it is a gentle, loving creature, and non-aggressive, so the quills are down unless trust is broken and fear grows. To choose this card, you have given yourself a gentle reminder not to get too caught up in the chaos of the adult world, where fear, greed and suffering are commonplace. Open your heart to those things that gave you joy as a child, such as your imagination, fantasy, the making of a toy from old scraps. Honour the playfulness in you, that lets everyone win.

But why is it upside down? I ask, intrigued. Does that mean something?

Oh yes, says my gentle friend.

When you take life too seriously, you cannot win the game. In some area of your life, you are feeling hurt, afraid of trusting again. It is possible that life has dealt you a hard blow recently. If so, this is a warning to begin again by placing your faith in your own ability to overcome with joy. Are you willing to trust yourself?

I look down at my hands. No, I say, not any more.

She smiles, waits for me to finish.

I fight the prick of tears and say, I imagine that I am upside down right now, vulnerable and defenceless!

We both chuckle. Yes, indeed, she says. But you can roll over.

In Glasgow, I buy a ticket for London. It's a city I know slightly, from my younger days when I worked at a West End theatre as a secretary, for all of three weeks. I call Alex who is out at sea and tell him I have left.

Don't try to find me, I say, and hang up.

I find my seat among other travellers who look like they know exactly where they are going and are excited about it.

They load their bags onto luggage racks, and their picnics and books onto the tables, chattering together, folding jackets and checking their pockets for their tickets. All I carry is an invisible burden of self-loathing, of anger and of fear as deep as the ocean, as raw as a winter wind, and this wind blows so hard that I couldn't roll over, even if I tried.

In London, I know one person.

Can I stay with you? I call Liz from an evil-smelling phone booth with shattered glass underfoot. I can hear it scrunch under my Doc Martens. After all, wandering the streets doesn't seem like a good idea for an island girl, even if that's the best she deserves. Although I haven't seen Liz for years, she was once one of Alex's students, and we became friends over those summer weeks. Now she is back in London, working part-time in a coffee bar. I don't really know her well enough to ask any such favour, but I plan it to be a short visit while I decide what to do next. I am way too frail to be alone, and she did say when she left the island that I could visit any time I liked.

Of course! she says, at first surprised, and then concerned, and no doubt intrigued to know more. She gives me directions to her flat in what she called 'the dodgy part of town'.

Cheap rent, she says, as we negotiate our way up the litter-ridden steps. Don't go out after dark, she adds, ever. Even I don't do that, and I know this place like the back of my hand.

She is kind to me and her kindness makes me cry even more.

Every day she heads off to work and every day I sit trapped inside, with only my thoughts for company. Night after night, I drink myself into the slow hours of dark dreams and aching limbs, not least as I am effectively sleeping on the floor in front of her wardrobe. All around me, through the skinny walls, I hear other lives being lived, full of conversation and music, laughter and cries; a dog barking and the high-pitched chatter of children. At night, the streets are loud with traffic, revellers, sirens. Cooking smells push through the cracks: the lemony scent of washing powder, the sweet tang of fragrant candles or the sharp spice of a curry.

And in here, a prisoner for hours while Liz is at work or out with friends, I feel more alone than I ever thought possible. She listens while I tell her how I feel, but how can she, a child herself, really understand? Each day, she fills the fridge with food I never touch, and, on the rare evenings she is home, she listens some more. I realise, as I hug the wine bottle, that my drinking is nothing compared to the amount the young folk swallow down, even on weekdays. She can come home a lot drunker than I ever am, but for her, life is still a party. Not so for me, and there's the difference. Where I am morose, she still thinks she will live forever, find her prince, live her long and happy life, just the way she sees it right now. Her biggest problem is what to wear for the next night out. That and the weepy woman on her bedroom floor.

I wonder how much pain a human body and mind can take before it just gives up the ghost? I ask her, and she looks at me sympathetically, and with no idea what I am talking about.

As if to find the answer, I take myself to a downtrodden hairdressing salon that tells me I can have multiple piercing in one session.

Four each side, I tell the blowsy bottle blonde who won't see fifty again. She clasps her taloned fingers under her bosom and raises one painted eyebrow, gathering in the room for effect. The inmates, beneath blue dye, rollers and dryers, eye me in silence.

You sure, lovey? she queries. It'll hurt like stink!

I nod. Do it, I say and she does, although if she had ever pierced before today, is up for questioning.

Now my nights become days, for I can get no sleep at all. Most of the piercings fester, but I only give in, and wrench out the metal when the pain is beyond bearing. Now I have a shaved head and huge red ears, and if anything touches them I almost faint clean away. And still I stay, and still I lose myself in a bottle.

One Saturday night Liz is invited to a party, and she asks me to come along.

It'll get you out, she says, some fun, some dancing, to meet new folk. What d'you think?

I can't, I say, because I cannot face the world like this. I can walk for miles through anonymous streets in my black leather, talking to no one, a nobody in a land that couldn't care less, but I can't go to a party where someone half my age will ask me about me.

That's way too close for comfort.

An hour or so after Liz has breezed out the door, looking like a dancing queen, I lie in my lonely bath and regret my decision. There is a sad song playing on the radio and the sounds of happy families playing out behind the walls. I decide to go after all. Did Liz give me the address? Place began with a B I think, and was the street called Henley, or Friendly, or Fenley, perhaps?

I dress in Liz's clothes, party clothes, and paint my face for the disco lights. I call a taxi and teeter down the dark smelly staircase, past graffiti threats, and puddles of something suspicious, broken glass and a child's satin pump that might once have been pink.

I tell the taxi driver to head for somewhere that sounded a bit as Liz had told me.

He is not convinced. London is a big place, luv, he says into the rear-view. Got an address?

I shake my head, clearing it enough to see his face. It's kindly, with a halo of white hair and nice old eyes.

I give him the general sound of the various street names and nothing rings his bell. I'll know it when I get there, I say confidently. With reluctance he pulls out into the road. For forty minutes we travel through streets and sights I have only seen on a wide screen. Women, children actually, wearing almost nothing hover in dark corners or litter-filled gardens, if you can call them gardens. Drunks weave along black pavements, and kids in noisy groups move towards bars and clubs, where wide-shouldered bouncers with less hair than I on their heads talk into radios, their faces set like concrete. There is not one inch of free space.

Every so often I suggest that this might be the place. Look at the people going in – hear the dance music, see the lights?

It must be here, the party, the one Liz is at. Shall I just pop in and check, while you wait?

The driver pulls into the kerb and turns to face me. I can see his eyes properly now, and they are kind. I am not afraid.

Listen lovey, he says, we're lost. Your friend isn't here, and even if she is, you shouldn't be joining her, not like this. I am going to take you back now, to where you will be safe.

And I know he is right.

When we arrive at the flat, he refuses any payment. He waits, his engine ticking over, till I wave at him from the window. I see him nod his head and smile. As I lie on Liz's floor, I hold that smile close, like a child holds her teddy bear.

Sometimes I speak to Alex on the phone, but mostly I walk the streets of London alone. Alex asks me to come home, but I am not ready for that, for him. To just step back into what I have left would be unbearable.

How can we change it? Alex asks, his voice heavy with weariness, and I can tell he has no answer to that either.

After a few weeks with Liz, I am acutely aware that I am taking advantage of her hospitality, not to mention cramping her style. With sick old me in the flat, there is no room to breathe – and certainly no room for a boyfriend. Shrugging off her kind protests, I take the short journey to my parents' home in Norfolk, for now there is nowhere else to go. I must face them and beg shelter. I know they will say yes, but my arrival will require explanations and answers to questions I don't even want to think about.

They are shocked at the look of me; I can tell it in their eyes. For I am their eldest, their talented, pretty, gifted, clever first-born; the one with loads of promise and freckles on her nose and long auburn hair falling down her back. I stand on the doorstep, almost bald, thin as a lamppost and coated in black leather. Lack of sleep has bruised my eyelids and there is a shake in my hands. My ears look like I strayed into a firing range.

I tell them basic facts, and they both let me know that my place is at home with my husband and children, no matter what. My own mother, regardless of how she felt, would never have abandoned her post. We don't talk a lot after that, not in any depth, for I am altogether too much for them like this. They let me be, running me hot baths, feeding me up, encouraging me from behind troubled eyes and skirting round me in wide circles. They are loving and hopelessly lost.

One day Alex calls to speak to my father. He is desperate, juggling miserable children, fending off neighbourly curiosity, running daily boat trips, and explaining, explaining, explaining.

Can I send Rhua down? he asks.

Rhua is distraught and inconsolable and noisy about it, he says. The others have turned in, and the silence is dreadful around them.

Of course, says my father, without hesitation and we go together to the airport. Rhua walks towards me beside a pretty stewardess, his minder for the flight – although at fourteen he hardly needs one.

Here he is! she beams, and I wrap my boy in my arms, holding him close. He is taller than I remember, a sudden growth spurt while we were apart, and we bump together awkwardly, as if I have forgotten how we fit.

Mum, you look amazing! he laughs, once he can breathe again. He takes in the skin-tight clothes, my shaved head, my weary face.

And suddenly I know I can do this. In that extraordinary moment, inside those ordinary airport walls, Rhua sees me, really sees, and his words lift me above myself, above the sadness and the dark, and something like butterfly wings flutter deep in my heart.

I can go back.

I can go back for my children.

The following week we make the train journey together, back to the island. I am nervous, yes, unsure, yes, but for the first time since I walked out on my family, some three months ago, I can see a light ahead. Perhaps I can roll over after all.

40

Restoration (Work)

⟡

Over time I gradually gain strength in my new independence, while still building a new friendship with Alex. And he does change – slowly, but surely, learning to accept what I have needed for years.

Freedom within marriage.

How can you have freedom within marriage? Alex asks me, one morning over his coffee cup.

I snort. Kahlil Gibran should be here.

I'm not free, he continues. I would live very differently if I was so-called *free*.

I nod. He's right, he would. He would live aboard a solid teak ketch with six miles of canvas to catch whatever wind he needed to move on. He would wear a fisherman's oiled wool jumper and deck shoes and wash occasionally in a bucket of salty water. He would avoid meeting anyone, which would be a given, considering.

Yes, he says, I would, and grins.

But that's not the sort of freedom I mean, Alex. I mean freedom to do what I want, when I want it . . .

He leans forward to interrupt and meets my warning stare.

And – I go on – that means even if you don't want me to want it.

Like what?

Like going to somebody's disco in the village, when you want to collapse on the sofa.

You can go, if you want, he says, a bit huffy. No one stopping you!

Ah, but I meant with your blessing! Like, have-a-lovely-time-my-darling kind of blessing.

Don't write my script for me, he says.

I have obviously asked for too much. But we have time and I am the eternal optimist.

When he has left for the day, I think more on that conversation. It is actually quite a long one for us, although it did end on the usual note. B Flat, I think.

Notwithstanding said note, I will still quietly push for my freedom.

Not just freedom to go here or there without him, but to think and speak for myself, no longer reciting his opinions as though they were my own – or worse, as though I had none myself. He learns that I will not say 'we' or 'ours' just because he does and wishes me to do the same. I send little notes to people, letters too, and sign only my name, feeling scared and deliciously brave all at once. He still tells me he doesn't like it, but accepts my shrug in reply and no longer says what he might want to say, and I respect him for that, even though I still long for a conversation around all these little rebellions. In my head I imagine good meaty communication, with both parties free to speak their mind, with or without theatrical gesturing, raised voices, or fiery explosions, but in my heart I doubt that will ever be our way. Perhaps too many years of my compliance, my suppression of myself, has set into the foundations of our life together, like concrete. But we persevere in rebuilding our relationship, albeit shakily and on rocky ground, and there is a growing peace within the walls of our new house.

As the weeks and months pass, the children learn to trust me again and we find a new dynamic friendship rising from the ashes of the woman I was before I ran away, before I left them, before I got myself red-eyed and sick in the green depths of a wine bottle. My new independence grows my confidence and I feel a seed of freedom germinate inside me, like a baby in my now redundant womb. Alex watches me change. Some of it he doesn't like at all, but he faced his worst nightmare when I left him, and is prepared, like the children, to trust me in this new way of things. I may be awkward, touchy, difficult, but at least I am here.

When Bryn takes over the whale-watching business, after his training as a merchant seaman, Alex works for a while on the mainland and I join him. He's doing something to do with Communications, which makes me smile to myself a lot. We have had to sell the new house, as we just don't have any money left to run it, and besides, the older four children have already left home to grow their own lives. I expect to be sadder to leave our new home. But there is something about the dark clouds of debt around my head that makes me think that any other sky would be a better one to live under. We rent a place on the mainland and we stay with Granny on the island. It seems to work – for now, at least.

With my new freedom, I enrol for a year-long course – an Art Higher and an NVQ in Art and Design at Falkirk College – and end up qualifying top of the class.

Early the following year, Granny-at-the-Gate is taken ill while we are all in the South spending Christmas with my parents. It's the first time in all our married life that we have left the island at such a time, and Granny-at-the-Gate, now a widow, is not best pleased. She tells me I am cruel, so when we get the call to say Come Home Quick, my guilt tank fills right up again. She is taken to the mainland hospital for evaluation.

She won't much like that! Alex says. Being evaluated at her age.

We stay in her house, the gatehouse, and travel over each day to sit at her side. She is troubled and not herself at all, but they can tell us nothing to explain her demise. I think she is tired of life and lonely without us just up the road, even though we visit most weekends. She has lost her purpose in life. No husband left, no orders for warm woolly jumpers, no buttons to sew back on or gingham napkins to iron. All this has made her ill and tired of life.

When Alex has to return to the city to work, I stay behind with Sol, who has left his job at a call centre to be with me. Each morning I leave him to look after the dogs while I travel across the water to be with the old lady, who daily dwindles before my eyes. One day, she beckons for me to come close.

You were always loyal, she says. To Alex.

I have to turn away to hide the stab of tears. A compliment like that from Granny is a rare gift indeed, one I treasure to this day.

One day, three weeks later, she sleeps without waking and I am happy to see her peaceful for once. As I am preparing to leave, she awakens and struggles to breathe. Her breaths are short and sound painful.

Should I stay? I ask the nurse. I have my overnight bag. I bring it every day, just in case.

No need, dearie, she says, pulling round the screens. Off you go! See you tomorrow!

I dash for the ferry and that night we get the call. Alex sets off immediately from the city with Cassie, and they make the nightmare journey through lashing rain, arriving in the early hours, too late to say goodbye to Granny. I think back over my conversation with the nurse and know I should have stayed.

We gather in the family for her funeral.

I return to art school, where the teachers generously supported me in my long absence from class, leaving Granny's little home empty – but only until I graduate the following June. My plan is to return to their house and paint full-time. Alex is not delighted about my decision, but he knows he cannot stop me; nor would he try, not with all we have gone through. And it isn't far to come for weekends, in the short term.

I pack up my car with all my paints and canvases on a warm sunny June morning to make the return journey. As I pull into the driveway, I stop for a moment. Last time I came here, Granny sat in that big picture window, looking out, waving. In the big wingback chair, she spent her days knitting, sewing, repairing, or just looking out across the sea-loch. This is where she lived out her life, watching us come and watching us go and watching us tear apart in a way all her threads, needles and bandages could never mend.

We have to do that for ourselves.

That summer is a hot one. In the early mornings I paint, and later I rest, and I love the freedom. Alex comes home at weekends, most of them anyway, and I know he wants to move back.

Can I come home? he asks me. He knows I love my solitude, and I am unsure of how I will hold onto it and my independence if he moved back for good.

I agree with reservations. We are still awkward with each other, clumsy.

Perhaps we can learn a new way, I say, sounding brighter than I feel.

Yes, Alex says. Why not? Besides, the boys could use me as skipper.

At this, I am genuinely delighted. The concrete life is not for Alex, and his buoyancy is deflating. I know it every time he comes home in his city trousers and his uncomfortable black shoes, and if I can do what I want to do, why not him too?

We have launched our children, pretty much, and so there is time for us.

It's like it was at the beginning, Alex says one evening as we eat our supper in the still warm garden, early enough to avoid the inevitable swarms of midges. Alex is tanned again, wind-blown, in faded jeans and a checked shirt with a collar that needs turning.

I don't remember how that felt, I smile. We were so young and naïve; or at least I was. It can never be as it was back then – too much past to answer for.

To answer for? he challenges.

Yes, I say, standing my ground. To answer for.

When he comes home, we struggle for a while over many things, like Granny's stuff, the stuff I haven't yet managed to clear out. Alex wants to hold onto it. I want a clean slate. Alex is untidy. I am tidy. I like Radio 2 and he likes Radio 4 and this house is very small. But, in the main, we know we both want this to work, and besides, we made our vows at the altar, and that means something. We try to talk things through, and although we're unpractised at this and often get it wrong, there is a sense of moving along in the right direction. For we both know that what we have may be imperfect, but it is also irreplaceable.

Alex begins to skipper the boat for Jake, now that Bryn has gone abroad, and bar a few bumps and scratches they seem to work pretty well together.

One sunny afternoon I decide to weed the gravel. After a snatched lunch of half an avocado and a slice of bread that felt like a panty-liner in my mouth, I change into my bikini top and shorts and grab Granny's little foam weeding pad.

I begin. The sun beats down on me and feels quite delightful. My tan should be well on its way by teatime. My little radio is by my side and I am humming along to the tunes under a blue sky and the happy buzzing of the insects. The weeding moves me closer to my car, my beloved old car – my friend, my escape, my independence. From down here I can see the rust spots, which I really should do something about. A new picture begins to form in my head, and, as you might imagine, it is a colourful one.

I can see big red and yellow daisies all over my car.

By teatime, my baby is looking extremely chic.

What on earth have you been up to? Alex swings into his parking place after a day at sea. His face is darkly tanned, as are his arms. The rest of him will be white as snow. As for me, I am covered in blobs of colour, and so are the remaining weeds.

Painting my car, I explain, although you'd think he'd have guessed as much.

Supper is late that evening, but I am delighted with my work, and keep running to the window to admire her. She now looks like a real head-turner. I will never again have to wonder where my car is parked.

To my amazement, the paint stays on, even after the rains. I drive to town and everyone smiles and waves. Visitors ask if they can take a photo, to show the family back home. Oncoming cars and vans now pull over into passing places to let me by; mouths open, fingers point. I am famous; practically a local celebrity.

What the DVLA will say about this, I wonder? smirks Mr Ordinary, as he stomps by, outside the Co-op.

I never thought of that.

Sensible cars, I would have told him had he stopped to listen, are for sensible people, and I have been sensible in my time, when my children were all around me and there was a certain requirement to be sensible.

In the sensible car, a boot was needed, a wide back for the Labradors, seats for three, four, five small people, space for the shopping, the schoolbags and so on. Attention to how the car looked was never important. What mattered was that it started in the mornings and kept going until we arrived at our destination. It had to navigate deep pot-holes and remain upright, to pull a trailer filled with cattle or sheep, to remain on the road when the ice was thick and there was no such thing as a gritting machine.

Now my car is just for me, and the odd soft toy. I no longer arrive exhausted and furious, wondering if I will ever be enough for all the demands of my life as a wife and a mother. In those crazy days, every now and then would come the surprise of a wild moment, and as I looked towards it, I caught myself wondering if anyone else was looking at it too.

41

The Exhibition

⌒

A year on, I have an exhibition to prepare for in a castle overlooking the wide Atlantic.

Would you like this slot? they asked me, and I agreed to it with no hesitation, with a new sort of gung-ho confidence. As the date looms, I am beside myself with panic. I know not one thing about setting up an exhibition.

Alex helps me to hang my work, for now I can call it work and look you straight in the eye as I do so. Actually it's me who helps Alex, for although I can paint these swirling crazy explosions of colour, I have no eye for design. Together we load up Miss Daisy and set off on the winding switch-back road that leads to the castle.

Hammer, cord, picture hooks, tape, list of work . . . ?

Alex nods, driving round the large black bottom of a highland bull.

I watch him drive. He knows it and smiles.

When I joined your life, I said, I thought I had lost me.

But the wild woman never moved out, however carefully I tried to bury her. She kept rising like bile in my mouth until, one grey morning, through a grimy window, I opened my mouth wide and let her out. I never felt better in all my life.

Good, says Alex. I fell in love with that wild woman, remember?

I send invitations out to everyone I know on the island. I am sure they will all come.

They know me after all. We have bumped trolleys in the island Co-op for almost thirty years, exchanged chatter about husbands, babies, the weather, the state of the roads, the cost of ferry tickets.

I never knew you painted, Nicky said to me the week before when we collided at Shampoos and Conditioners.

I have just begun, I told her, looking down at the sea of upturned faces. I never had time when my kids were this age, although I did paint furniture, holes in the wall, damage marks and other such things.

Nicky smiled and I saw the first soft age lines around her eyes.

What sort of paintings? she asked, not wanting me to move away.

Big abstracts. Colourful, wild, all from inside my head. I paint how I feel about what I see, and what I have seen before.

Wow! she breathed and I know what she was thinking. In that moment, she saw chances and freedoms for herself too, for perhaps somehow I have freed her. One day her many little ones will leave her, and when they do she will have a heart bursting with memories and colours and experiences, both happy and sad. And, if she has a mind to, she can turn her whole life into a new song, and sing it out any way she pleases, for no one but her has seen it in quite the way she has.

No one.

We women can do all that is demanded of us, with devotion, dedication and enthusiasm. All we need are moments like that one, and the singular courage (although Nicky has no idea how much she will need yet) to walk our dream out into the light. That, and a chance meeting with an older woman, one further down the track of life, one who has stepped out of her brown dress, and donned a peacock.

On opening night, as the room fills with curious island dwellers, I feel like a demented hen. It took all day to hang my work, label and price it.

How much!? I squeal at Alex, who is adding noughts like they were on offer. I can't believe anyone will buy a single one. Why would they? It's just mad shapes and swirls and if there hadn't been edges to the canvases I could have gone for miles without drawing breath.

What does this one mean? asks the smartly dressed woman from the bank.

Startled, I flounder. Alex shrugs.

It's a sunset! I say confidently after reading the label. Sunshine and Red.

It was at full moon, I continue, over the loch. We have wonderful sunsets on the island, as you know.

She nods and sort of smiles, inching away. Obviously she has different sunsets wherever she lives; ones without purple blobs and squiggly black lines where the brush kept dribbling. I had mixed the Mars Black with egg white, which made for long feathery strings of colour I could never have created by hand however light my touch.

And besides, the island weather can be extremely odd.

Sometimes I turn paintings upside down if I can't make any sense of them. It's a trick I was taught at the mainland college I attended the year before as a mature student.

Flip the canvas! they said.

So I do and it works.

There you are! I say to the painting that now makes perfect sense, although how on earth I manage to paint it the wrong way up . . .

Trust your inner eye, they said, even if yours might have faulty wiring, and I loved the way they really talked to me, the fruitcake me who does most things differently, and the fact they encouraged any spontaneous eruption of creativity, like the kite I fashioned from a charity-shop bra collection.

It has to fly for you to pass this assignment, they said.

It did. As I watched it rise into the grubby sky, and heard the laughter all around me, I just knew I could fly too. All I had to do was grow wings.

A woman twists her head round for illumination. I watch her through the sea of moving bodies, the murmur of people with drinks in a hollow space. I can see, as she bobs about like Little Weed, looking this way and that, sideways and then the other sideways, that illumination is not forthcoming. I consider telling her it is already three times flipped, the job is done, but I have learned enough about art to know that no amount of chat will sell a painting that hasn't immediately captured the heart. She moves on to the next piece and I suddenly feel naked, as though I am baring my breasts in public – and not just any public, but one that has watched me make various pigs' ears of various things over quite a number of years. Perhaps they think this is just another disaster-in-waiting.

What is the story behind this one? a man asks me. His face is whiskery and I recognise it, but can't remember his name.

Ah, this one is easy. This one is obviously something.

It was a stormy night, I begin, and the wind was behaving like a hooligan, crashing branches against the windows and moaning round the corners of the house . . .

I am warming to this tale, and, on checking the painting once again, I take us right out into the big-ass waves.

See the little red boat? Well, I think it's a boat. Yes, it's definitely a boat.

A little crowd is gathering. Must be all this arm waving and eye flashing as I marinade us all deep into the storm. Alex watches from the outskirts, grinning. It gives me confidence.

Marinade? he asks.

Well . . . yes . . . it's 'serenade' with a marine flavour . . .

The group laughs at our wit and re-settles itself around me like parenthesis.

What are your influences? asks a man with a moon face and big black-rimmed glasses on his wide nose.

My breath freezes, just as I am drawing in a lungful to blow the bracket further out.

Mind empty; mouth open.

They're all peering at me. Waiting.

Picasso? he prompts. Kandinsky?

Yes, I nod.

Pollock?

Yes, him too.

Barbara Rae?

Who?

I sell seven paintings that night, including the stormy one to Mr Whiskers. Illumination obviously did come to the woman with the rubber neck, as she put a red spot on both paintings. I am tempted to ask her to explain them to me, but decide against it.

Seven sales! On the first night!

Seven homes will now be adorned with my crazy abstracts, each of which will become a talking point when friends or family come to visit. The feeling of this is one of both elation and disbelief. My self-confidence racks up another few notches and I float out of the castle on a magic carpet.

Well done, lass, Alex says. I am so proud of you.

I can't stop smiling all the way home. At last I am me.

Well, that's all fine and dandy, but what now? One exhibition is not going to be enough to call myself an artist. Seven paintings sold is not fame, nor is it fortune, although it sure feels like it. From now on I will have to push my work out there, into a world bristling with lively competition, with critics, with egos and with big ponds; with wild people, outrageously dressed with blue hair and tattoos; people who work crazy hours, who talk excitedly together about imagery and concepts, about mediums and movement, about the shape of instinct and the colour of sound.

My sort of people.

The next morning I am up and running. I run all the way down the stairs and grab my cup of coffee. Excitement is wild inside me and my brain is fizzing with opportunities and adventure.

Until I step up to my desk, that is.

Selling me is much harder than selling someone else. It was easy to bring Alex into the limelight with his pioneering work among whales and dolphins, or with his recording studio. I just picked up the phone and, in my plummy English accent found my way to the top decision maker within the national press, the BBC, or wherever. I took no put-downs, no dithering about, and I was consistently and powerfully good. I can wax lyrical on pretty much anything once I have mugged up on the subject, and I can spin any size of web required to tempt you in and hold you fast. I can bring in funding, publicity and success to you, with my quick brain, pretty face, disarmingly charming telephone manner and my ability to close the deal. But just look at me now, sitting on my chair like a dumpling, watching the phone grow teeth and horns. It takes more courage than ever before to pick it up and begin to speak, and it's worse the next morning. Any rejection is agony, especially if I am holding out my work to a gallery owner and he is shaking his head.

* * *

But in the main, I enjoy a measure of success, not least in the way I can change from the inside. I now have permission to wear the outrageous clothes I have always worn inside my head – but better, for now I design them myself, which can, in itself, be a highly precarious process. My 'upcycled' garments (found in charity shops and personalised) often tell me I should have paid more attention in dressmaking classes. Nonetheless, they make me sassy as hell. Now I can be moody and difficult, demand space and time for my 'work' and draw new boundaries. I can wear one earring, or twelve, depending on my mood. I can meet other artists and not feel an outsider. I can keep odd hours and even odder company. I am an artist now. I can dance in the mornings and forget lunch entirely and hog the bathroom as I study the swirls bathwater creates as it drains away. I can talk to Alex about the rhythm of space. I can be bonkers.

You were always bonkers, lass, he says, and this time I can smile with him.

And it's not just Alex who thinks so. I know it makes people smile when I tell them how I could never remember where my car was parked, pre-Daisy days, and how long I spent trying not to look like I was looking for it. Or that I never finish what I started; nor can I remember what it was I started, in order to give myself any chance of being able to finish it. They might laugh at my quick wit, my spontaneity, the suddenness with which I might rush outside, barefoot, to stack some logs, or dash upstairs to paint the bathroom floorboards just because I have found some bright red paint in the garage. They might even envy me these things from where they stand, over there in the right clothes, with shoes on their feet, a plan in their hands and knowing exactly where they parked their car. But sometimes I feel like a sparkler on bonfire night, fun to hold for a little, while I sparkle and spit, a dazzling white light, a handful of shooting stars. And yet when the fire has died and the sparkler is dead, they will dispose of it in the dustbin, taking care to ensure that it is quite cold, so as not to melt the plastic.

But being bonkers with a purpose is a different thing altogether, for now I am doing something with my creativity, instead of wasting it in frustrated dreaming. I have sold paintings from here to London Town and out across the world from France to Canada, to New Zealand and beyond, if you can go beyond New Zealand.

And I will again, I tell myself, when I dive into the trough of a fallow period.

I can make you some frames, Alex says, and I squint at him across the table.

Frames? I ask, remembering his schoolboy attempts at woodwork.

He disappears into the garage, emerging hours later with something pretty sound. Together we fit the block canvas into the surround and the textile painting of boats is transformed.

A gallery calls the following morning.

They want the same, but in blue.

No, I say. Sorry, but no. Every painting is itself; a one-off. However low my bank account might be, there is absolutely no chance of my ever painting the same but in blue.

Alex grins from where he sits behind his coffee.

Tell her to go to Ikea!

I may be temporarily felled after the call, but please don't imagine I will be seduced by ordinariness, with its old teeth and its sensible shoes and its music trapped inside, for I am wild with all the colours in my veins and you will see them all for yourself once my arm gets better and the doubt inside me is booted into the loch at the very top of a spring tide. Then the dishes will sit and the carpet will wheeze and the vacuum will squat in silent darkness and I will take myself behind the upstairs door and begin, and there will be nothing in the fridge and no plans for supper. And Alex won't mind a bit. Now that the children have grown and gone, we have just us to feed. For years after they had all finally left, I cooked enough for a whole battalion. It took years to calm down, to pace myself. An empty fridge is no longer frightening, nor is it judgement on me. Alex will just make an omelette for supper, using four pans, and dripping egg white all the way from the cooker to the hob.

And that is fine with both of us.

42
New Beginnings

～

The next day is grey and yellow and raining, like it's been grey and yellow and raining for weeks.

It's not always fun being me, I say to Alex, as I watch the vacuum bounce backwards down the stairs, having lost contact with its Darth Vader breathing tube.

Oops, he says, and I know he is wondering where on earth that came from, but I am in my usual rush, as though time is running out, and Alex, standing calmly at the bottom, makes me even more bad-tempered.

He removes himself from the stairwell in a wise silence, and I hear the kettle flicking into life.

Alex has learned since being home again that I am dangerous in such a mood. When we lived at Tapsalteerie, I kept it all in, and the only way I showed my anger around him was in loud silences, a lot of huffing and puffing and even more slamming of doors. Once, after a particularly frustrating interchange, when he was gone up the hill, I flipped the broom upside down and smashed all the big kitchen windows.

We women respond to all this, I mutter, furiously jamming bits back on the vacuum. A small thin brush I have never seen before refuses to fit in place. I whack it with my fist until it does.

Being taken for granted, I mean. We grow quiet, you know, and submissive, stepping back into the pattern of the wallpaper and we can do this for many years until folk really think they know us, what we can do, how well we bake or make jam, or how clever we are with bunting. But deep inside us all, there is another woman with a voice, and a way of rising to the surface at the most inconvenient times.

Oh I know about HER! Alex calls back from the kitchen, but I ignore him.

And so, I continue, the years roll on the same, until one day the scales fall away from our eyes and we see what we have allowed ourselves to become. There is an explosion – a polite one at first, kept under the skin, but it cannot be contained for long. Once a woman senses the fresh tang of wild freedom on its way to her, she will find someone to help her turn and I don't mean towards another husband. One in a lifetime, it is generally agreed, is quite enough. This woman with new lights sparkling in her eyes and her soul bubbling like champagne and the 'running' in her bright as bluebells on a sunshine day, will find her first guide – in a book, perhaps, or at a bus stop, or on the train – and one will lead to another until she can see, with a clear and ancient look-ing, the dividing of paths. One path leads back to defeat, to try no more, to accept the picture painted by others as the definitive blueprint of her life, and to silence forever her own song of rebellion.

This way is the safest one. She knows it; we all know it well. We have already walked it for years, after all. We have seen our mothers walk down it before us, and we can trace its line in the eyes of a stranger. It is the sensible path, and there are plenty of women waiting at the crossroads to welcome her back!

I peep round the corner to see if Alex has run away, but he's still there. I feel the hot sting of tears. The drama queen is rising in me. Alex is silent, listening, and nowhere near his laptop. I can't let this opportunity go.

Come with us! they cry, these sensible women . . . (centre stage now) . . . in their regulation skirts and aprons. This is the right way, they say. This is for the best. And if a woman has too much fear, she will go with them, obediently, as all nice girls should. And I did go with them . . . you know Alex, often over the years. It was so different for you. You were always just Alex!

Did you hate me for that? he asks.

Yes, I say, sometimes I did.

And yet I loved him too.

Alex the explorer, Alex the pioneer, Alex who set sail for America with £10 in his pocket and the wildness quite at home in him. Alex the traveller, who moved through countries, over borders and along dangerous streets, working where he could, sleeping on beaches in his only set of clothing, sharing beef jerky with other homeless wanderers. Alex the frozen lumberjack. Making music around a camp fire with Baez, Dylan, McQueen and Julie Christie. Alex the beach bum. Starving, he stole a chocolate Hershey bar, landing himself in jail with no money for bail. Alex the jailbird.

And then he came home and spun me off my feet.

Alex the Impossible.

He comes back into the room, and hands me a mug of tea.

I am sorry I got so many things wrong, he says. I always loved you, so very much.

He touches my face.

Behind him, a bumble-bee knocks against the glass in the big picture window and we both turn. A shaft of sunlight pushes through the clouds.

I smile. See, that, Alex? It's stopped raining.

Epilogue

⌒

Alex and I still live here in Granny's house on the island. Neither of us have the slightest wish to be anywhere else, and for the children this is home, a place they love to come back to, even if none of them ever lived within its walls. Perhaps, after all, home is not a place. Perhaps it's us. Me and Alex, together.

Alex is forever the old sea dog, and he still skippers the whale-watching boat for Jake throughout the summer months and loves it. He keeps bees in the woods at the back of the house and the honey is like nothing I have ever bought off a shelf. It tastes wild.

Bryn and his new wife live and work abroad on super yachts.

Cassie is a qualified counsellor and lives with her family in Scotland.

Jake runs the whale-watch business, is second coxswain of the lifeboat and a qualified yachtmaster instructor. He and his wife and family live on the island.

Rhua is a successful broker and he and his wife live in London. They expect their first child at Hogmanay.

Sol is head of social media in a prestigious digital perform-ance company. He and his fiancée live in Cape Town.

Our children adventure on.

Maddy lives in Scotland working on collaborative projects in music and stage performance with a passion.

After Jenny left us for bigger challenges, she met her husband while leading a whale-watching tour in Iceland. Diagnosed with breast cancer whilst carrying her second child, she died, before he really knew his wonderful crazy wild mother. I am glad I did, and so is Alex. She was an extraordinary young woman with a passion for wildlife I have never encountered since.

And me? Well, I still paint, although I absolutely will not ever do the same but in blue. I write a monthly piece for the local paper, a wave away from my own window, and I get many smiles and hoorahs for them, touching as I do, on things others know well, but probably never mention in polite society. I cook for pleasure now, and for Old Harry, who has been our handyman for a hundred years and deserves to be spoiled. I help out with Saturday changeovers from time to time, as I know that job pretty well, and I have many friends on the island. On Sundays I go to church, and sing my praises to my God, who guided me right through this book and whom I didn't let down in the end. I work a lot with textile pieces, such as wall hangings or brightly coloured cushions, and suchlike. I sing for pleasure, working out new songs, new melodies, new interpretations of ones I know well and singing them at every opportunity.

My daily walks around the Tapsalteerie estate, those walks through woods and across rocks we used to call our own, is a constant joy to me. As we no longer carry its burden of care, Alex and I can wander among the trees, watch the deer, listen to the birdsong and jump over the pot-holes with a childlike enthusiasm. We walk at different speeds, Alex and I, so he sets off with his crook and his little dog one way around the loop, while I march off like I was late for something, at a frightening lick, the other way. We meet somewhere in the middle and take our time strolling back together.

Perhaps that is the story of our life.

Acknowledgements

There are many places a story can go, although it belongs to only one. It can lodge in the bones and the sinews, all the good and all the bad, and die in silence. Although it colours and flavours a whole life, it can still hide in the dark. But that way is not for me. Life is not easy, not for anyone, but we all have a choice and all we need is one person to reach out a hand of hope, with the twinkle of humour in their eyes, and the words – you can do it. Perhaps, for you, this person is me.

I have so many angel guides to thank, from the first chance encounter of a woman on a train, to the finished book you have in your hand. The words, you can do it, resonate strongly with me, and those words gave me the courage for just one more step, and then another, and another, until I had walked the miles in my own shoes with my head high, full of grace and laughter.

My forever thanks to:

Joy, the woman on the train.

Janet, for giving me my first spiritual book, for her open mind, warm heart and all the books since.

My mother, the Silver Fox, with her wicked sense of humour, who thinks I'm barmy.

Sorrel, whose wild child recognised mine across a busy pub and whose sparkle is catching.

Maddy, who danced with me through many difficult times.

Jenny, who told me I could wear mini skirts and grow my own independence.

Isobel, who taught me songs of the sea and kept me up late learning the words.

My father, the wordsmith, who brought me music and language, and who showed me how to consider every word in a sentence, and to lay each one down artfully.

Pete Urpeth of Hi-Arts, Inverness, who took my first draft, a noisy tome of yellings and angst, and guided me patiently towards a readable draft. Without you, there would be no book. My tutors at O.C.A. who saw me through my Creative Writing Course.

Acknowledgements

Falkirk College tutors and Cathy Sneddon, who saw the frightful drawing of my own left foot and still offered me a place on an art course.

Annie Lennox, whose voice sang me courage as I went through every new challenge.

Marie-Christine, who gave me just the right words at just the right time.

June Anderson, whose gentle encouragement and boundless wisdom guided me through the early stages of *Island Wife*.

My brother and sisters, whose quick wit and honesty keep me the right way up.

My beautiful agent Jenny of Jenny Brown Associates, Edinburgh, who loved my story right away and whose tenacity and encouragement never fails.

Lisa Highton, of Two Roads, who squared her shoulders in her determination to find me a publishing deal. To all the Hodder team and to Tara for her final edit.

Lex and Sophie, my lovely young girlfriends, who make me realise that age means nothing.

Dr Clegg and Nurse Campbell, who cared for me through the years, and whose skills and humour kept a whole island safe from harm.

And all those brave, sensitive women, whose smiles and words have lifted me more than you will ever know.

My five fabulous children, all grown now into strong, peaceful warriors, true to their own hearts. You have enriched my life beyond belief.

To Alex who stayed close through all the hard times, and who has loved me over 40 years. It is he who made this book possible, the wild man, who taught me to overcome myself, who always believed I could do whatever I tried to do, and who first led me out into an adventure I am still living today.

And, lastly, to the island and all her people, tough, plucky and always ready with laughter and a pocketful of silver linings.

TWO
ROADS

stories ... voices ... places ... lives

Two Roads is the home of great storytelling and reader
enjoyment. We publish stories from the heart, told in strong
voices about lives lived. Two Roads books come from
everywhere and take you into other worlds.

We hope you enjoyed *Island Wife*. If you'd like to
know more about this book or any other title on our list,
please go to www.tworoadsbooks.com or scan this
code with your smartphone to go straight to our site:

For news on forthcoming Two Roads titles,
please sign up for our newsletter

We'd love to hear from you

enquiries@tworoadsbooks.com

Twitter (@tworoadsbooks)   facebook.com/TwoRoadsBooks

www.pinterest.com/tworoadsbooks